The Complete Guide to Certification for Computing Professionals

Drake Prometric

Lawrence Gilius, Writer
Tracy Downing and Alan Hupp, Editors

McGraw-Hill

New York   San Francisco   Washington, D.C.   Auckland   Bogotá
Caracas   Lisbon   London   Madrid   Mexico City   Milan
Montreal   New Delhi   San Juan   Singapore
Sydney   Tokyo   Toronto

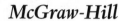

McGraw-Hill

*A Division of The **McGraw·Hill** Companies*

pbk   1 2 3 4 5 6 7 8 9 0 DOC/DOC 9 0 0 9 8 7 6 5
hc   1 2 3 4 5 6 7 8 9 0 DOC/DOC 9 0 0 9 8 7 6 5

Library of Congress Cataloging-in-Publication Data
Drake Prometric.
    The complete guide to certification for computing professionals/ by Drake Prometric.
       p. cm.
    Includes index.
    ISBN 0-07-017948-4 ISBN 0-07-017949-2 (pbk.)
    1. Information technology. 2. Technologists—Certification.
    I. Title.
    T58.5.D73 1995
    004'.068'3—dc20   95-9204
                                                             CIP

McGraw-Hill books are available at special quantity discount to use as premiums and sales
promotions, or for use in corporate training programs. For more information, please write
to the Director of Special Sales, McGraw-Hill, 11 West 19th Street, New York, NY 10011.
Or contact your local bookstore.

Acquisitions editor: Brad J. Schepp
Editorial team: Susan J. Bonthron, Book Editor
                Susan W. Kagey, Managing Editor
                Joanne Slike, Executive Editor
Production team: Katherine G. Brown, Director
                 Rhonda E. Baker, Coding
                 Jeffrey Miles Hall, Computer Artist
                 Rhonda E. Baker, Desktop Operator
                 Joann Woy, Indexer
Design team: Jaclyn J. Boone, Designer   WK2
             Katherine Stefanski, Associate Designer   0179492

Contents

Preface

Drake Prometric is the pioneer and global leader in computerized certification testing. Drake offers expert exam development services and program administration to leading companies, professional associations, and government agencies. As part of its services, Drake operates a growing network of more than 700 testing centers in major markets around the globe.

Vendors and associations within the information technology (IT) industry rely on Drake to help them create and administer powerful and prestigious certification programs as well as to deliver their certification exams throughout the world. Today, most of the certification programs in the IT industry are administered by Drake Prometric.

As the leading supplier of computerized testing in the world, Drake offers state-of-the-art testing programs. Its clients enjoy benefits such as same-day testing, localized language support, and efficient communication of tests and test results from a centralized database. Candidates taking the exam benefit from easy-to-use computerized testing, efficient registration and administration, secure testing environments, and accurate record-keeping.

Both IT certification and Drake's involvement with it have grown dramatically over the past six years. In 1989, Drake administered certification for one vendor, Novell. Today, Drake serves more than 40 major IT industry vendors and computer industry associations with exams for 75 individual programs.

Drake receives more than 60,000 calls a month from people asking about or registering for certification exams, double the number of last year's calls. Each month, Drake's testing network delivers tens of thousands of certification examinations; in January 1995, Drake delivered its millionth exam.

Drake Prometric believes that certification is not a fad. It's here to stay because it is an increasingly important answer to real business problems. The information technology industry in particular has found certification an essential tool in advancing the interests of individual professionals and the industry as a whole.

This book has been written in response to the calls Drake receives every day asking for a single source of information describing its programs for information technology professionals. The book explains how certification is useful to all those in the market for IT services. It also gives detailed program descriptions to help IT professionals select appropriate programs for themselves or for their companies.

Introduction

On July 15, 1994, the mainframe computer system that runs the NASDAQ stock exchange collapsed. Two and one-half hours later, when the market's brain revived, the damage was tallied: Traders were outraged, customer confidence was shaken, and the day's trading volume had been cut from 300 to 206 million shares.

Arthur Pacheco, a former chairman of the Security Traders Association says, "Everything in this system depends on the computer. If this breaks down, you're crippled, and millions of dollars are at stake."

The possibility of serious loss through computer failure is now a fact of life in almost all American organizations. Computer use is no longer a back-office activity for tallying the week's receipts and expenditures. Computers help track business transactions, plan the use of capital and human resources, and make just-in-time decisions. The computer network is the electronic nervous system; when it fails, the organization falters and stops.

Computer failure, of course, is often tied to human failure. Qualified people are needed to make technology work, allowing it to grow the business rather than weaken it. Organizations need high-level

technical skills from the people who sell, configure, and service their computer systems. They need them even from the employees who use their systems. Organizations cannot take the chance that their computers will fail. But how can they know what level of skill they have access to?

Experience, of course, is one indicator. In the fast-changing information technology world, experience with new technologies and related products is often more important than a degree in computer science. But the change and complexity in the information technology arena also makes the value of experience difficult to gauge.

Six months of networking experience in one environment is vastly different from six months experience in another. The technology used, as well as the size and complexity of networks, varies greatly. The precise level of skill that any worker has attained with particular hardware, software, or networking tools is difficult to determine.

Using experience to judge expertise can be a costly exercise in trial and error. It's costly for technical managers who have hired the wrong staff member or consultant. It's costly for users who can't find adequate technical support. It's costly for software and hardware vendors who can't find skilled workers to service and support their products.

It even costs training departments when they can't determine what a worker knows versus what he or she needs to know. It also costs human resource departments when they face lawsuits and can't document the skills that led them to hire or promote one person rather than another.

Human skills are often an organization's greatest asset. But to apply them effectively, organizations need to define and catalogue them like other assets, such as money, equipment, and real estate. This is particularly important in the "information age" in which knowledge and skill are emerging as the chief factors for competitive advantage. Even the federal government is working to define very specifically the skills needed in every area of work if America is to compete forcefully in the world marketplace.

Certification has emerged as a winning answer for making better use of human resources. Certification programs help define very specifically the skills needed to perform given jobs. The successful certification candidate must pass a rigorous exam that tests for those skills. Holders of certification have hard evidence of their qualifications to show to employers and customers.

Certification helps organizations with a variety of critical tasks including hiring, contracting, training, promoting, developing teams, and redesigning the organization for greater productivity. In fact, as this book explains, the usefulness of certification in solving business problems is growing over time as a variety of forces combine to promote it—technological changes, business pressures, and government initiatives.

Certification is solving business problems in a variety of industries. In the information technology (IT) industry, dozens of vendors have created certification programs over the past five years, and several industry organizations have recently developed or are now developing certification programs of their own. Some organizations are even developing in-house certification programs for their technical staff.

Certification is helping all of the players in the IT industry solve problems. Vendors benefit from trained users, resellers, and service people who use their technology for its full potential. Resellers use certification to meet increasing customer demands for qualified service providers and to set themselves apart from the competition. Individual IT professionals choose certification to document the specific knowledge and skill they can bring to a job and find the credential increasingly important as skill demands for IT professionals change rapidly.

End-user organizations rely on the credential to help them distinguish who has the skills needed for particular technical jobs and to more efficiently recruit, train, and deploy technical staff. Some businesses are using certification to restructure their information technology departments or their entire organization, which they could not do without a precise understanding of who knows what.

This book explains how certification is serving the information technology industry by making its complex and rapidly changing marketplace of skills more understandable for everyone. The book is written for you: the IT professional, vendor, reseller, technical manager, training or HR manager. Whatever your role, if you offer or use information technology services, you can benefit from certification. This book tells you how.

The first two chapters consider the forces promoting certification throughout American organizations, particularly in the information technology industry. They help you understand some of the opportunities presented by certification as well as the possible consequences of not using those opportunities.

Chapters 3 and 4 give you an insider's view of who is benefiting from certification and how they've used it strategically for their own careers or for their companies. All of the major players share their advice. Chapter 3 gives you the experience of vendors and resellers; Chapter 4, the experience of professionals and managers in departments throughout the organization.

These chapters answer the most commonly asked questions about certification: Why should I invest in certification for myself or for my employees? What are the benefits of hiring or contracting with a certified professional? How can I convince top management that certification is worthwhile? What are the benefits of multiple certifications?

Chapters 5 and 6 examine the heart of the certification process: the exam and its delivery system. Only well-constructed exams delivered the same way all over the globe can satisfy the market's need for dependable results that can be relied on for critical decisions. This material tells you what constitutes a dependable, legally defensible exam; how performance-based exams are revolutionizing the certification process; and what's coming in the near future for testing. It also describes Drake's highly effective test delivery system and worldwide network of testing centers.

Chapter 7 guides you to individual certification programs offered by 29 of the major vendors and associations in the information

technology industry. Included are all of the programs for which Drake Prometric administers the certification exam—a listing that constitutes most of the IT certification programs available in the marketplace today. Chapter 7 helps you quickly determine if a program is right for you or for your employees. It presents detailed information about exam requirements, training opportunities, and individual program benefits. In this final chapter, you learn where you need to go to become certified, how much you need to invest in time and resources, and where you can go for still more detailed information on any particular program.

The Complete Guide to Certification for Computing Professionals gives you all you need to know about why certification can benefit you or your organization and how to put appropriate certification programs to use without delay.

What is certification?

CHAPTER 1

C ERTIFICATION is a formal validation of knowledge or skill. Validation is given based on performance on a qualifying examination developed by subject matter experts. The goal of any certification program is to ensure that an individual has the skill and knowledge to perform a particular job.

The examination actually substitutes for direct observation of the candidate performing the job. Instead of assigning an expert to watch the individual work over a period of time (as, for example, in flight instruction), the certifying agency uses a test to determine knowledge or skill. Tests are less expensive than direct observation, and some believe that they are often superior to direct observation because they are objective and impartial.

The goal of any test-based certification program is to produce results that are as dependable or more dependable than those that could be gained by direct observation. To do this, the job is first characterized by defining skill and knowledge objectives that must be mastered if the job is to be performed adequately. Next, a test is developed to

Figure 1-1

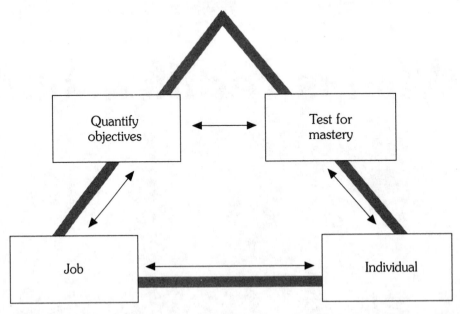

Certification tests must accurately reflect job requirements, measure mastery, and ensure reliable results.

assess whether a candidate has mastered these objectives. Finally, the test is administered to the candidate.

For the certification exam to give results that can be depended upon, three requirements must be met. First, the test objectives must accurately reflect the knowledge and skills required by the job. To ensure this, a test development organization typically surveys experts in a given field to define the crucial knowledge and skill that candidates need. These become the test objectives, which experts also help to rank in terms of importance and difficulty.

Second, the test must accurately measure mastery of the objectives. This is ensured through a process in which the test is delivered to a group of candidates who span the range from novice to expert in the field. Test questions are added, modified, or deleted until the test effectively distinguishes between those who know the material and those who do not.

Finally, the test must be delivered to the candidate in a way that ensures reliable results. This requires careful attention to candidate identification, proctoring, test center security, and data security.

Increasingly, certification exams are being administered by computer. Computerized testing offers advantages over paper-and-pencil-based tests in convenience, efficiency, and dependability. Computerized testing and the test development process are discussed in detail in Chapter 5. Test delivery to ensure reliability of results is discussed in Chapter 6.

Certification fulfills the training and development promise

The purpose of certification is to verify that a candidate has the particular knowledge or skill for performing a job. In some cases, that knowledge has been acquired through formal training programs; in other cases, through real-world experience. Most certification programs, therefore, require only that the candidate pass an exam. Formal training for the exam is generally optional, not required.

Certification, then, is not to be confused with training. Certification is different from training. It complements training and experience, adds value to training programs, and in some ways completes the training and development process.

For example, training materials are often developed concurrently with the certification exam. Thus, training is enhanced because the curriculum is designed to develop the same real-world job skills that the certification exam measures. The exam communicates to both the candidate and the trainer what is to be learned. At the same time, it enables both to verify that learning has taken place. Candidates also work harder during a training program when they know that their learning will be assessed at the end.

But wouldn't informal testing after training accomplish the same objective? The questions remain: Are we testing the right things? Do the people who test high at the end of a course also demonstrate that higher level of knowledge and skill on the job? Even if we decide that we can depend on the test results to predict more effectiveness on the job, will the exam always be given the same way, even if delivered at different test sites? If not, however well the exam has been constructed, it might not provide dependable distinctions between one test-taker's ability and another's.

This is where certification programs add value. In a rigorous test development process, the certification exam is designed to test the right things, and to test them in a consistent and therefore dependable way. In the information technology (IT) industry, the "right things to test" are those things that relate to a particular technology or product and also to the tasks to be done related to that technology. The two together define the crucial job skills, knowledge, and abilities.

The certification exam tests for knowledge and skill related both to the technology and to the tasks to be done with it. The expertise in both areas can come from the same source. For example, tests developed by information technology vendors capture the product expertise of the vendor as well as the vendor's understanding of the demands on professionals using that technology in a variety of business environments.

Certification exams test both technology and task knowledge and are also expertly designed to capture valid and reliable information about

that knowledge. Organizations offering new certification programs may contribute their own test development expertise or work with companies such as Drake Prometric for expert test development.

Certification exams also give reliable results because they are delivered in consistent formats and consistent environments. Testing sites will have very similar exam equipment and test-taking rules. Where various forms of the exam are delivered, those forms have been tested statistically to ensure that they are of equal degrees of difficulty.

High security also plays a role in ensuring dependable results from certification exams. Continuous monitoring is offered throughout the exam, and a variety of safeguards, both high-tech and low, ensure that exam results are in fact accurately measuring the test taker's knowledge.

With these advantages, there is a significant difference between a certification and a course completion certificate or even a post-training assessment. The certification shows in a valid and reliable way that the candidate has a particular skill. That skill is tied to the real-world demands of using a specific technology in specific environments. The exam has been administered so consistently, even in varying locations around the world, that it can be depended on to distinguish between the skills of one candidate and those of another, even in high-stakes decisions of hiring and promotions.

The link between certification exam results and ability to do a job makes certification an indispensable tool for a knowledge society. A certification manager at the former WordPerfect corporation says, "The attitude that I don't want to be certified, just teach me how to do x, y, or z is passing out of existence as the link between credentialling and productivity is more and more closely made."

What needs does certification answer?

Knowledge and skill have emerged in recent times as the key to business success or failure. As the information age advances, what we

know takes center stage, pushing to the background the concerns for financial and material resources.

According to business writer Peter F. Drucker, for the past 20 centuries the vast majority of the developed world has earned its wages by physical labor in one form or another. In the near future that will change, and for the first time in history, the largest part of the work force will consist of individuals whose status comes from knowledge rather than the strength of their backs.

The place of the traditional industrial worker, Drucker says, is being taken by the "technologist"—someone who works with both hands and technical knowledge. Technologists include computer technicians, X-ray technicians, and physical therapists, among others. Technologists, taken collectively, are now the fastest growing segment of the U.S. labor force. By the end of the century, knowledge workers such as these will make up a third or more of the U.S. work force.

According to Drucker, the change implies that the key competitive factor now is how well one does in acquiring and applying knowledge. This is true for an individual, an organization, an industry, or a nation. To succeed, he says, we need to improve the quality of knowledge and the productivity of knowledge, neither of which has even been well defined so far.

The October 3, 1994, issue of *Fortune* magazine announced that leading businesses are beginning to define and inventory the knowledge held by their workers. They are doing this because they believe that "the value of intellectual assets exceeds by many times the value of assets that appear on the balance sheet."

According to the American Institute of Certified Public Accountants, the components of cost in a product today are largely research and development (R&D), intellectual assets, and services. The old accounting system, which tells the cost of material and labor, gives only half the picture.

To capture the full picture, companies are trying to quantify their intellectual capital. Only then can they begin to make full use of it. According to *Fortune*, when CEOs are asked how much of the

knowledge in their companies is used, they typically answer, "about 20 percent." But making fuller use of knowledge is complicated by the fact that the quantity of information to be known is growing explosively. For example, between 1950 and 1970, a span of only 20 years, all published information in the world doubled. By 1985 it had doubled again. Between 1985 and 1995, in just 10 years, the amount of information has tripled.

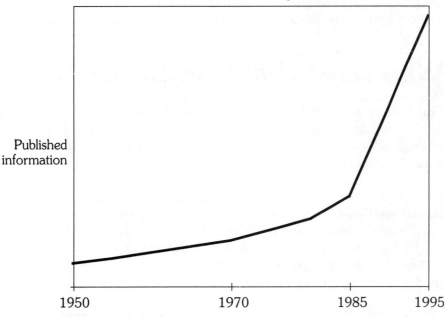

The information explosion

Figure 1-2

The information explosion

In the information explosion, organizations need to define two things: What part of the total universe of information is really useful (that is, what is really "knowledge"), and who has that knowledge. Then, because of constant change, organizations need to administer a process of continually redefining relevant knowledge and identifying knowledge holders.

Certification is emerging as a useful answer to each of these needs. Certification programs in a variety of industries are defining what is important for professionals to know and who, based on certification

exam results, has that knowledge or skill to bring to the job. Certification programs keep organizations up-to-date on knowledge or skill by continually updating exams and by requiring recertification.

Certification addresses Drucker's concern for the "quality and productivity" of knowledge and the needs of organizations to inventory their intellectual capital. It not only helps us define what is useful to know, it also motivates many to gain that knowledge in order to be more productive. At the same time, it helps organizations identify the job candidates and employees with needed skills and so helps it to hire, promote, and deploy skills for better productivity.

 # Who cares about certification?

Certification meets the needs of a knowledge-based society by helping to identify relevant knowledge and the holders of that knowledge. All of those who are offering or employing knowledge and skill are potential beneficiaries of certification programs.

Beneficiaries of certification include vendors that are producing goods; resellers that are marketing and servicing those goods; the professionals whose livelihood depends on those goods and the services related to them; end-user organizations that buy the goods and employ the professionals; and the associations that represent the professionals or the relevant industry as a whole.

Certification helps vendors ensure quality service and support to their products. It helps industry resellers set themselves apart from the competition with superior product knowledge and service. Certification helps professionals to verify to potential employers the knowledge and skill they can bring to a job. It helps end-user organizations to select, train, and deploy workers more effectively. It also helps associations to protect the integrity of the industry and to advance the interests of individual professionals through standards of professionalism.

The interests in certification of vendors, resellers, professionals, and end-user organizations in the IT industry are discussed in

Chapters 3 and 4. The involvement of two of the IT industry's major associations—The Network Professional Association (NPA) and CompTIA—are featured in case studies. The NPA story appears at the end of this chapter; the CompTIA story appears in Chapter 3.

 # What's driving certification growth?

Stakeholders in certification find the argument for it growing stronger every year as a variety of new social and market forces promote it. Most agree that the main forces driving certification growth today are the influence of technology changes, business pressures, and government initiatives.

Figure 1-3

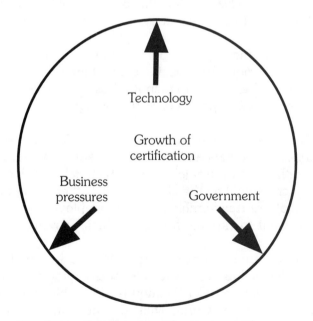

The forces that drive certification growth

 # Changes in technology promote certification

The nature of technical work in the information age is contributing to certification's popularity. According to a *Fortune* magazine article in August 1994, technical workers—those with the specialized information and skills to perform technical tasks—are quickly becoming the new "worker elite." Technical competence rather than place in the hierarchy now defines an employee's value, and certification helps to develop and verify key technical competencies.

Since 1950, the number of technical workers in America has increased nearly 300 percent to some 20 million—triple the growth rate for the work force as a whole. One out of four new jobs is now going to a technical worker, and job growth for technicians is expected to far outpace the need for other workers in the foreseeable future. The number of college graduates who take jobs in technical fields might grow by 75 percent to 2.2 million over the coming decade.

As technicians assume larger responsibilities, employers have a greater need to pinpoint the specific competencies that a technician holds. Certification exams help identify those with specific skills and knowledge on particular products or technologies.

To properly manage the new technical worker, *Fortune* argues, companies need to understand that that worker is increasingly a "careerist" rather than just a job holder. Technicians will define themselves increasingly by the cluster of skills they bring to their work, skills that are transferable from one employer to another and that they will want to expand throughout their working lives.

Certification programs can provide technical workers with concrete markers of skill development. They can be stepping stones toward building a varied skill set. Certification is a portable credential of value to employers all over the world. Thus, certification programs can be used to motivate and better manage the new worker elite.

The rapid pace of change in technology is also pushing business toward a concern for skills definition, skills development, and the certification of job-critical skills. Technology changes so fast that certifications might be more helpful to some than a two- or four-year degree just because they're current and up-to-date. Old qualifications don't measure whether an individual has up-to-date skills, hence a need for frequent recertification.

With new technologies coming out so fast, it's difficult even for the practitioner to know what he or she can really do. Certification gives a reality check on skills and a comparison with others practicing in the field.

 # Business pressures promote certification

Other forces from within the marketplace itself are pushing the need for certification to the forefront. For example, pressures for increased productivity are causing U.S. businesses to reorganize. Many organizations today have fewer levels of management and have pushed decision-making responsibilities down to the front lines. Workers are increasingly asked to use judgment and to make decisions. They are assuming responsibility for many of the tasks— from quality control to production scheduling—that formerly belonged to upper management.

According to the National Center on Education and the Economy, this new kind of work organization is the key to higher productivity and higher wages for the U.S. work force, and it is needed if we are to avoid a freefall in productivity in the coming years. The Center points out that the national economy has continued to grow over the last several decades only because more people have been working. The actual gross national product (GNP) per worker has been declining steadily. As a result, earnings have also been declining since 1969.

We can no longer depend on growing the economy by adding new workers, since work force growth is slowing.

The way to grow the economy now, the Center says, is to grow the skills of workers rather than the number of workers. While high-performance work organizations require large investments in training

Figure 1-4

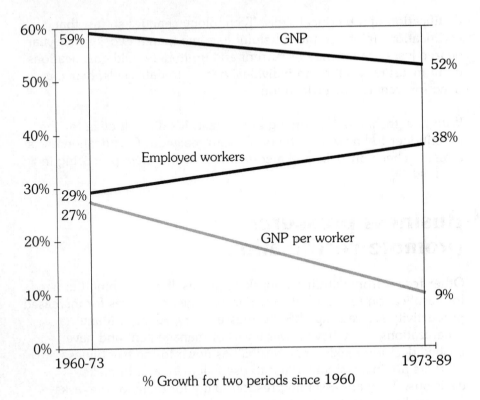

% Growth for two periods since 1960

Source: Bureau of Economic Analysis
Bureau of Labor Stastics

The GNP per worker has steadily declined since 1960.

and increased pay (to reward workers for their greater qualifications and responsibilities), the quality and productivity gains more than offset the costs.

To create the new work organization, and with it a more prosperous future, the Center says that we need to fundamentally change our approach to work and education. Today, "Education is rarely connected to training, and both are rarely connected to an effective job service function." The Center also recommends the creation of new performance-based exams for the schools, and technical and professional certificates for the entire range of service and manufacturing occupations.

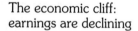

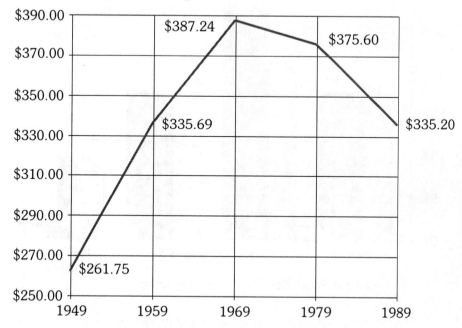

The economic cliff:
earnings are declining

Figure 1-5

Average weekly earnings
Total private non-agricultural workforce
(1989 Dollars)

Source: Bureau of Labor Statistics

The economic cliff: Earnings are declining.

Certification programs can play an important role in addressing these concerns. For example, certification programs typically make well-defined connections between the skill demands of particular jobs and the performance requirements to pass the certification exam. These programs thus encourage the growth of precisely the skills needed to make workers more productive in specific real-world jobs.

The connection between job demands and certification requirements is enhanced by performance-based exams, which vendors, associations, and end-user companies in the IT field are increasingly using as part of certification programs. Certification is already

Figure 1-6

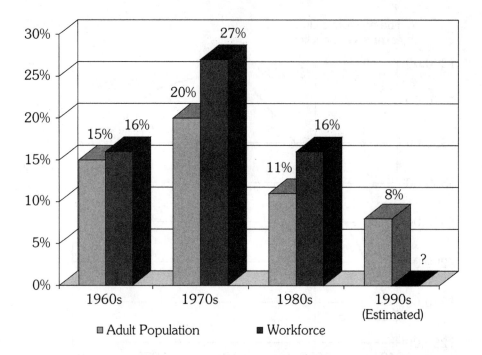

% Growth of Adult Population and Workforce
Source: Bureau of Labor Statistics

The economic cliff: Workforce growth is slowing.

playing an important role in the move to new work forms in the U.S. It is smoothing the path to reallocation of responsibilities by providing objective verification of particular knowledge and abilities.

Beyond the creation of the high-performance work organization, a variety of other business trends are contributing to the certification movement. For example, workers typically change jobs many times in a lifetime. Certification can help in the transition because it is a portable credential valued anywhere in the world. Certification also protects against unemployment when one's employer is downsizing.

The trend toward total quality management requires companies to collect objective data about key processes and resources—particularly

human resources. The pressures for better quality of product and service requires companies to demonstrate to investors and to the marketplace that they have the skills needed for top-quality performance. Certifications are one valuable indicator of work force skills.

For the managers of technical professionals, certification is an important screening tool. It's an objective, consistent test of technical proficiency. For the human resources department, using certification as an additional criterion in the hiring process adds a further objective basis for hiring decisions and helps avoid lawsuits.

Training departments are under increasing pressures to justify their expenditures by measuring their results. Learning goals established by certification programs and certification tests help identify who needs to be trained in what, as well as showing objectively what the outcomes of training have been.

Companies are contracting out more and more activities, keeping only their core business functions in-house. Certification helps businesses know that their contractors have the skills required. As commerce goes international, businesses need to depend on people all over the world to deliver the same level of skilled product support. Certification is a valuable safeguard for quality work performed anywhere around the world.

 # Government influence promotes certification

The federal government has formally recognized that lifelong learning is increasingly important to the competitiveness of the nation and the success and well-being of U.S. citizens. It is promoting the idea that at all levels and in all professions, growth in skills and knowledge will be increasingly important as technological change accelerates.

The Goals 2000: Educate America Act introduced by the Clinton Administration involved government in a process of defining skill standards for both workers and students and advancing certification of skills through voluntary partnerships.

The move is viewed as pivotal by many involved with training and assessment because, they argue, America is behind most of the industrialized world in developing skill standards, and without effective standards it will be difficult or impossible for the nation to have the right skills at hand.

Since 1992, a variety of departments, led by the Departments of Labor and Education, have collaborated to begin creating a "national skills infrastructure." The Secretary of Labor's Commission for Assessing Necessary Skills (SCANS) has begun to look at the kinds of jobs that will be available in the 1990s and beyond and has identified a set of basic skills and knowledge that every worker should have.

It has also stressed the importance of continuous evaluation as an important part of the learning process and has set out criteria for effective assessment programs. The Commission recommends that:

➢ Assessment should apply to adults in the workplace, not just to students.

➢ Assessment should use new techniques for judging performance so that tests are not perceived in the traditional way, but as a set of tools tied to learning goals.

➢ Employment-based assessments should be locally developed for specific tasks and should permit evaluation of individual learning needs.

➢ Public and private employers should define requirements for higher-level competencies.

Following the SCANS recommendations, federal government agencies are steadily developing voluntary skill standards for workers in various roles in several different industries. To date, they have begun defining detailed skill standards for 24 different occupational fields, with new ones to be added by the recently established National Skill Standards Board (NSSB). Some represent relatively small vertical niches, such as hazardous materials management technician and photonics technician, while others represent broad industry concerns, such as computer-aided drafting and design (CADD) and advanced high-performance manufacturing.

According to Joan Knapp, a consultant on certification programs in Princeton, New Jersey, a number of industries such as retail, electronics, printing, laundering, and hospitality are involved in these projects, and others have developed skill standards and are now designing methods of assessing a person's performance against those standards.

Knapp says that none of the industries represented in the government skill development projects has yet certified their workers, but, she says, "That time is near." A number of trade associations and organizations are joining the national skills standards initiative by planning to finance and develop their own programs.

Knapp says, "The jump start that federal policy and agencies envisioned that the pilots would engender has occurred—a national movement that recognizes the value of skills standards for workers and employers and a highly skilled work force for the U.S. economy has begun."

Wayne Hodgins, technical director for customer learning, education, and training for Autodesk, Inc., is observing the government's skill development efforts from his seat on technical, executive, and steering committees for several of the National Skills Standards projects (including CADD and advanced high-performance manufacturing). His dream is that one day, when given a business project to manage, project team leaders will have resources to tell them exactly what skill sets they need on their project team. Then referring to a database of skills currently held by the company, they will build teams from the available pool of skill resources, and know precisely whom they need to train in what, and whom they need to hire or contract with to provide the missing skills.

The National Security Agency (NSA) has called for a further step—a widely accepted mechanism to "tag" training products to indicate that they will successfully teach a specific set of skills. The NSA argues that we need a rating system, including a seal of approval in combination with a description of the purpose of the course, in consistent skills-related language. This would provide an objective, quantitative basis for systematically selecting performance-relevant courses to match an individual's training needs. What is missing, says

the NSA, is "an agreed-upon certifying mechanism that will enable the government and large corporations to acquire training that guarantees a high probability that the employees will become more productive in the workplace."

Government initiatives are stimulating the work of leading-edge researchers and training providers to develop performance- and technology-based training, and to prepare to deliver it over the electronic "information superhighway." Initiatives have fostered a climate that encourages individuals and organizations to plan for developing specific job-related skills. They have promoted the idea of standards as the key to ensuring that the right skills are available at the right time to get the job done.

This atmosphere is encouraging the growth of certification programs, programs that address the government's call for connecting training to well-defined, real-world job skills, as well as the need for objective evaluation of skills and knowledge. Certification programs—private sector initiatives driven by the demands of the marketplace—are evolving to keep pace with new and emerging technologies. As such, they also fulfill government concerns to define job requirements for both today and tomorrow.

Certification—A happy medium

Certification is more formal than simple training assessment. But certification is less formal than government-controlled licensing programs that serve as absolute hurdles to leap before one is allowed to practice a profession. Certification could be seen as standing midway on a continuum of formality between training verification at one end and licensing at the other.

Figure 1-7

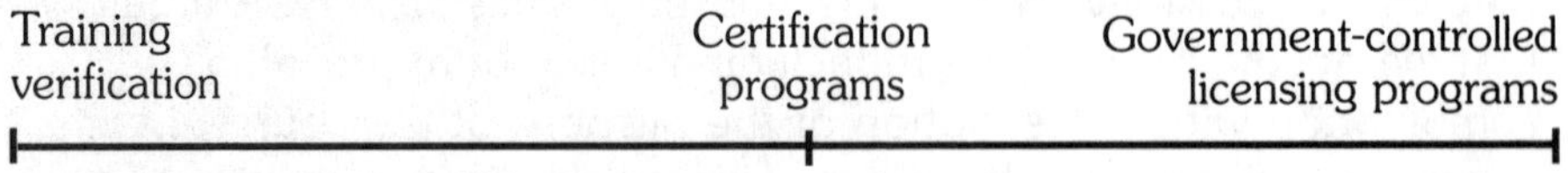

| Training verification | Certification programs | Government-controlled licensing programs |

Certification can be viewed as the final gateway before actual licensure in the professional development process.

All three kinds of programs—training verification, certification, and licensure—coexist in the marketplace and influence one another. Training verification programs are commonly found in the hospitality industry serving hotel and restaurant workers. The industry offers a number of courses to the public and awards certificates upon completion. These recognitions, while short of formal certifications, nevertheless serve as standards of performance in the industry.

Some programs in the early, informal stages might only verify that the candidate has completed a course. Over time, however, pressures for greater accountability might push such programs into becoming national and standardized certification programs.

As part of the move to greater accountability, some programs that began as voluntary and self-regulating might become mandatory licensing programs regulated by the state, particularly where the public health or safety is concerned. Programs for acupuncturists and massage therapists are two examples. Or, the industry might do such a good job with self-regulation that a state might decide that government regulation is unnecessary. State licensing programs also sometimes adopt successful certification programs as part of their regulatory requirements.

Among professions, health care has been and continues to be among the most heavily regulated and tied to licensing requirements. The health care profession is so concerned about its actions, both real and perceived, that it sometimes regulates itself far more strictly than is required by the state. For example, a hospital might choose to exclude anesthetists without certain credentials even where the state does not require that credential.

Other fields in which practitioners make life-and-death decisions are heavily regulated by licensing requirements. Examples include air traffic controllers, nuclear power plant workers, and handlers of hazardous chemicals.

In between the extremes of training verification and state-controlled licensure lies the growing number of American professions seeking to define themselves, regulate themselves, and build customer loyalty through certification.

While certification, by definition, is not mandated by government, the results of certification exams offer the kind of hard evidence of skill that make them an asset to those offering skills or looking for skills in the marketplace. They are increasingly demanded, therefore, not only by government, but by vendors, associations, professionals, and end-user organizations. They are becoming increasingly important over time.

 # Making the move to certification

Many industries are moving from informal standards of self-regulation to more formal certifications. Some even welcome state licensure to enhance the credibility of the profession. No complete list of organizations offering certification programs in the United States exists; however, estimates range from 400 to 1000 organizations. The numbers are growing dramatically each year, particularly in health care—a field including a great variety of licensing and certification requirements.

According to Joan Knapp, certifying organizations have created programs for *every* type of occupation and profession imaginable, including travel agent, picture framer, and professional tennis player. Knapp says that in a sense, these organizations have appointed themselves to represent a particular occupation or profession in order to develop and maintain knowledge and practice standards. In occupations or professions such as health care, real estate, and finance, where the safety and protection of the public is involved, says Knapp, certification is an attempt at self-regulation—a proactive strategy to fend off the possibility of federal and state regulation.

According to Knapp, "The history of certification in this country reveals that most programs are spawned from the efforts of membership or trade associations." As required by law, however, the certifying agency is created to be administratively and fiscally independent from the parent association, to avoid conflict of interest or restraint of trade.

Examples abound of industries making the move to certification. The National Association of Purchasing Management (NAPM), as one

illustration, began in 1914 as a place for discussion of productivity among purchasing managers, originally only in the manufacturing area, but later also in service and government. Over the years, as its membership grew, it evolved ethical principles and standards of behavior for the profession that it continues to update and publish today.

Discussions about certification at NAPM began in the 1960s and culminated in 1974 with the creation of the Certified Purchasing Manager (C.P.M.) certification. An association spokesperson commented that "Purchasing had reached such a point of sophistication and level of value to the organization that it was time to define the knowledge, skills, and abilities that would be necessary for a purchasing professional. Now one of the things that's happened is that we've become sophisticated in understanding our common core of knowledge."

NAPM now tests for that knowledge in an exam worth 35 of the total 70 points required for the C.P.M. certification. The other 35 points are earned from education, contributions to the profession, and experience. The certification program is open to the public; membership in NAPM is not required.

Today, many purchasing manager job openings announce that the C.P.M. is preferred or required. About 25,000 people have been certified to date, and that number will increase. An industry consultant comments that it is becoming increasingly difficult to hold a purchasing management position in a major company without holding this credential. The C.P.M. certification gives a further benefit to business: Its definition of the common body of knowledge for the profession provides a way for any organization to focus education and training for its purchasing staff.

The sales profession has also recently taken to certification. For example, the National Automobile Dealer's Association (NADA) is developing a certification program. Anna Arnone of NADA says, "We would like to tell consumers that if they ask for a certified sales professional, they can have the confidence of working with a person who is knowledgeable about the product, who deals in an ethical manner, and who is experienced with satisfying their needs."

The NADA training program covers ethics, legal aspects of selling, selling techniques, listening skills, and practical strategies for building customer loyalty. Similar programs are being considered or have been recently developed by other major organizations of salespeople, including the Certified Medical Representative Institute within the pharmaceutical industry; the Prudential, among insurance agents; the National Association for Professional Saleswomen, and the Sales and Marketing Executives of Greater New York.

Two organizations fueling the drive to certification are the American Society of Association Executives (ASAE) and the National Organization for Competency Assurance (NOCA). ASAE provides the Certified Association Executive Program to raise professional standards in the large field of association management. NOCA has a commission that accredits certification programs. Their accreditation criteria and standards are the only national and voluntary standards for certification agencies.

While certification has been pushed by a variety of industry associations, including some specific to the information technology industry, certification is also driven by vendors and even end-user organizations. The role of IT vendors in certification is discussed in detail in Chapter 3. The role of the end user in the certification process is discussed in Chapter 4.

Case study: Starting a certification program from scratch at the Network Professional Association

The Network Professional Association (NPA) wants to lead the information technology industry in a way that only a not-for-profit association can. The NPA is a self-regulating association that sets standards of technical expertise, professionalism, and ethical behavior.

The NPA plans to sponsor certification programs and expects those programs to play an important role in its future. NPA President Berkeley Geddes says, "If the association is going to help each of us advance as professionals, it must responsibly advance and manage a common professional certification." For the NPA, "responsibly advancing" has meant thoughtfully considering the fundamentals:

How have other professions developed certification? Should the NPA be involved with it at all, and if so, what are its objectives? What organizational structure is needed to represent all of the interests that the certification will serve?

According to Geddes, a not-for-profit organization is the logical, perhaps inevitable, choice as a standard-bearer for an industry. The accounting profession, he says, rallied around for-profit training providers and university accounting programs before finding its identity with the American Institute of Certified Public Accountants (AICPA), a not-for-profit group.

Similarly, the medical profession experienced education and certification leadership provided by for-profit companies before the not-for-profit American Medical Association (AMA) rose to provide industry leadership. Geddes believes that a variety of social forces combine to pass the mantle of leadership to the not-for-profit association.

Geddes says that in the medical profession, doctors united themselves within the AMA and took responsibility as a group to regulate themselves with a code of conduct, a code of ethics, and certification to safeguard their customers' interest. Doctors felt that they, and not the for-profit educational companies, had the interest and the ability to do that. Geddes believes that, like the for-profit educational companies, vendors in the IT industry today cannot provide impartial industry leadership as an association could.

Government also prefers to relate to an industry through a single group, according to Geddes, and it prefers that group to be a not-for-profit industry association. Were the government to deal with an industry through a single company, the government would risk appearing prejudiced; at the worst, it could even risk creating a monopoly.

Geddes says, "From a historical perspective, we concluded that certification and education leadership for the information technology industry rightfully belongs in the hands of a not-for-profit organization. In fact, there are society pressures that will cause that to happen whether it happens in two or in twenty years."

As to whether the NPA should provide that leadership and provide it using certification programs, the NPA put the question to its 6500 members in 90 chapters around the world. Their answer, according to

Geddes was "yes" on both counts. Members wanted an NPA certification to help the customer identify networking specialists and to help members develop their technical proficiency. Geddes says that members also asked the NPA to help reduce the redundancy among the several dozen certifications already available in the industry.

As to what kind of program to offer—course completion certificates, certification for work on particular products or using certain skill sets only, or a full-fledged professional certification—the NPA members said they wanted a multivendor professional certification. The NPA is now working to create one.

What makes up a professional certification? NPA research revealed seven major components. First is testing for proficiencies in particular areas to determine a base level of competency. Second is a legal component: binding oneself to a code of good practice. Third is an experience requirement: Candidates must have hands-on learning and experience in key areas. Fourth is exposure to the industry. Before being certified, candidates usually associate with the industry for a period of time. Many industries have created apprenticeship programs to provide that opportunity. These four categories are precertification requirements.

The fifth requirement is continuing education and training to retain the certification. Sixth is continuing activity and experience. Many professionals must demonstrate an ongoing stream of activity in their area of specialization. Seventh is membership in a professional association to demonstrate commitment to advancing one's profession.

The seven categories became for the NPA a model of the concepts their certification program would have to include. But how best to apply those concepts to a new certification for the IT industry? The NPA decided that before it could answer this question, it needed to create the infrastructure of a certifying organization that would systematically consider the issues. For the appropriate infrastructure, the NPA again looked to industry examples.

Eventually, the NPA Board of Directors established the following groups to guide the process. A certification review counsel (CRC) and a certification advisory committee (CAC) were formed in late 1993. The CRC's technical specialists are analyzing certification programs already in the marketplace. They will review any certification proposals submitted to the board of directors by the CAC.

The CAC's job is to involve the six groups that the NPA believes itself best suited to represent: customers and end users, IT professionals, vendors and manufacturers, other associations, educational institutions, and government. While the ways in which the NPA can serve these groups will evolve over time, the initial emphasis for each is clear.

The needs of the customer and the users of technology are an important starting point for the association to address. The NPA wants to better understand what customers are looking for in a computer professional and what challenges they face as they try to use technology productively.

What challenges are IT professionals—the individual members of the NPA—facing, and how can those be addressed through certification? According to Bruce Law, NPA's director of marketing, the NPA has chosen to focus on the individual because it believes that he or she is the "lowest common denominator" in the industry, or the point at which service actually happens.

Some associations link vendors or other associations or channels. Law says, "The NPA focuses on individuals and empowers them by providing the services they need to be current and active in their profession." For that reason, the NPA emphasizes meetings of professionals at the local level.

Still, IT vendors are among the most important audiences for NPA programs. As Law says, "Vendors are critical to the whole puzzle because they have the technology. You can't make a certification relevant to the needs of society without that link."

Geddes says that vendors such as Microsoft, Banyan, Novell, Lotus, and others are responsible for much of the activity within the CAC. "Vendors understand that their technologies are part of a larger picture. Each has its own certification, but now they are searching for the synergies between their individual programs."

Regarding other associations, Geddes says that information technology affects many professions and many associations, some within the IT industry and some not. Many of their concerns, he believes, can be addressed through certification. "Our responsibility," he says, "is to determine where we have synergy with these associations and to partner with them."

As to educational institutions, Geddes says that no one organization has been providing leadership to higher education institutions. As a result, "Educational institutions hang their hat on IT vendors, associations, or their own research and study. Some follow a single vendor and some follow a major service provider." To bring some consistency to networking as a profession, the NPA hopes to become an organizer of information technology knowledge for universities.

To accomplish this, the NPA is providing IT laboratories to universities. Geddes believes that offering faculty an opportunity to work with advanced technology gives them the understanding they need to reshape IT curricula for the future.

Government is a final and essential customer of an NPA certification program. Geddes says, "As governments try to advance their societies, they need the help of information architecture supported by IT professionals. The NPA is asking, 'How can we help government meet their challenges through a professional certification?'"

The NPA also hopes to promote self-regulation of the information technology industry through certification so that, where possible, government regulation of the industry can be avoided. "We want to provide leadership to IT professionals and help them to take the future into their own hands," says Geddes. Bruce Law agrees. "The NPA aims to keep the profession off the government worry list," he says.

Still, as a worldwide organization, the NPA recognizes that government regulation of IT professionals is inevitable for some of its members. Where government proposes regulations, the NPA hopes to be an important advisor about what those regulations should be. The NPA message to governments, says Geddes, is "Please have us involved in legislation. We understand the issues and the challenges of the profession."

When can we expect an NPA certification? According to Geddes, as of January 1995, "We're coming down the stretch to launch the certification program itself. But we're still concerned about the process and advancing things responsibly. We haven't locked on a date yet."

The thoughtful beginnings of the NPA certification bode well for its future. They also suggest the organization's seriousness of purpose in becoming an organizing force for the whole of the IT industry—one that works well for each of its varied and wide-spread constituent groups.

Forces promoting
certification

CHAPTER 2

T HE number of certification testing programs has grown rapidly in the information technology (IT) industry within the past five years. Today, more than 40 leading computer-industry vendors and their customers use certification results to help manage their businesses.

Vendors and many IT associations offer a wide range of exams that test fundamental technical skills as well as product-specific knowledge. IT certifications test skills in networking technologies, operating systems, client/server, databases, developmental tools, and many applications.

The IT certifications in the marketplace represent 11 professions common to the industry. These are network administrator, network engineer, service technician, instructor, sales representative, office personnel, application specialist, application developer, system administrator, system operator, and system engineer.

The popularity of certification is suggested by the number of professionals being certified by Novell and Microsoft, the first and second most active vendors in the certification arena. Novell has certified more than 90,000 IT professionals on Novell products and technologies as of January 1995. It certifies approximately 7500 more each month, and Novell reports that the growth curve has steepened dramatically over the last year. Microsoft counts more than 13,000 Microsoft-certified professionals as of October 1994 and is certifying another 1000 every month.

Drake's growth figures from first quarter 1993 to first quarter 1994 represent well the explosion of interest in certification programs across technologies, particularly in the areas of networking and operating systems.

Computer industry certification is driven by the same forces promoting certification elsewhere: technology changes, business pressures, and government initiatives. For the IT industry, rapid changes in technology are the most significant factors spurring the growth of certification. These three forces create pressures for performance on vendors of software and hardware, their resellers, individual professionals, and end-user organizations. They also

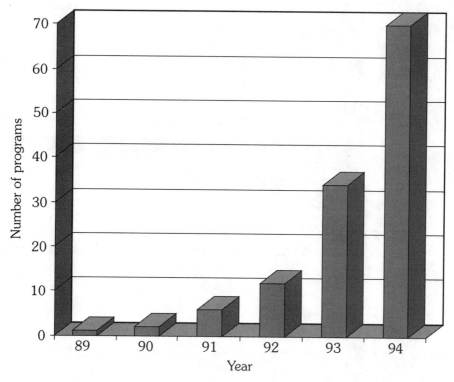

Figure 2-1

Drake certification program growth from 1989 to 1994

strongly influence the industry associations that represent individual professionals and those that represent the industry as a whole.

Technology changes

For many companies the days of mainframes are long gone. Soon the days of personal computers operating independently on the desktops of workers will be gone, too. The introduction of PCs by IBM in the early 1980s revolutionized computer use and increased productivity. At the same time, however, it created islands of software, custom applications, and data. For companies to realize the full potential of these resources, they needed to connect them so that access to the software, data, and applications could be shared among users.

Figure 2-2

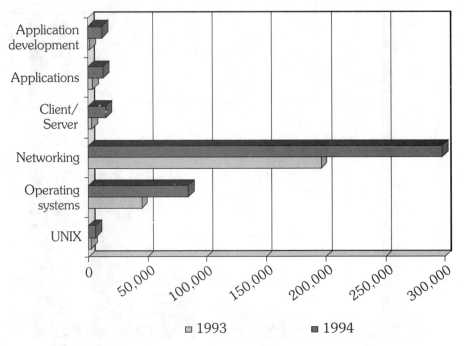

□ 1993   ■ 1994

Drake certification testing growth in seven areas from 1993 to 1994

LANs, WANs, and client/server architectures have developed over the past decade to answer the need for shared resources, creating demand for new skills for IT professionals. At the same time, more software packages and more hardware are being offered by a growing number of vendors, and the life cycles of those products are shrinking down to months rather than years. The result is that networks are becoming more complex as the elements to be linked together multiply. Programmers and network administrators are now faced with the increasingly difficult job of making a galaxy of diverse elements work well with one another as if they had been designed to do that all along.

One solution to these complex issues is the advent of new client/server tools, like PowerBuilder and Microsoft Access. These tools allow hundreds of PC users to access a central computer, which acts as a traffic cop directing each of the users to the programs and data they need without interfering with the work of other users. With

Figure 2-3

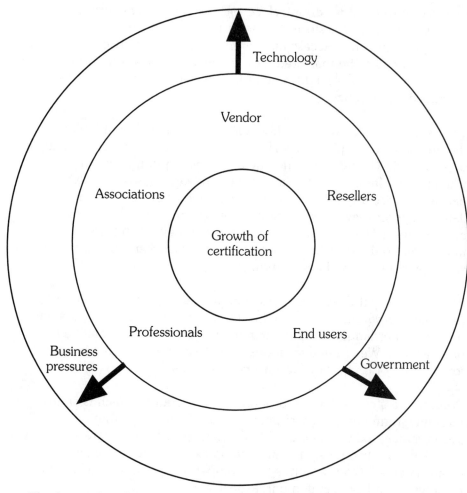

The forces that drive certification growth in the information technology (IT) industry

these tools, the central file server even mediates the work of other database servers that might already reside on the network, such as Oracle, Sybase, DB2, or SQL Server.

Using tools like Access requires programmers, service technicians, and network administrators to learn a variety of new skills. For example, Access uses its own programming language, another language for creating macros, and SQL Query Language. It also

requires learning a design interface for onscreen forms, printed reports, and tables for storing information. At the same time, many of the programs that Access must work with on the network also have tools that need to be mastered. For example, to use a graphics program with Access might require knowledge of special tools for downloading graphics.

This is just one illustration of how technological evolution multiplies the demands being placed on IT professionals. Elliott Masie, president of The Masie Center, a technology and learning think tank in Cambridge, Massachusetts, says, "Every release of a new software package, every upgrade to a suite, every migration to a new form of database access, every expansion of networking capacity, every consideration of a new operating system, and every shift from mainframe to desktop focus yields a need for workers to learn new skills, procedures, and even attitudes."

Paul Brook of HRSoft says that when he began programming 18 years ago, programmers needed to know only one operating system, one computer language, and a few utilities already integrated, all from one vendor. "We created solutions in that system with little concern for how to coordinate the various components."

Programmers can still write programs from scratch, which is simpler than integrating existing technologies. But Brook says that programmers today rarely do. More often, they build programs on top of existing applications, "hooking complex tools into complex environments." One reason is that competitive pressures today often make working from scratch unreasonable.

For example, Brook tells how programmers at HRSoft decided to undertake a complex development effort. They had been writing a human resource software package in C++ until they realized that many of the features they wished to build into the product were available in the already existing Access package. In the race to get their product to market, they bootstrapped Access onto their product—a job that required a dozen programmers to train themselves to Access literacy within one month. The demands of competition force companies to embrace the new technologies, despite their increasing complexity. But the technologies cannot

deliver on their promise without qualified people to operate and to service them.

The burden of interconnectivity rests mainly with the software vendors who write applications for networks. But computer professionals at every level, including programmers, administrators, and service technicians, share responsibility for making networks usable. The organization called Open User Recommended Solutions (OURS)—a group of vendors, solution providers, and end users—puts it this way: "If organizations ignore the human factor in the client/server equation, they risk building a 'house of cards' that, in the long-term, might not be able to support the initiatives that the business requires."

Certification is one way to address "the human factor." As Brook says, "There are now so many details to be aware of. It doesn't help to know the details coming out of school either, because very soon the details you've learned are out of date."

While experience can be a good teacher, experience on paper can be misleading. Brook says, for example, that one could claim eight months experience working with Access but have worked on only a few small areas of it. Certification shows the range of skills an individual has with a particular technology. "The certificate doesn't prove that you know how to solve problems," he says, "but it shows that you've studied all the details and you've got all the nuts and bolts together to solve problems."

One vendor representative takes the problem to a higher level of seriousness when he says, "Vendors, resellers, and even service technicians will all be out of business soon if we don't find some way to certify all of our knowledge, because the systems are just becoming that complicated."

Meeting the need for new skills

Robert Half International, in its 1995 Salary Guide, reports that "the hiring outlook in the information technology employment area is bright. The need for professionals who can design and implement

advanced systems will remain strong as companies of all sizes continue investing more freely in technology."

"Nationally, companies are reporting demand for microcomputer programmers, programmer analysts, and systems administrators. Not surprisingly, these positions will experience the highest salary increases in 1995."

Robert Half finds firms investing in network technology in record numbers, resulting in very strong demand for administrators and engineers who specialize in local area network (LAN) and wide area network (WAN) environments. In regions with a shortage of these experts, firms are paying higher salaries and, in many cases, at least a portion of relocation costs for top candidates. The demand for networking skills is predicted to grow.

The U.S. Department of Labor also sees a bright future for information technology skills. It considers computing the nation's second fastest-growing industry, with a projected annual growth rate of 4.4 percent through the year 2005.

Opportunities abound for well-trained computer professionals. But professionals in the near future will need more skills than ever before. The OURS Multivendor Education Task Force study highlights the rapidly changing skill needs in the computer industry. Its July 1993 study surveyed 150 information technology professionals from a variety of job roles, including executives, front-line managers, and staff. Respondents represented a variety of organizations including banks, insurance companies, manufacturers, service providers, and state and local government agencies. The study also drew from the Gartner Group's survey of 15,000 IT professionals.

The results point to a dramatic shift in the roles and responsibilities of computing professionals. They strongly suggest a need for training and for the certification of skills. Here are some of the key findings of the study for five areas of operation:

✳ 1. Data center operation

IT departments will be changing their skills along with their tools to better exploit advanced technologies. For example, the new corporate

environments are both smaller and more open, in the sense that computing is no longer an isolated function, but one that connects every worker in the enterprise. IT professionals within the corporation need to become more responsive and service-oriented, able to deliver the solutions their corporate users require.

At the same time, respondents to the survey expect that the importance and complexity of networks will soon force their companies to consolidate data centers with LAN and WAN groups.

Data center managers see themselves as increasingly responsible for LAN, WAN, and data processing simultaneously. They believe these services will not be provided through traditional mainframe technologies, but more often through server operating systems such as UNIX and Microsoft's Windows NT. To support the transition, OURS concludes that the new IT professional will have to be "retrained in programming disciplines, management disciplines, and the tools that will enable this new architecture."

The top skills that respondents felt they would need in the data center of the future are:

➤ UNIX operating systems and systems programming

➤ Capacity planning in distributed environments

➤ Host and server scheduling procedures

➤ Disaster recovery and backup for PCs

➤ Graphical user interfaces and artificial intelligence for automated operations

✳ 2. Applications development

Respondents to the survey predicted a change in job roles for applications developers between 1993 and 1997. For example, programmers are increasingly able to program through pictures, icons, and objects. In essence, the system generates the code. This rise of computer-aided software engineering (CASE) will decrease the programmer's need to code and test, while increasing his or her need to understand the business; plan, analyze, and design software; and measure the results in productivity.

✳ 3. LAN operations

LAN administrators expect to be increasingly viewed as "mission critical." The LAN is the first layer of access into the corporate computing hierarchy and will need the same level of integrity, security, recoverability, and scalability offered on today's mainframes. To accomplish this, LAN professionals will need new technical abilities along with management skills.

Respondents expect to spend less time on rote, labor-intensive functions such as adds, moves, and changes. They expect to spend more time on strategy, including measuring performance; handling software distribution; and managing applications, disaster recovery, and security.

The top skills needed to support the LAN environment will be:

> ➤ LAN process/traffic flow analysis

> ➤ Directory services maintenance

> ➤ PC and network operating systems skills

✳ 4. WAN operations

Those working with WAN communications will need to learn a variety of skills for working with client/server, internetwork, and LAN technologies. At the same time, like the LAN professional, the WAN operator will rise in strategic perspective.

For example, new technologies such as asynchronous transfer mode (ATM) and switched multimegabit data service (SMDS) will compel WAN managers to rethink the sources of their services, the designs of their networks, and the financial impact of redesigning their WANs. In the future, they will be less concerned with ordering bandwidth and more concerned with understanding the applications requirements of the business.

The top skills in this area will include:

> ➤ Negotiation

> ➤ Network management tools

> ➤ Business project management

✳ **5. Architecture and planning**

Systems architects of the near future will need to create "nontechnical" systems to better communicate with users. They'll need to build systems that work easily and promote productivity.

Among the top skills needed in this area will be:

➤ Business modeling

➤ Technology transfer

➤ Migration planning

⇨ OURS report calls for retraining

Respondents said they see their skills retraining needs increasing, but 49 percent didn't expect their company's budget to expand to meet this need. Most also felt that their company's training plans were focused on product training rather than training in process and concepts.

The OURS/Gartner Group report found comfort in the respondents' recognition of the need for training and the fact that the skills needed for the future are definable. However, it lamented that budgets might not support the coming demand for training, and that today's training programs don't meet all of the needs to come.

According to OURS, "The technology shift is undeniable and unstoppable, and many of the new technologies that will comprise these new applications will be new to IT organizations. With these innovations, IT organizations will need to retrain their existing staff and seek new employees with skill sets that are currently in rare supply."

The report cautioned that failure to train properly for the future might lead to serious consequences, including failure to assimilate the new technologies, unproductive users and IT professionals, and a fall-off in productivity.

OURS recommends that managers and trainers design training programs for IT professionals that are relevant, timely, and flexible. It

encourages senior managers to recognize that training is a necessary investment for the long run.

Certification is one answer to OURS study concerns

Elaine Bond, a Chase Fellow and former chairperson of OURS, says, "Certification can play a very important role in implying, if not guaranteeing, that the desired skill levels have been achieved." Bond says that certification has not yet proven its full potential; she believes that potential will emerge in the coming years and that certification will continue to grow in importance for the information technology industry.

Certification is a valuable response to the OURS report's concerns about the training needs for IT professionals. For example, the report calls on organizations to "find innovative new ways to leverage training dollars to reach all those that require retraining."

Certification has shown itself to be a powerful way to leverage training dollars. Training is most cost-effective when the organization is clear about what skills it requires, what skills it has, and what skills it needs to bring into the organization. Certification helps clarify all three issues for the IT department.

Skills competency as defined by certification programs helps organizations understand exactly what skills are needed to perform particular tasks. At the same time, the product and systems certifications held by its employees and contractors are a powerful aid in inventorying the skills at hand. When bringing new skills into the organization, applicants with certifications have an added credential that helps the hiring official understand their true capabilities.

Business pressures

Many key players in the IT industry are responding to business pressures by using certification programs. Certification's usefulness in

addressing a variety of business pressures is illustrated in responses by vendors, resellers, and end users to focus group interviews sponsored by the International Data Corporation (IDC). The study from early 1994 identified five factors contributing to the growth of certification in the IT industry:

➤ Vendors' desires to ensure a level of quality from parties who sell, service, and support their products

➤ Reseller complaints regarding the redundant training and certification they must receive on vendor products

➤ User demands for a screening tool or "gatekeeper" of service skills

➤ The federal government mandate for the United States to be more competitive by developing standards of competency

➤ Increased integration of rapidly changing technologies, and the need for computing professionals to update their skill sets frequently

In a separate study conducted by Dataquest Worldwide Services Group, information technology managers were asked to rate the importance of having certified computing professionals and reasons for investing in certification. They answered:

➤ To improve productivity

➤ To improve access to vendor support services

➤ To gain a service marketing advantage

➤ Because it's required by vendors

➤ Because it's required by customers

➤ To achieve lower operating costs

The responses to both the IDC and Dataquest studies suggest that business pressures impact each of the IT industries major players: vendors and resellers, individual professionals, end-user organizations, and the associations representing these interests. Pressures for higher productivity and better use of human resources are pushing these groups to embrace certification. The motivations of each group are discussed in detail in Chapters 3 and 4.

 # Vendors and resellers

The ability of vendors to survive and thrive in the coming years will depend on the ability of their customers to buy more sophisticated, complicated, interwoven products. Service quality must be high to support customers' use of those new products. If the marketplace is not receiving adequate technical support, resales will suffer and business will dry up.

Channel managers of vendor products use certification as quality control on agents who are selling, servicing, and supporting their information technology. But certification not only controls service providers, it also empowers them by making them more competitive.

Empowering the service channel is increasingly important because profits in the industry are shifting away from hardware and software toward service and consulting. Professionals in service can gain advantage by developing and marketing an inventory of skills required by demanding customers with increasing service requirements. For that reason, certification of reseller staff is encouraged and sometimes required by vendors. Where it is not required, resellers often pursue it on their own to gain competitive advantage.

Certification programs can also reduce operating costs for vendors by allowing them to offload technical support to more highly qualified resellers. It can also reduce operating costs for resellers by identifying for them the crucial pieces of knowledge needed for success in selling or servicing particular products or technologies. Some industry programs such as the A+ certification program also test fundamental service skills common to servicing a great variety of products. Preparing for the A+ exam can therefore save a reseller the effort of pursuing several other training programs with redundant curricula.

 # Professionals

IT industry professionals have personal reasons for seeking certification. The designation is an additional, objective indicator that

they can produce the specific results that employers are demanding. Many professionals and many companies believe that certified IT professionals have a competitive advantage for advancing in their profession, advancing in their current job, and preparing for new jobs. Certified professionals are also often rewarded with higher salaries.

End users

End users are another powerful force driving certification growth. The president of Drake Prometric, William Dorman, says that certification will grow because organizations want to take advantage of emerging technologies to boost their own productivity.

The hunger for those technologies is shown in industry sales figures. For example, the market for client/server products and services alone is forecasted to reach $44 billion in 1995. As sales figures for new technologies continue to grow, so will the number of end users requiring technical certifications from their own staffs and from service providers.

Associations

In the IT industry, associations mirror the concerns of all of the players mentioned here, though the emphasis varies. For example, the concern for the interests of vendors and resellers, while evident in all IT industry associations, are particularly evident in CompTIA. Their A+ certification program, described in Chapter 3, is designed to satisfy the needs of service providers for higher skill sets.

The concerns of individual IT professionals in a variety of professional roles is represented by the Network Professional Association, described in Chapter 1. Inevitably, though, each of the IT industry associations represents the needs of all of the industry players, and certification programs begun by the associations help all those players to handle business pressures and grow their competitive advantage and profitability.

 # Productivity pressures: Closing the competency gap

Research shows, surprisingly, that we have thus far gained little real increase in productivity by using computer technology. The problem, however, might be less the fault of technology and more the fault of our inability to use it to its full potential.

According to Alan Hupp, vice president of marketing for Drake Prometric, end-user organizations fail to make full use of the potential of information technology already in the marketplace. The gap between technology potential and the benefits that organizations are deriving from technology is what Hupp calls the "competency gap." By industry estimates, this gap is costing American business millions in lost productivity each year.

Figure 2-4

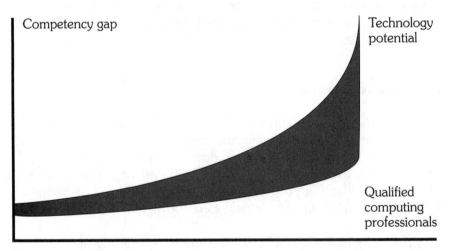

The competency gap

The competency gap, Hupp says, can be closed only when organizations have access to the right skills at the right time in the right place. Certified IT professionals, he believes, are the needed ingredient for ensuring access to those skills.

Randy Biggs of Training Services International agrees with Hupp. He says, "If we don't get more people out there to integrate the technology we already have, we won't grow the technology business. We need to have trained people in place to grow the industry. Certification is taking us in this direction."

Using technology's full potential is a more complex challenge today than in the recent past. According to Hupp, the needs of the end user have become more sophisticated and increasingly hard to satisfy. "In the Sixties, it was simple," he says. "We bought from one vendor, using one platform, with few solutions available to choose from, and MIS was a centralized function within the organization. In the Nineties we have multiple vendors that we work with, using multiple platforms, providing multiple solutions, and each department wants to do its own thing. They don't want an MIS department to dictate to them about standards and what systems they should use." The expanding technical needs, he says, might go unfulfilled because of insufficient numbers of qualified individuals who can service, support, install, and maintain the systems.

The current need for downsizing while increasing productivity also demands access to the right technical skills. Pauline Mustazza of Hewlett-Packard says that certification is becoming increasingly important as companies are downsizing. Companies are trying to increase productivity, and people are being asked to do more with seemingly fewer resources. She says, "The end user is investing a lot of dollars, and they have to be sure that solutions will fit their needs and allow them to grow. They don't want to be put in a position where they will have to spend money to undo mistakes."

While the demand for specialized skills grows, the lack of skilled IT professionals is becoming increasingly apparent. For example, a recent study in *Client/Server Economics* magazine asked technical managers, "If you're going to be moving to client/server technology, what is the single biggest obstacle you face in making that migration?" Issues that surfaced included costs, security, and lack of standards. The chief concern, however, was lack of qualified personnel.

The demand is far outstripping the supply of qualified computer people. Robert Half International commented on this in a recent

salary guide: "As recessionary impacts fade, investment is likely to accelerate and to increase the demand for IT experts in the next few years. The best will be hired very quickly."

What companies are really looking for are job-relevant, up-to-date skills that can be put to use immediately. The value of computing degrees is somewhat diminished in the current environment. In contrast, certification programs are proliferating to verify attainment of skills on the emerging technologies.

For example, certification was initially promoted as a way to ensure the skills of networking professionals, and there are still many networking-focused programs in the marketplace today. Of the 75 IT certification programs administered by Drake today, 24 are networking related.

But the growth in terms of percentage increase has been in the area of applications development tools, client/server, UNIX, and open systems. Certification is also starting to mirror the growth in different technologies; as new products become popular, certification on those products follows.

Certification is helping to increase the supply of IT professionals with skills on a broad range of current and emerging technologies. It is also helping organizations to identify those professionals and to use their skills to close the competency gap and to achieve competitive advantage.

Government influence

IT industry certification programs have gained impetus from federal government initiatives to define and to develop the skills needed to improve America's productivity. But IT industry certification is, at the same time, growing in response to another set of potential government initiatives, primarily at the state level. These are initiatives that would impose government licensing requirements on the industry.

All industries either regulate themselves adequately to protect the public welfare or have government regulations imposed on them to help them in that job. As the information technology industry has become more

complex and also more important in the life of society, the issue of potential government regulation for the industry is surfacing.

The industry might be at a crossroads where it needs to choose either improved self-regulation or government regulation. Many believe that self-regulation is the preferred alternative and that certification programs are a valuable and effective means of self-regulation for the IT industry.

One way or another, the public interest needs to be protected. With the advent of networks, the public is increasingly concerned that local mistakes could create widespread problems. Nuclear power plants, chemical factories, hospitals, and other crucial facilities are increasingly run by computers and computer networks. Computer mistakes in a hospital can cause harm or even death to patients. Computer mistakes in government can cause the loss of data worth millions of dollars to the public.

The flow of information, controlled by computers, is lifeblood to business; its interruption, even briefly, can cause significant losses. For the public well-being, much of what computer professionals do is now "mission-critical."

The public has been repeatedly shocked in recent years by the immensity of damage that can be caused by errors of an individual or small group of individuals. The nuclear power plant disaster at Three Mile Island, the oil spill from the Exxon *Valdez*, and the contamination of Bhopal, India, from a chemical accident have increased awareness of the need for highly trained people operating in mission-critical environments.

As a result, the public has called for tighter regulation of industries and jobs that affect the public welfare. Some have even proposed mandatory licensing for computer professionals. The issue was raised in 1991 when the New Jersey State Assembly presented a bill to regulate and license "software designers." The bill was killed in the state senate after IT managers, vendors, and independent programmers teamed up to oppose it. AT&T, which employs about 5000 information technology managers in New Jersey, even threatened to remove them all from the state if the bill had passed.

But Robert J. Melford, chairman of the public policy committee at the Institute of Electrical and Electronics Engineers (IEEE) says, "I expect some form of mandatory competency validation is inevitable, at least for safety-critical software, because society will want some control of the profession."

Some believe that over the next decade the information technology industry will see a variety of approaches to performance standards. Included might be state licensing, certification, regulation of specific industries, and quality standards from the International Organization for Standardization.

A joint task force of the IEEE and the Association for Computing Machinery (ACM) is studying such issues as skills, education, reeducation, and standards of professional practice. The target date for a report is October 1995. The ACM's Special Interest Group on Computers and Society also has a task force studying certification and licensing, and it plans to report in June 1995.

Other organizations looking at the need for training and quality control for the IT industry include the Network Professionals Association (NPA), the Computing Technology Industry Association (CompTIA), and the Institute for Certification of Computer Professionals (ICCP). Certification programs of these industry associations are designed to complement vendor-initiated certification programs in order to advance the skill levels and, in some cases, also the ethical standards for the profession. These programs are being created with a keen awareness of the potential for government intervention. They aim to raise standards of professionalism in order to both grow the profession and better protect the public interest.

Case study: Defending the network at Fort Leavenworth

"Fort Leavenworth is like a small city," says Robert Wright, director of information management for the complex. The fort includes dozens of "activities"—small companies commanded by a general officer or a colonel. Most of these are connected to the fort's computer network, and each has between 50 and 300 workstations. The fort also includes an army college, whose students and administrators also use

Wright's enterprise network system. The network for which Wright is responsible connects to other forts throughout the country. A mistake made by anyone on the larger network can affect the use of information anywhere throughout the system.

Wright is concerned about the prospect for widespread problems, partly because the scenario has already occurred. Wright tells how an applications developer at a distant fort changed an application. That change caused other applications throughout the network, including at Fort Leavenworth, to suddenly stop working. "It took a long time to find that one out," Wright says.

To deal with the possibly disastrous effects caused by people unqualified to work on networks, Wright turned to certification. He believes that only certification can guarantee the level of network performance he requires from his staff. Wright says that Leavenworth includes every kind of network and every kind of computer sold to the government. A worker here might move from one department to another, having knowledge of one network and be expected to have knowledge of another. "We have no way of knowing if they really do," he says, "unless we certify."

Wright tried years ago to set performance standards to keep the hundreds of workers on the network from causing problems. "We've written down performance standards in the past," he says, "and that helped. But what if workers don't understand the standards?" Certification, he says, shows that they understand what the standards mean and how important they are.

Novell network software is now the main operating software for the fort, and those in responsible positions who are working on the network must be Novell certified. Leavenworth is also considering certifications for those who work with applications such as WordPerfect.

Certification helps Wright as a manager. For example, the credential helps ensure that those assigned to jobs involving crucial work on the network can do the job. If they are not certified when hired and fail to become certified when given the chance, they will not work on the network.

Wright says this is particularly important to him now, as the military and the government are downsizing. When there are reductions in force, he says, the personnel division "stretches qualifications to place into a vacancy someone who would otherwise lose a job." Having

certification requirements ensures that the "stretch of qualifications" will not cause disaster, and that Wright won't have someone placed in a job "whom it takes years to get rid of."

When making hiring decisions, Wright considers certifications and experience. "Real-world experience is the most important feature you can have," he says, "but it's hard to judge it on what people tell you." Wright tells how he hired someone several years ago (before the certification requirement) who claimed extensive network experience. The worker performed poorly and eventually admitted that he'd never worked on a true network but only on computers connected by modem.

For Wright, the results of certification exams are important hard evidence of knowledge and skill. "I've been to a lot of software classes, and I always think I've learned it all. But when I get back to work I find that I haven't. A certification test proves what you've really learned."

Novell's three levels of certification in combination with other information about a person's skill and judgment help create a knowledge-based hierarchy of job functions in the information department. Only those in the networking section actually get to be certified. Within that group, those performing the basic administrative tasks on the network hold the Certified Novell Administrator certification (CNA). The next level of responsibility—designing and maintaining the networks—goes to those with the Certified Novell Engineer certification (CNE). The highest level of administration and troubleshooting responsibility goes to the holders of Novell's Enterprise CNE certificate (ECNE). At Leavenworth, certification requirements are written right into the job description and help the personnel division define the government pay grade attached to it.

Wright believes training dollars spent on certifications have been good investments. He's never been disappointed with the knowledge of a worker returning with a Novell certification. He credits this partly to the training company they use and partly to his decision to send only the best candidates to certification programs.

Certification is a good use of training dollars for one other reason. Wright has found that if a worker can't be certified, it's a good indicator that he won't work out in that environment. After that, the worker is likely to leave before further training dollars are invested in him.

Wright's employees like certification. In fact, he says that they all seem to want it. People working in career fields that lead to

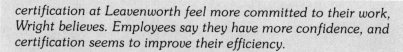
certification at Leavenworth feel more committed to their work, Wright believes. Employees say they have more confidence, and certification seems to improve their efficiency.

Wright has found only one negative consequence of certifying his workers— the certified ones are in such demand that business and industry sometimes snatch them away. He is, unfortunately, not the only manager to have discovered the benefits of certification. Rather, his experience shows what is true for many.

Certification is a positive help for managers when hiring and assigning jobs, particularly in a time of downsizing. It can be used to structure responsibility and pay, and employees like it. More importantly for Wright and many others, certification not only helps conduct the daily course of mundane work, but steers the enterprise away from mistakes that can seriously disrupt it or bring it to a halt.

3

Vendors and resellers

CHAPTER 3

C ERTIFICATION programs serve the interests of all players in the information technology (IT) industry. This chapter examines the interlocking interests of IT industry vendors and their resellers in the distribution chain. Vendors have been among the first into the IT certification arena, and they have used certification strategically to grow their businesses. Resellers have figured prominently in vendor planning because they are the crucial link with the marketplace.

Certification programs help vendors better manage the distribution channel and gain a variety of business advantages. But every benefit enjoyed by vendors—enhanced image, improved customer confidence, reduced costs—accrues as well to resellers who invest in certifying their staffs. For that reason, vendors have found resellers to be willing participants in their certification programs, and the two have become partners in certification. That partnership has been formalized in the A+ certification program, described at the end of this chapter.

 # The vendor perspective

In the past five years, the rapid growth of interest in certification programs for IT professionals has been led in large part by software and hardware vendors. Leading IT development vendors have created certification programs on their technologies in order to develop expertise in both the reseller community and the end-user community. Certification has served vendors well, and the number of vendor-sponsored programs continues to increase.

International Data Corporation, which has studied certification, reports: "Ever since Novell established the Certified Novell Engineer (CNE) and Certified Novell Instructor (CNI) programs in 1989, the industry has latched onto the idea of certification as a reliable measurement for product expertise."

Dozens of other technology vendors have followed Novell's lead and developed certification programs on their own products. Certification has emerged as an important way for vendors to control quality throughout their distribution channels, ensuring that resellers, service

providers, and even their customers have the knowledge to use the products to their full potential. For these vendors, certification means a successful distribution chain and satisfied customers.

Certification helps vendors manage distribution

Sales and service revenues from the distribution chain are the lifeblood of vendors. Vendors rely on distributors, resellers, value-added resellers (VARs), and dealers to represent their products in the marketplace and provide quality service to their end users. Ensuring quality in resellers is more important today than ever because vendors increasingly depend upon new distribution channels to expand their markets and gain broader coverage at a lower cost.

Vendors have discovered that by using certification to qualify individuals who service their customers, repeat and referral business has been improved—both accounting for increased revenues. For example, Carolyn G. Rose, vice president and general manager of Novell Education, says that end-user perceptions of Novell have grown more positive as they've had increasing contact with and support by the "growing army" of Novell certification holders. She says, "The larger the group who understand and support our products, the larger the group who will buy them."

The importance of resellers is also increasing as the market for hardware is becoming saturated and the demand for quality service is growing dramatically. Pauline Mustazza of Hewlett-Packard says that the channel partner is crucial to HP and to the whole industry. She says, "All of us are deciding, as the market changes, that our money will come more and more from the service area, not from hardware. Our resellers add value on top of the hardware in terms of software and systems integration. Having them certified in the product is so important to us."

Certification is an important means of increasing product knowledge as well as specific service and support skills. The importance of such programs increases as the systems increase in complexity. Vendors

need to be assured that their current and future channel partners are up to speed on products and can represent them well to existing and prospective customers.

Clients need resellers who understand the products and how they can produce the results customers are looking for. Mustazza says, "If a channel partner is certified, the customer can have greater confidence that the right system solution will be recommended. When channel partners know the HP products well, they can help integrate them into heterogeneous environments, thereby protecting the customers' investment."

The increase in the number of certified professionals means not only that the service provider is more likely to be knowledgeable about the products, but that he or she is also likely to be familiar with the client's own environment. Vendors say that certification allows their customers to have an expert to work with on a local basis. Certified service providers, they believe, have a more detailed knowledge of the environment they're supporting, and so provide better support.

Vendor certification programs also try to include those most familiar with their end users—corporate MIS departments. Elliott Masie, president of The Masie Center, a technology think tank in Cambridge, Massachusetts, says, "If you have a problem with a database or network and can't get good support from your internal MIS department, you might end up blaming the product developer. Certification programs are aiming to build an envelope of competency and support surrounding each major system and application suite."

Quality service from certified technicians, however, is a must, since the vendor's reputation is on the line. One network systems architect comments that when a service provider is certified, it's no longer only the service provider's name that will be judged by his or her work, but the vendor's name as well. Nancy Lewis, director of education and certification for Microsoft, speaks for many when she says, "The risks are greater if we don't certify our channel partner because then there's no assurance of success."

Vendors understand that they need to build ties with resellers so that the reseller is a more nearly perfect extension of the vendor into the marketplace. Novell, for example, developed its certification programs both to ensure that its products performed in the marketplace and to establish a link between Novell standards and policies and the service provider community.

Channel partners are encouraged, through a variety of means, to go the certification route. Often, the vendor stratifies channel partners based on the number of certified professionals on their staff. For example, Banyan has created two main categories for its resellers: Premier Network Integrators (PNIs) and Authorized Network Integrators (ANIs). To earn the higher-level PNI designation, a reseller needs to have two Certified Banyan Engineers (CBEs) on staff. To earn the ANI designation, the reseller needs to have two Certified Banyan Specialists (CBSs) on staff.

According to Carol Greer, Banyan's manager of marketing services, only PNIs typically service the larger clients or those with complex needs. Providing higher-level support to customers who need it has helped keep customers happy. But Greer says that the resellers have also taken to the designations enthusiastically and use them to differentiate themselves from their competition.

 # Certification helps vendors distribute technical support

Certification of resellers is also an important means to share the growing responsibility of technical support. As sales of products increase, so does the demand for qualified technical support associated with the product.

As the number of product users increases, the responsibility for supporting them all becomes too much for vendors to handle alone. If vendors assume the responsibility for answering service calls directly, support costs skyrocket and profitability suffers. This is especially true as systems and the questions concerning them become more complex. So vendors use certification to empower both the channel

and end-user organizations with skills and knowledge to address increasingly complex support questions.

Scott Edwards of Cisco Systems says that the bottom line of certification is to identify professionals who can be self-supporting. Cisco-certified professionals, he says, lower costs for Cisco by handling technical support calls themselves in the field. Also, he says, when they use the privileged access to Cisco technical support staff that the certification provides them, the certified professionals "give us better information to work with so that the problem is easier and quicker for us to resolve." Edwards says that the reseller also has service support costs lowered by identifying, through certification, the people qualified to front customer calls.

Novell has also reduced its support responsibilities significantly through certification. The company estimates, for example, that each CNE in the field manages 15 calls per year that would otherwise have come in to the Novell call center. With more than 60,000 CNEs (as of January 1995), this spares Novell approximately 900,000 calls each year.

Microsoft has off-loaded some of their technical support demands through certification programs as well. Celeste Boyer says that Microsoft classifies and tries to cost out each customer technical support problem. She says that the number of problems surfacing is reduced as more Microsoft certified professionals enter the field.

Certification exams test for the knowledge needed to resolve customer concerns. Microsoft hopes that in time, with more certified service providers, whole classes of problems will stop ringing into the Microsoft call center.

By reducing technical support calls, certification streamlines operations for vendors. One respondent to an International Data Corporation survey said, "Essentially, the dollars spent on training and certification testing represent a cost savings by having the support off-loaded. We can concentrate on developing best-in-class products, and our solution providers can concentrate on offering best-in-class service and support. It's a win-win situation."

Certification helps vendors make the best use of training dollars

Another force encouraging certification is the need for vendors to get a better return from their training dollars. With budgets squeezed, vendors want their training to have the most impact with the least expenditure.

Carolyn Rose says that market research connected with certification training has helped Novell focus on the tasks that people actually perform in their jobs to create courses more focused on job tasks. Those courses are helping Novell to support its worldwide expansion plans. For example, when Novell developed its CNE program, it decided that while it would not require CNE candidates to take training, those candidates who desired training should take it through a network of Novell-authorized training centers. These centers employ Certified Novell Instructors using Novell-developed courseware. Carolyn Rose says, "We needed this system in place so that when people went for CNE training, that training would be high-level."

Microsoft benefited from similar market research two years ago. At that time Microsoft took a close look at its new certification program as well as the tasks and requirements of its clients. It asked some hard questions. For example, if someone was a Microsoft Certified professional on Excel, what did that really mean? Could they use Excel? Support others on Excel? Develop with Excel?

The research findings led Microsoft to abandon the emphasis in its certification programs on product features and functions and to reorient the emphasis toward job functions. Today, all Microsoft certifications and their related training programs are focused on the tasks that a professional performs. For example, a Microsoft Certified Systems Engineer needs to show skill in implementing, maintaining, troubleshooting, and supporting Microsoft products. "There is a tie-in to the products," Celeste Boyer says, "but always from a job function perspective."

Boyer says that the new angle pleases both candidates and end-user companies. She says candidates are thankful to find themselves measured on the right things, and the companies who certify their technicians on Microsoft products are seeing more of the value in certification. According to Boyer, "They see that it's not just a marketing ploy, but that we're giving them a tool they can use."

Certification also provides focus and efficiency to reseller training departments. Nancy Lewis says that Microsoft's Authorized Support Centers really value certification for the way it sets goals for their training programs. She says that the centers are telling Microsoft, "Now we know what to train our people on and, with certification, we know when we are done." Lewis says, "That sounds like a simple thing, but it can help you to be much more efficient with your money."

Training curricula of certification programs can tell trainers when they are done with training. Just as importantly, for some experienced candidates, it can tell them that no training is required. They already have the knowledge and skill to pass the certification exam.

To require or not to require training as a prerequisite for certification is sometimes a difficult question for vendors. Certification training generates some incremental revenues for vendors, but most have chosen not to require courses for completion of their certification programs.

Rather, most certification programs recognize that experience has been an adequate teacher for some of their test candidates and, in those cases, the certifying organization can make the most efficient use of training dollars by requiring only that certification candidates pass their exams rather than sit through their training programs.

For example, Digital Equipment Corporation's Bruce Betz says, "We encourage people to take the training; however, if they feel that they have the product knowledge, then we certainly don't want them in the course; they should just take the test."

Microsoft, too, does not require training to earn its certifications. Susan Dwyer, certification marketing group manager, says that

Microsoft's only interest is in whether the individual can perform the job. How the individual gets that knowledge is less important.

Microsoft also wants to serve customers better by acknowledging what they have learned elsewhere. One way to do that is to avoid redundancy not only in training but in certification exams. Microsoft is talking with CompTIA about how future versions of the A+ exam (discussed in a case study at the end of this chapter) could fit into Microsoft certification testing. Boyer says, "Our goal will always be to give our customers a measurement tool that makes sense to them."

As to ethics, Boyer says that training for ethics would have to include valid and reliable test instruments to determine if ethics are indeed being developed. She says that since certification in the IT industry is so new, the most efficient thing to do now is to concentrate on developing valid and reliable measures of technical core competencies.

Certification programs have clarified training goals for the IT industry by creating training curricula and standards of performance that make sense in the real world. By doing so, they have saved money for vendors and resellers alike. Certification programs have also stimulated discussion about the most meaningful components of knowledge and skill for IT professionals, including the issue of ethics. The industry might be moving to more efficient sharing of training responsibility as new vendor and association-led programs emerge and learn how to work with one another.

At the same time, certification program training curricula and certification exams are helping candidates determine for themselves if they need training or not. This too, is helping vendors and resellers, as well as the candidates themselves, to make more efficient use of their training dollars.

Certification helps vendors by creating knowledgeable end users

So far, certification of IT professionals—those who help others to use IT technologies—has played a more significant role than the certification

of end users. Some believe, however, that certification programs for end users will increase in number. Vendors perceive the end user as part of the skilled community of technology users they hope to create.

Becky Howland of the Software Publishers Association (SPA) says her organization's goal was to create a community of computer professionals that would be well-versed in piracy and software-management issues. She says their programs are for "anyone who has to manage software assets." Those people include microcomputer, MIS/DP, end-user computing, and department managers; computer specialists; computer services and tech support personnel; auditors; and counsel. She says the most common titles for those pursuing SPA certifications are MIS or network administrator.

Susan Dwyer says that Microsoft doesn't view certification as something only for the channel. She says, "We're looking to certify people not only in the channel but in end-customer organizations. While certification is of great value to our solution-provider program, it's not limited to that." An important reason for certifying end users is to increase the number of trained and competent people in the marketplace. Trained end users are more effective and hence more satisfied with the product—an important fact for vendors hoping for resales.

Grace Yeung of Powersoft says that client/server development is a complex and emerging business. "The purpose of the Certified PowerBuilder Developer (CPD) program is to provide a framework for measuring PowerBuilder skills and to help organizations select qualified individuals."

Powersoft goes beyond question-and-answer testing by requiring CPDs to build an application. This approach enables Powersoft to assess application design skills, knowledge of client/server disciplines, and real-world development experience. Powersoft hopes to save customer time and effort and increase their satisfaction with the vendor and the product.

Powersoft has several programs to address the demand for quality developers. The Consulting Partners program ensures that projects for clients are led by Certified PowerBuilder Developers. Organizations can identify CPDs through a public referral list.

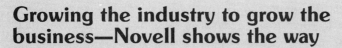

Growing the industry to grow the business—Novell shows the way

Novell has been the front-runner among IT vendors in leveraging certification as a business tactic since it introduced the IT industry's first certification program in 1989. In fact, the company recently certified its 60,000th CNE; another 90,000 CNEs are in training. The company has also recently unveiled ambitious plans for expansion. It hopes to increase the number of users of Novell products and technologies to one billion by the year 2000. Novell is counting on certification to play a key role in supporting that growth.

While certification is a tactic for growth at Novell, it is best understood as part of an underlying strategy. Carolyn G. Rose, vice president and general manager of Novell Education, sums up that strategy this way: "Since this was and still is an industry in its infancy, we have to grow the industry in order to grow our business."

Certification has emerged as one way for Novell to achieve its strategic objectives. Novell's certification programs have benefited all of the players in the IT industry and increased its own revenues as a direct result. Their programs have also become a model followed by dozens of other IT vendors hoping to grow their business through certification while simultaneously promoting the interests of IT professionals, the distributor chain, and end-user organizations.

The grow-the-industry strategy at Novell dates back at least to the time when former president Ray Noorda took the company briefly into the hardware business. Novell produced network interface cards in the early 1980s—just long enough to drive the price down from approximately $300–$400 to $39 each. As the cost of hardware fell, networks became much more accessible and widespread. With that trend underway, Noorda took Novell out of the hardware business and focused it on producing software for the rapidly growing number of networks.

By doing so, Novell soon found itself in the business of educating resellers about its networking technologies. In 1985 Novell created an education department to offer a three-day training course for resellers and system administrators. Education has played a key role in Novell expansion efforts ever since. Its importance emerged forcefully as sales of Novell products doubled and tripled each quarter in the late 1980s.

At that time, the customer support group found itself overwhelmed by incoming calls. Carolyn Rose says Novell recognized at that time that they couldn't continue to do it all by themselves through investing directly in the infrastructure of facilities and personnel. Instead, they decided to leverage their business by empowering resellers to field all but the most difficult support questions.

But relinquishing support responsibilities to the resellers increased the need for educating those resellers properly. Novell had to address new questions: "If the resellers are now going to play a larger role in representing us to the public, how can we ensure that they represent us at a high level of quality? Do they really know our products? Can they solve the customers' problems?" According to Rose, those questions gave birth to the Certified Novell Engineer (CNE) program, the industry's first certification program, in January 1989. The program provides a standard of competence for professionals giving technical support to Novell networks.

The sales organization soon required resellers servicing Novell networks to maintain at least one CNE on staff for fielding customer support calls. In later years, Novell stratified its resellers, based primarily upon the number of CNEs on staff. According to Drake Prometric president William Dorman, setting such stringent requirements on resellers was unheard of, and much of the IT industry believed that resellers wouldn't willingly comply.

But resellers didn't balk at the requirements, and Carolyn Rose says the popularity of certification continues strong today among resellers. They embrace the new stratifications, she says, because the label of authorized, gold, or platinum helps to separate the resellers from their competition.

Novell certification was welcomed not only by reseller management but by the professionals themselves. An industry observer says, "What the CNE program accomplished for this industry was to help unite people who are providing the service and support. The designation of CNE has become a common point of entry for these folks. It's helped them understand that they're in a new career, a new profession, and helped them learn not only the technical proficiencies but also the professional skills for success in that career." The end user of IT services enjoyed a corresponding benefit by identifying people in the field with that higher level of professional competency.

The CNE owed its success not only to the interest of managers and professionals in the reseller channel, but also to professionals in end-user organizations who found it useful in servicing and supporting their internal customers. The interest of this latter group took Novell by surprise and drove the number of CNE candidates to much higher levels than Novell ever expected.

With the influx of candidates, Novell had difficulty keeping up with the demand. Novell realized that the early-education model of Novell-proprietary education centers couldn't meet the company's goals for rapid worldwide expansion.

So Novell again chose the path of partnering—this time with existing training facilities—and created an international network of Novell Authorized Education Centers (NAECs). To become an NAEC, each center had to meet a triangle of requirements: It must offer quality hardware, software, and facilities; use Novell Education-developed courseware; and employ certified Novell instructors to teach all networking classes.

To enable the third leg of this triangle, Novell launched its second certification program, the Certified Novell Instructor (CNI) program, in April 1989. The NAECs were required to use CNIs to teach certification-preparation courses. Although the instructors are not on the Novell payroll and do not contribute to Novell overhead, they're considered reliable representatives of the company, just as employees would be.

Rose believes that the partnership benefited not only Novell but also the education centers. As of mid-1995, more than 1.6 million students had been trained through 1300 NAECs worldwide, and Novell expects to add another 750,000 to that number by year-end. In working with Novell, these centers were required to continually raise their level of quality.

While Novell's educational direction promoted sales and supported education centers around the world, some industry observers also credit it with raising the educational level of the IT workforce. For example, CNE training, they say, while basically product-focused, nevertheless teaches many fundamental concepts and provides an important general education in information technology.

Also, as the industry has changed and grown, Novell has continued to adapt its exams and training. The number of exams and standards of

performance have been raised repeatedly in the CNE and CNI programs, and those programs have been joined by two others: the Enterprise CNE (ECNE), which has evolved into the Master CNE, and Certified Novell Administrator (CNA).

The ECNE, added in December 1991, trains professionals to higher levels of proficiency on Novell networking technologies. The CNA program, launched in August 1992, seeks out an entirely new audience: the network manager, rather than the technical-support professional. The skills taught to CNAs are the skills of network maintenance, including such things as adding and subtracting users and adding applications to the network. The CNA is typically an office manager with many other responsibilities unrelated to the network. There are currently 50,000 CNAs, and that number could double within the next year.

The growing numbers of Novell-certified professionals and the growing importance of those certifications to professionals and end users have added to Novell's responsibilities. The CNE came to be perceived as almost a bachelor's degree for the industry, and people's careers increasingly depended on it. As that happened, Novell focused hard on the quality of the certification exam to be certain it was worthy of the "gatekeeper" function it was beginning to assume.

Novell adopted computer-based testing to add quality to the exams and to provide certification candidates with immediate results. In 1989, Novell turned to Drake Prometric, and together the two companies worked to develop more sound exams based on psychometric principles.

While rigorous tests were being developed for qualifying exams in other industries, Novell became in many ways a pioneer in the use of computer-based testing. The company was unique for using psychometrics on such a large scale, testing large numbers of candidates through a network of testing centers, and testing knowledge of rapidly evolving technical material.

Since 1989, in its work with Drake, Novell has pioneered adaptive testing (electronic exams that automatically adapt the difficulty of questions to the skill of the candidate) and performance-based testing to gauge knowledge and skill in handling real-world job responsibilities. Drake's president, William Dorman, says that in pioneering these areas of testing, "Novell has blazed a trail that dozens of other vendors are following to create more valid and meaningful exams in support of their certification programs."

Novell's support of the IT industry has included offering the industry's first certification program and building the infrastructure for certification, including a stronger chain of training centers and a stronger chain of testing centers. It has also pioneered the realm of valid and reliable certification exams. But Novell has gone further still in hopes of growing the industry in order to grow Novell.

For example, the company regularly joins with other vendors and industry associations to discuss issues of education and certification, freely sharing lessons from its successes and failures. Forums for discussion include the Network Professional Association and CompTIA, as well as conferences sponsored by Drake Prometric.

In fact, Novell has helped to found major IT industry associations, including Open Users Recommended Solutions (OURS), the Network Professional Association (NPA), and the Computer Education Managers Association (CEdMA). Novell is an active supporter of many of these and other associations today.

Rose believes that sharing knowledge to strengthen other vendors is as important today as it has been in the past. She says, "We recognize that networking is inherently multivendor, and we support multivendor education and certification solutions. It's in the best interest of our customers that other programs are solid."

Novell has demonstrated many lessons to the industry about the value of partnering for success, particularly in the realm of certification. Many observers of the company feel that lessons on building ties to resellers and to end users through certification have been the most important. Dennis Samuelson, director of education at MicroAge Learning Center, a Novell Authorized Education Center, says that Novell's "certification programs create a large group in the marketplace who can support users with their current Novell products and recommend new ones."

Doug McBride, executive director of the Information Technology Training Association, agrees. He says, "Essentially, Novell certification has created almost 100,000 'salespeople' who work day to day in the business of their customers. As a result, Novell has established tremendous long-term customer loyalty and the ability to directly communicate with their customers without directly selling to them."

But benefits of certification extend even beyond resellers and end users. Novell made clear to the industry that certification works because it benefits all those who offer or employ skills in information

technology. Novell has also helped other IT vendors and organizations to reap the benefits of certification through their own unique programs.

As the industry matures, vendors and associations increasingly seek alliances that support the interest of all the players in the industry. Certification is emerging as one important tool in the effort. The Novell experience offers lessons both on the tactic of certification and on the larger strategy of partnering for success. By demonstrating the effectiveness of both, the Novell example will be important to the IT industry for years to come.

 # The reseller perspective

Resellers are embracing certification with enthusiasm. Certification helps them meet their most pressing needs: satisfying customers, winning competitive advantage, enjoying managerial benefits, and fulfilling vendor requirements.

 # Customers prefer certified resellers

According to IT managers attending focus groups sponsored by International Data Corporation in October 1993, customers prefer to receive service from value-added resellers (VARs) that hold formal vendor certifications. The study revealed that users believe certified VARs "tend to know their products better, have more training, and can provide better training when we need it."

Users also indicated to IDC that they appreciate their certified resellers because they believe these resellers have a closer relationship with manufacturers. They believe that certified resellers get better support from the manufacturer and thus have the ability to provide superior support to the customer. One user commented, "At least I know that person is qualified by the vendor."

IDC found that users believe certification is proof of the level of a reseller's knowledge. IDC's interviews also suggest that resellers are acutely attuned to the demand for reliable service from their customers. Their business success depends on customer confidence in their ability to give "value-added" service, which basically means their

ability to handle technical problems satisfactorily. As one reseller put it, "People don't buy computers anymore, they buy people and the organizations behind them."

Bruce Betz of Digital Equipment Corporation says, "Customers see real value in certification. They want a business relationship with a company that strives for excellence and has invested in its people. They want to interact with an individual they're confident in, someone who has the ability to be an effective product consultant."

Betz says the customer isn't interested in distinctions of value-added resellers, master resellers, or distributors. But, they want to deal with someone they know can solve their problems. "Certification supports that," Betz says. "It reflects positively on the commitment of the certified professional and also on the company that the professional represents."

Phil Symcas, president of Symcas, Inc., a value-added reseller in Rancho Cucamonga, California, says, "Having our people certified is just as important to us as passing the bar exam is to a lawyer. Our Digital Certification will tell prospective clients that, when they choose us, they're getting superior professional training they can count on."

Apex Computer is certifying technicians who complete its series of courses, which cover repair, installation, and diagnosis of hardware and operating systems from Sun Microsystems. Clint Morese, president of Apex, says that certifying technicians is a growing trend in the service industry. "As the industry matures, more people are going to be trying to set themselves apart. Having field engineers certified on one brand of hardware gives an independent service company credibility in a user's mind."

One spokesperson for a reseller comments, "If you've made advancements with certifications, especially with national accounts, it's to a service vendor's advantage. If you have 300 sites across the country, you can talk about certification accomplishments in that area. It speaks to the customer's needs and to your desire to make an investment in quality service."

Setting oneself apart with certification is important to both sales people and service providers alike. For example, Jim Lund, owner of Fox

Business Systems in Manhattan, Kansas says, "It's difficult to sell in the high-end networking arena unless you have certified sales people."

Elaine Hamilton of International Network Services says it takes the highest quality service person to address the needs of the same market. "Because of the size and expense of today's network," she says, "you can't learn on the job. You can't send junior people. Certifications are very important to the client and very important to us. They offer a piece of assurance to the client and confidence to the technician going in that the job will be handled well."

 # Certification provides managerial benefits to resellers

Jim Lund, like many other resellers, also benefits from certifications in his role as a manager. He says that while he is a certified technician himself, the main benefit of certification for him is in the area of hiring. He says, "Certification helps me to know that the people I hire can follow set procedures." Lund has hired CNEs and A+ certified technicians. He says he might hire and begin training them before they actually complete their certifications.

Managers at the reseller often want to inventory the skills of their staff. They want their certified talent to be well distributed geographically and to offer, collectively, all of the skills each region requires. Bruce Betz says he sees resellers building their support teams around who is certified on what.

Certifications also help the manager in the distribution chain to advance employees and to discriminate among them regarding their long-term worth. Stana Steen at Laser Express in Houston says that a toner delivery driver was given the chance to be certified in servicing Epson products. He passed the test, was trained by Laser Express to be a technician, and is successful today.

Steen gets other managerial benefits from certification: She uses it in the strategic positioning of Laser Express. For example, Toshiba requires A+ certification, and Laser Express is applying to be a Toshiba service center. "Our goal," she says, "is to have everyone A+ certified."

The parent company of Laser Express is a leasing company. Laser Express itself is an authorized sales center, but not yet an authorized service center. Steen hopes that A+ certification will also help to convince a number of vendors, including AST, Dell, and Lexmark, to authorize her company to both sell and service their products.

Resellers use certification in another simple but strategic context: referrals. For example, Bill Heck of the Technology Resource Center of Brookfield, Wisconsin, says his company's involvement with A+ certification is winning them referrals from other resellers and service centers who don't work on Toshibas.

Certification even makes managing client relations easier when the client itself has certified staff. For example, Jim Lund has found that he prefers selling to end users who employ certified professionals. "Knowledgeable end users make purchasing decisions more easily," he says. "If they know what they want, our sales job is easier."

Such end users are also easier to satisfy in the area of technical service. Lund has found that communications are enhanced and conflicts between his organization and the client are less likely to arise. Another advantage he has found is that more knowledgeable end users don't require the higher levels of technical support as often, so, "I can often send a Certified Novell Administrator out to help them rather than the higher-level Certified Novell Engineer."

 ## Certification as a vendor requirement helps resellers

Service-oriented resellers are increasingly required by vendors to have certified technicians on staff to service vendor products. Among the sample in the 1994 Dataquest study (discussed later), 29 percent of resellers indicated that vendors required them to have certified technicians on staff.

From the vendor's perspective, professional certification can be a measure of the reseller's commitment to the vendor's products. It shows that the reseller is committed to delivering real-world solutions using those products.

As Bruce Betz of Digital puts it, "Just as certification gives credibility to a professional from a customer point of view, so it does with the Digital sales force. It is the proof of expertise based on effective training. I'm sure that those of our Business Partners who go back to school and invest in Digital Business Partner University, will find they receive more business referrals from Digital."

John Young, a manager with the Technology Resource Center, says that after some of their technicians received certifications from Epson, the Center found Epson referring quite a lot of new business.

Similarly, Sun Microsystems encourages resellers like Apex Computer to go the certification route. From the Sun Microsystem perspective, certification of Apex technicians allows their customers to have another way to determine ahead of time how well trained their independent service vendor is going to be.

Certification popularity among resellers

The popularity of certification is clearly drawn in IDC's reseller survey. The first chart that follows shows the percentage of employees certified by reseller size in 1993. All resellers in the survey said they would significantly increase the number of certified staff in 1994. The second chart shows reseller perceptions about certification as a competitive advantage.

The popularity of certification was also confirmed in a major research study released in the autumn of 1994, called "Technical Training and Certification: Outlook and Opportunities." The study was commissioned by Drake Prometric, Novell Inc., IBM Corp., Microsoft Corp., Lotus Development Corp., and Compaq Computer Corp. It was conducted by Dataquest Worldwide Services of Framingham, Massachusetts. Alan Hupp of Drake says, "The study is a rigorous piece of work; nothing like it has ever been done before."

The study drew from online interviews with certification candidates as well as telephone interviews with managers responsible for staff technical training and certification. Participants included corporate customers representing a mix of small, medium, and large corporations,

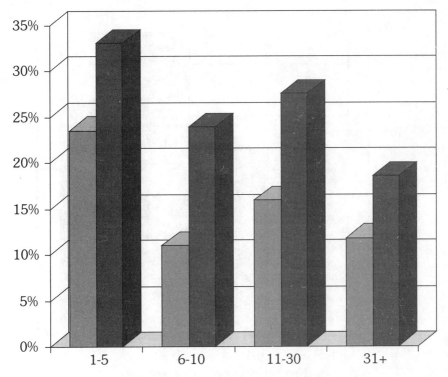

Figure 3-1

■ % of staff with advanced network certification
■ % of staff to be certified within 12 months

Percent of employees certified, by reseller size, 1993

along with resellers and system integrators. Candidate surveys were administered to certification candidates at Drake Authorized Testing Centers. A total of 8535 surveys were completed in July 1994.

Dataquest drew contact information on corporate and reseller managers from the Computer Intelligence and Paratechnology databases. Dataquest's Primary Research Services group administered a manager survey of 400 interviews in July 1994; 249 of these interviews were with corporate customers, 151 with resellers and system integrators.

The results are helpful in understanding the attitudes of resellers toward certification and comparing their attitudes with those of

Figure 3-2

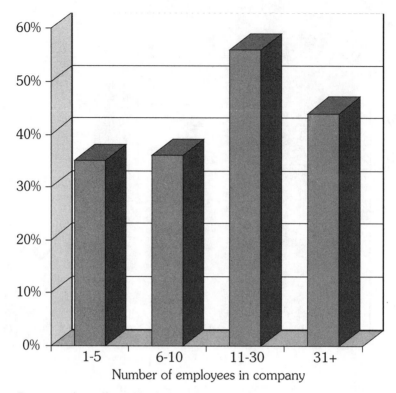

Percent of resellers that believe certification offers a competitive advantage, by reseller size, 1993

corporate end users. The results indicate that resellers are more enthusiastic in their endorsement of certification. For example, nearly half of the resellers surveyed consider certification a requirement; however, most corporate customers consider it "nice to have." Nearly 60 percent of the resellers surveyed require certification for everyone on staff, and 25 percent require it for their most senior employees. Only one-third of the corporate customers require certification for their entire staff; one-third reserve it for their most senior employees. Resellers rate certification higher in value compared to corporate customers, as shown in the following chart.

Both corporate customers and resellers are looking for organizational and market positioning benefits to certification, but resellers are also

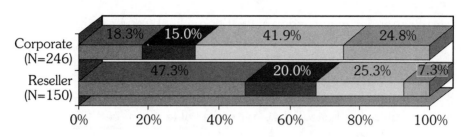

Figure 3-3

- ▨ Very valuable ▪ Fairly valuable ▢ Somewhat valuable ▨ Not at all valuable

Importance of certification (resellers vs. corporate customers)

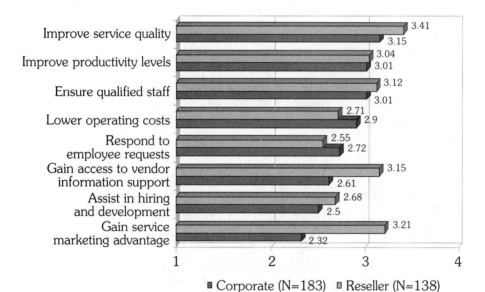

Figure 3-4

- ▪ Corporate (N=183) ▨ Reseller (N=138)

Importance of reasons for investing in technical certification (resellers vs. corporate customers)

looking to increase access to vendor support and gain a service marketing advantage, as shown in the following bar graph.

Corporate and reseller managers also differ in their preferences for certification topics of the future. While certification for network management is a priority for both, resellers also emphasize

73

certification for multivendor networking, client/server architecture, systems administration, and operating systems.

Other findings:

> ➤ A higher percentage of resellers, as compared to corporate customers, believe they get more value out of certified employees.

> ➤ Resellers are willing to invest more in employee training for certification and more in certification itself.

> ➤ Few corporations, but more resellers, are actively measuring the benefits of certification.

> ➤ Resellers are more likely to have used certification as a basis for hiring and promotions, as well as to have higher compensation levels for certified employees.

Resellers believe in and will continue to endorse certification. They show a high acceptance and perceived value for certification and view it as a requirement for doing business. Their involvement with certification will clearly increase as time goes on.

Case study:
Building from a common ground through the A+ certification program

"It's a win-win situation," says David Bossi about the A+ certification program. Bossi, worldwide warranty and service manager for IBM's PC Company, echoes the sentiments of the other major IT industry players who have worked together over a period of years to create the industry's first cross-vendor certification program.

Led by the not-for-profit Computing Technology Industry Association (CompTIA), the cooperating companies include manufacturers, distributors, resellers, maintenance companies, parts suppliers, publications, and industry associations.

Together, they have sought to improve industry health through a single certification program that addresses their most crucial needs. Those needs are to increase consumer confidence in the reseller

channel, to build individual competency, and to develop a framework for professional growth for service technicians.

The A+ program, launched on June 1, 1993, establishes a baseline level of competence for technicians who service microcomputer systems. The certification exam does not include vendor-specific procedures or product information, with the exception of client operating systems. Instead, the exam tests for command of the fundamental knowledge related to a set of core technologies.

The exam covers the technician's basic job functions, including configuring, installing, performing upgrades, diagnosing, repairing, performing preventive maintenance, interacting with customers, and maintaining safety.

The program emerges at a time when customer confidence in the distribution channels for IT products and services is wavering. Dataquest reported in its 1992 User Wants & Needs report that end users are "largely unwilling to brave seeking out external support" because service vendors are unable to consistently meet their expectations for quality service. The entire industry bears the cost of losing customer confidence because the industry is built on customer acceptance and use of new technologies. If the industry cannot adequately service those technologies, industry growth will suffer.

The A+ certification program seeks to restore customer confidence and thereby help the channel to hold on to current customers and more easily secure new ones. In effect, a respected outside agency is verifying that a vendor or reseller has the technical skills to back up its marketing promises with action.

Drake worked closely with CompTIA over a period of three years to help design, develop, and implement the program. The test concept was devised by CompTIA's Service Section and developed in partnership with Drake to ensure its validity. Alan Hupp of Drake says that the A+ certification program is "off to one of the fastest starts of any program we have administered in the information technology industry."

Support for the program comes from all corners of the industry and is growing steadily. Original "cornerstone members" included, among others, industry giants like Apple, Compaq, Hewlett-Packard, Toshiba, and Packard Bell, along with the industry's major service organization—the Association for Field Service Management

International. That group has been joined by 10 other financial contributors since January 1994. Newest supporters include, among others, Microsoft Corporation, IBM Education and Training, and Zenith Data Systems.

Sponsoring companies hope the program will give them an important competitive advantage, so they have contributed not only knowledge and cash, but have also jump-started the program by requiring their own employees to be A+ certified. For example, as of August 1994, Digital Equipment Corp. had more than 1600 A+ certified technicians; Bull Information Systems employed 560; and Packard Bell, 350. Several other companies count hundreds of A+ certified technicians on their payrolls.

Many organizations employing A+ certified technicians are also taking advantage of a new program designation, the A+ Service Center, by ensuring that at least 50 percent of their service professionals are certified. By September 15, 1994, the number of companies authorized as A+ Service Centers reached 589—and the number of new authorized centers is growing rapidly.

Yet the program's growth owes as much to the enthusiasm of individual technicians as to the support of companies. Bill York, a past cochair of the A+ Advisory Committee, says that the A+ program "is a step higher than certification on particular products because it is recognized throughout the industry by everyone." York reports that his own technicians embrace the program enthusiastically. "All of my technicians are standing in line," he says, "so they can prove their value to me and to their peers and clients."

The A+ program was originally projected to certify 5000 technicians by the end of its first year, or June 1, 1994. By July, however, there were more than 6785 A+ certified technicians. This is a significant fraction of the estimated 60,000 PC hardware field-service technicians in the U.S. who could benefit from the program. That 60,000 excludes technicians working on application software, UNIX hardware and software, LANs, and hotline/help desk telephone staff.

As to the program's effects on customer confidence, David Bossi of IBM says that A+ has helped IBM deliver better service both internally and through their reseller organizations. Service, he says, is a logistics problem. "It's the right personnel with the right part at the right time with the proper professionalism." Good professionalism, he believes, can make up for lateness of parts and other logistical problems. A+, he says, has improved IBM's rating on professionalism.

Glen Boulton, who manages training for Technology Service Solutions (TSS) in Valley Forge, Pennsylvania, says, "The most important thing about A+ certification to a large third-party service and support company is that it allows us to compete on the basis of quality of service." TSS employs 2500 service representatives nationwide and is creating a telephone support center. Within a year, all of these people will be A+ certified.

Boulton says, "Certification allows me to promote quality of service on several different levels and helps me to build solid relationships." He says that without these relationships, an independent service company cannot prosper.

In addition to bolstering consumer confidence, A+ certification strengthens the channel in another important way: It significantly reduces costs. Costs for service at all levels—end user, reseller, and manufacturer—have been skyrocketing in recent years. An important component of those costs has been the training expense to bring sales and service reps up to speed on the variety of new products entering the marketplace.

Through A+ certification, training costs are significantly lowered. Preparation for the A+ exam teaches candidates the fundamental technology and human relations skills needed to service IT products. Once technicians master the fundamentals, they need not retrain on them with each new product release.

A manager at a nationwide reseller praises A+ for helping them avoid redundant costs. "I have to be authorized on all of the different manufacturers' products," he says. "To do that, I have to spend a lot of time and money to go to all of the different training events across the country. The cost of training and travel and time away from the job is very critical to us. The A+ program allows us to eliminate the base level of training. Then we can concentrate on learning the specific technology required by the different manufacturers."

Many hardware vendors also save time and money by relying on A+ certification training to cover "the basics." The vendor no longer has to teach the fundamentals of laser printers or color displays when their classes consist of A+ certified technicians. This allows vendors to spend training time on the features that differentiate their products.

Dan Burn, a vice president at Apple, says, "The A+ program is critical both to Apple and to our resellers. It allows our resellers to reduce training time while increasing productivity for their service technicians.

Knowing our resellers are A+ certified, in turn, allows Apple to focus our training on meeting the specific needs of our customers."

A+ certification has been embraced as well by end-user organizations, who also benefit from improved professionalism of service staff and reduced training costs. Increasingly, organizations require their own technicians, and even telephone support and sales people, to be A+ certified. Many also structure internal training programs around A+ certification requirements and use A+ as a useful reference when hiring.

The program serves a variety of needs common to the IT industry, not least of which could be strengthening industry self-regulation in a way that avoids government controls. Nathan Morton, president and CEO of Open Environment Corp. and former CEO of CompUSA, says that the A+ program has established important "self-policing" mechanisms for the industry.

As for the future, John A. Venator, executive vice president and CEO of CompTIA, says that the A+ certification program could broaden over time to include new technologies and new professions within the IT industry. It will also expand participation to more industry players, whether small, medium, or large.

Alan Hupp of Drake believes that so many powerful supporters are behind the program that its influence as a de facto industry standard will continue to grow. But he says that A+, while successful in its own right, also represents "a model for any group of companies or organizations in the information technology industry who want to rally around certification." Hupp believes that A+ could be the first in a series of vendor-independent computer-related certifications on which the rest of the industry can build.

Professionals
and end-user
organizations

CERTIFICATION programs are ultimately directed at individual professionals because only individuals can be certified. However, the benefits of certification extend far beyond the individual deep into the organizations that employ their skills. Benefits to the individual include enhanced skills where training has preceded certification. But certification is also a valuable credential for finding jobs, building self-esteem and credibility within the organization, and being promoted.

The organization that is the ultimate end user of IT skills can be a business, association, or government agency. That organization usually includes a number of departments for technical work, training, and human resource management. Each of these departments and the organization as a whole benefits from the certification of IT professionals.

In fact, for every benefit to the individual professional, there is a corresponding benefit to one of these members of the end-user organization. For example, where individuals use certification to build their skills and potential for advancement, technical managers encourage certification to promote the productivity of the organization. Where individuals use certification to distinguish themselves from other job candidates, technical managers and human resource (HR) managers rely on certification to help make hiring decisions. Where individuals use certification to keep up with advancing technology and prepare for new job roles, training departments encourage the process and use certification as a formal mechanism in employee development. Where individuals hope that certification will give them a variety of skills for greater flexibility in their careers, management at the end-user organization relies on certification to deploy staff for greatest effect and to achieve strategic objectives.

This chapter examines these interlocking benefits of certification from the perspective both of the IT professional and of the end-user organization.

The perspective of the IT professional

 ## Hiring trends reflect a preference for certified candidates

Professionals are finding that specific technical skills—the kind addressed by certification—are increasingly demanded by HR departments. Consider, for example, Allan Karan, a very experienced computer professional who faced problems in his job search. Mr. Karan is an expert in managing OS/2 Presentation Manager and LAN technology development teams.

When Karan entered the job market, he found that his project management expertise was not exactly in high demand. "Unfortunately," he says, "most companies today are looking for hands-on technical experts, BAs in computer science, and CNE certification." Although Karan worked extensively with PCs, ran a department, oversaw networks, and managed developers and consultants, he did it from a managerial, not a technical, level.

After an extended job search, Karan finally landed a position as a manager of information technology. Though he got the position because of managerial skills, he has since taken training through certification programs to develop specific skills useful in his job. In the hiring he does today, he prefers candidates who have relevant certifications along with experience.

Vicki Balser of Kelly Services, Technical Division, says that overall, companies are looking for IT professionals either right out of school with very strong potential or else with very specific technical skills, for example with applications or client/server environments. Balser estimates that more than 50 percent of the technical skills sought today are network-related.

Figure 4-1

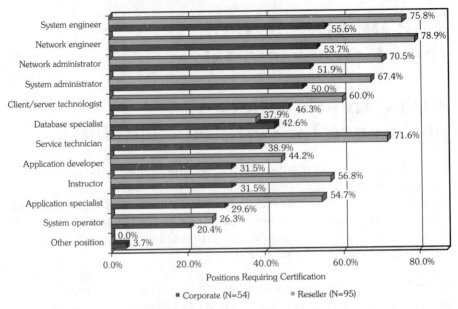

Positions requiring certification (corporate vs. reseller)

The Dataquest study suggests that the technical positions most likely to require certifications are system and network engineer.

"From a company perspective," Balser says, "we're moving into a more technical arena. People are focusing in on training and getting sponsored for certification by their employer."

Balser believes that certifications can play an important role in an IT professional's job search, but for most job seekers, she says, it's not the certification alone, but certification plus experience that does the trick. That belief was echoed by respondents in the Dataquest study, many of whom believe that certification does not substitute for experience.

➡ Certification gives benefits beyond finding employment

Certification provides a variety of benefits to professionals beyond just landing a job. For example, the certification process seems to

provide professionals with enhanced self-esteem. One holder of the CNE and CNX certifications says that attaining them was reward in itself for the sense of accomplishment it gave him.

Objective testing and measurement also build confidence by giving a powerful feedback on skills. Those who have been certified have a greater appreciation for their own skills and how those skills make them a valuable part of the information technology industry.

The exam can also make the candidate more aware of skills that need to be developed. David Lowe of Brown & Root, for example, says that certification gave him a way to gauge himself on his skills against other professionals. He says, "Even after six years working in the field, you're always learning something new. I just wanted to see how good I was." Lowe believes that even very experienced people lack some of the fundamentals, and certification programs can point out to them the gaps in their knowledge.

One network technician says that certification training and testing help you "cover the bases" by being exposed to the full range of relevant knowledge. Allan Morris, software analyst for Saskatchewan Government Insurance, says that preparing for the CNX exam helped him learn all of the problem areas in networking. Without such a program, he says, "You learn on the job based only on the problems in front of you."

Preparation for the exam can be a powerful way to fill knowledge gaps. John Rolf, a systems engineering manager with International Network Services, says that the preparation period is like readying yourself for a marathon run. "If you know you're going to run a marathon in six months, after five months of training, you're in pretty good shape."

Sometimes the feedback from the exam itself can spur one to develop deeper knowledge. For example, Richard Blackwell says of his CAD/CAM exam by Autodesk, "The certification exam was so thorough in analyzing my skills that I was able to improve my own weaknesses almost immediately. This resulted in a positive review and annual salary increase and the possibility to move into new

opportunities within the company that I otherwise would not have been qualified for."

Studying for certifications might also provide direction to one's career progress. For example, Allan Morris says that the CNX program gave an important goal to work toward. "CNX," he says, "gave me a way to measure my accomplishments and plan my growth."

The knowledge and skill developed while preparing for a certification exam pays off with improved problem-solving abilities on the job. Sometimes even a little new knowledge can go a long way, as Steve Kurz found while servicing a Compaq ProSignia server running Novell NetWare 3.11. The corporate client's just-in-time inventory system was locking up and corrupting their very large database file. The file was larger than 16MB and took more than three hours to reindex after crashing. The company's hardware staff and software staff were pointing fingers at each other, unable to solve the problem.

After Kurz arrived, he recognized right away that there wasn't enough RAM in the server to accommodate the large disk storage requirements and to cache the large files. The cache buffers were down from the recommended 70 percent to 21 percent because a second 1.2GB hard drive had been installed without allowing for the additional RAM requirements.

Kurz was able to resolve the problem immediately by installing another 16MB of RAM. He credits Compaq certification training for having demonstrated to him the effects of too little RAM in a Novell server, and he credits Compaq certification continuing education with giving him knowledge of the details of the correct memory configuration needed in this case.

The customer was more than satisfied. In fact, the company was so impressed with the quality and speed of the diagnosis that they awarded Kurz's organization a $100,000 purchase order to upgrade their network and rewire their entire plant.

Certification opens opportunities to the already-employed

Ben Eckart, an instructor at a technical school in Kansas, says that certification has opened new doors for his students even after they have landed a job. For example, one of his students applied to a company that had no interest in the A+ certification program. They hired him, but for other reasons. Within a few months, however, the company was so sold on the A+ program that they stopped providing training to any of their employees who weren't A+ certified.

Eckart has always encouraged his students to pursue A+ certification even before they find work. He says, "My students weren't all convinced of the value of certification, but they find now that when they get in a predicament, certification helps them. They get better jobs and advance more quickly. It has turned out, in fact, to be a necessity." Eckart says that whether you personally believe in the value of certification or not, you'll find that you need to be certified today to get ahead.

The benefits of certification might be more subtle than an offer of new training opportunities or a promotion, but no less significant. For example, David Lowe says that his CNX designation is separating him from the pack in the eyes of his employer. "When I speak about networking these days," he says, "people pay more attention. They know I've been through the program, and it's boosting my credibility." He says that he doesn't look for immediate payback, but he knows the payback will come.

In addition, certification is often cited as giving IT professionals more confidence in the interviewing process and more weight in the review process. When cutback or reorganization time comes around, some also find that certification is the life jacket keeping them afloat.

Certification might also open the door to additional part-time consulting assignments. Pat O'Connor, for one, looks to augment his federal government paycheck with moonlighting assignments as a Certified Banyan Engineer. O'Connor says, "Small companies out

there can't afford to have a CBE on staff, so I can subcontract for system integrations or setting up Internet gateways."

Others might use certifications as a launching point into a full-time career as a consultant. O'Connor knows someone who recently left the government to build a consulting company based on his several certifications in networking skills. The consultant will target the small to mid-sized companies who can't afford to have a full-time certified network engineer on staff.

 # The value of multiple certifications

In a time of proliferating technology, professionals—including administrators, technicians, consultants, and others—can open new opportunities for themselves and develop their competitive advantage by earning certifications on several products and technologies.

For example, David Lowe currently holds the CNE and CNX designations. He plans also to pursue certifications from Microsoft (for operating systems knowledge), from Powersoft (for applications knowledge), and from Cisco Systems (for routing skills). He says, "I need all of those in my current job. Each program has its own angle."

Doug Hall at Sun Microsystems agrees with Lowe about the value of multiple certifications. He says, "It used to be that you were required to do only one job. Now a person does many. You can't be good at just one thing anymore. Having different skill sets is very important."

This is especially true at large organizations, which often require knowledge of several different systems. Not all projects are as large in scope as the renovation at the Pentagon, but it is typical of the large organization's need for multiple skills and multiple certifications. Colonel John Barnes is overseeing the restructuring of the Pentagon telecommunications network. "We're dealing with a project," he says, "where you name a product or protocol, and we're dealing with it."

Among the certifications Barnes is looking for are Learning Tree International certifications in networking skills. He has also required the Registered Communications Distribution Designer certification

from Building Industry Consulting Service International for some jobs. "It is very difficult," he says "to find one engineer who has knowledge of all the different systems we use."

Barnes says that members of his staff are using the Learning Tree Passport Program opportunity to receive unlimited training at a fixed price. They are anxious to develop the variety of skills needed for the renovation project and other projects. In fact, though they are allowed some time off from work for training, many are also taking additional training at night on their own time.

Professionals can also use certification as a bridge into expanded job roles. For example, Kevin L. Johnson at Amtrak took a Local Area Networking certification from Learning Tree International. When his office started using wide area networks, he became certified in internetworking skills to keep up with the knowledge requirements of his increasing responsibilities.

More skills also mean more opportunities for consultants. For example, Pat O'Connor currently holds the Certified Banyan Engineer certificate, which he finds helps him subcontract his services to the Banyan market. That market, he says, is a smaller niche than Novell's market. But while it has fewer clients, those clients can be large.

Still, O'Connor wants as much opportunity as he can get, and he believes multiple certifications are crucial today for opening opportunities to consultants. So he's considering both the CNX certification and Novell's CNE. Ultimately, he wants his résumé to reflect high-level troubleshooting skills, along with knowledge of relevant applications packages like Network General's Sniffer.

The trend toward multiple certifications is likely to accelerate as the demands of technology increase. Randy Biggs of Training Services International, for example, says that the forces making computers easier to use and more powerful continue to make for increasing complexity "on the back end." The demands on IT professionals will escalate he says, and demands for certification will escalate with them. "That's the direction," he says. "It just makes sense. As technology gets more complex, people are forced to learn more and more."

Certifications help carry professionals from one stage of complexity to the next. Biggs says that you don't jump from a beginning DOS user to a systems integrator. The CNE, he believes, is a good transition. But, he says, the CNE used to put people "on the top of the heap." Now he says, it's become more of an entry-level requirement.

Other programs will evolve, he believes, to function as stepping stones to help IT professionals bridge their skills across a field posing increasingly demanding technical challenges. Professionals who can document their fluency with both current and emerging technologies—via multiple certifications—will open doors for themselves at every turn.

 # Attitudes of professionals toward certification

The Dataquest study suggests that certification candidates view certification as likely to bring them a variety of benefits, including opportunities for new jobs and promotions. Respondents also believe that employers and customers will respond to them more favorably as a result of their certification. Managers responding to the survey seemed willing to reward certified employees with higher wages.

Virtually all of the professionals in the Dataquest study considered certification to be of value to their careers; many considered it very valuable.

The majority (55.8 percent) of certification candidates responding also believe that certification will be a significant help in getting a desired job in the future. Most of them are pursuing certification as a ticket to advancement in their profession or in their current job, as well.

Many believe that certification will enhance their image within their organization and with customers.

The study suggests that not only will the professional's image be enhanced, but so will his or her salary and position. Managers in the

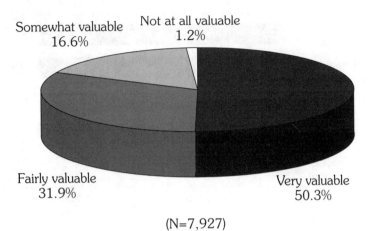

Figure 4-2

Somewhat valuable
16.6%

Not at all valuable
1.2%

Fairly valuable
31.9%

Very valuable
50.3%

(N=7,927)

Professionals' perception of value of technical certification

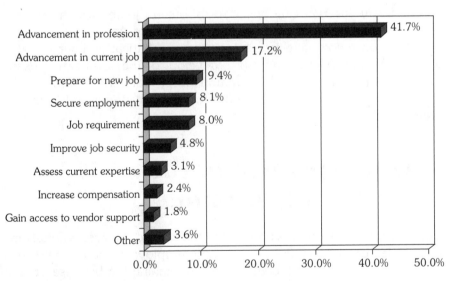

Figure 4-3

Candidates' reasons for seeking certification

study made comments such as these: "There is an automatic add-on to certified employees' salaries;" or "There is a salary increase or bonus for achieving certification;" or "We give certified employees more responsibility and higher pay."

Figure 4-4

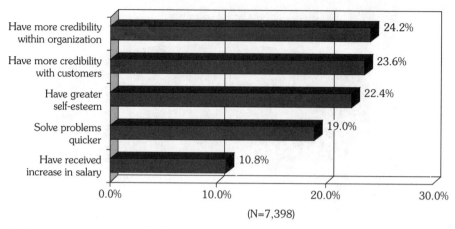

Achievements as a result of certification

One industry observer cautions: "You shouldn't jump into any course or pay testing fees without completely evaluating the program. However, once you have ascertained that a certification course teaches the same skills you wish to develop, or the certification exam measures the skills you wish to demonstrate, that certification program becomes a plus both to the technical manager and to the technical professional."

The perspective of the end-user organization

Certification helps those who employ the skills of IT professionals in two fundamental ways: first, in selecting employees and contractors with the specific skills needed; second, in making the best use of human resources.

Using human resources well means deploying them to advantage and also training and developing them further. Certification helps to accomplish these tasks for individual departments such as technical, training, and human resources departments, among others. Yet certification does more than benefit individual departments. It can

help the organization as a whole achieve its strategic objectives. Ideally, certification is an integral business solution.

 # Certification benefits technical managers

Skill measurement through certification often dramatically proves its worth when a technical manager hires employees or contracts with consultants or service providers. The need for accurate and quick hiring decisions is increasing as technology demands become more complex and support demands increase. Objective and consistent methods of evaluating employees, including certification, are increasingly important to managers and recruiters.

Pat O'Connor, microcomputer analyst, says that certification gives a good benchmark for hiring. It means, he says, that candidates have a way to document their knowledge or skill. "Without it," he says, "you don't know what they've done unless you go back to every previous employer and ask them."

One industry observer says, "Certification puts the onus on a third party— the certification house itself—to prove knowledge, rather than on your interview skills, however terrific they might be. Certification, at its best, allows you to weed out true support professionals from those who exaggerate their experience or capabilities."

Managers also know that when they have certified people in their departments, in many cases they gain access to training, events, information, and technical support from the vendor or other certifying agency. For example, those certified under the Microsoft Certified Professional program receive technical information from Microsoft via monthly CD-ROM discs and a dedicated CompuServe forum. Newsletters, conferences, special events, and hands-on sessions provide additional support. These benefits give the certified professional, and his or her employer, access to information otherwise difficult to obtain. Supports like these can help build a stronger technical organization.

Figure 4-5

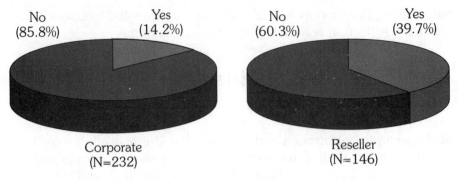

| No (85.8%) | Yes (14.2%) | No (60.3%) | Yes (39.7%) |

Corporate (N=232)

Reseller (N=146)

Managers' perception of value of certification

The Dataquest study indicated that the majority of resellers and corporate customers believe they get more value out of certified employees. Those employees are seen as having greater self-esteem, providing higher levels of service and productivity, and playing a leadership role for other employees.

 # Certification segments the profession into recognizable skill levels

Chris Sulentic, a systems engineer with International Network Services, agrees that certification is an important differentiator of skill. The actual problem-solving ability of many in the field is far less than they lead their clients to believe: "Many can talk in this business," he says, "but when it comes to hands-on and making it happen, quite honestly, there aren't that many who can." Sulentic says certification serves the profession by segmenting it into recognizable skill levels.

Speaking of the networking area that is his specialty, Sulentic says that the particular form that certification takes, whether Cisco Systems CCIE or Novell's CNE, is less important. What is important, he says, is that some certification mechanism be in place "to serve the needs of the people who buy and sell networking services."

Valda Hilley, computer consultant and author of *Windows Configuration Secrets* (1994, IDG Books), agrees. One problem found by Hilley is that often computer consultants offer their services as generalists. In fact, they might have narrow areas of expertise and don't understand the limits of their knowledge or the importance of filling in the gaps.

Hilley says that while consultants can solve certain problems, as the problems get deeper, their lack of knowledge in that area becomes apparent. She gives an example of working with a consultant who was skilled in the Excel applications package, but who had no knowledge of or interest in operating systems.

Hilley points out that when "the General Protection Faults started flying all over the place," this consultant turned to others for guidance. Hilley says that certification is a real help when hiring consultants. It helps sort out the particular skills a consultant has and where those qualifications begin and end.

Randy Biggs, president of Training Services International, has met the same problem described by Hilley. When he hired someone to upgrade the company's hard drives, the technician "got lost in the process" and TSI's computers were down for three days. Biggs let the technician go and hired another, who, he says, did a wonderful job. Soon they were back in operation, and the data was reloaded.

Biggs liked the new technician so much that he ordered an upgraded system from him. The new system soon failed, however; the technician was unable to help, and TSI's computers were down for another three days. Biggs says the problem was that they had "stumbled into a deeper layer. First came the hardware issues which this technician could handle, then came the networking issues, which he couldn't."

Biggs says that the information technology field must define a hierarchy of skills much as the medical profession has. He says "If I'm sick, I might go first to a general practitioner. That doctor in turn might refer me on to a specialist. If the specialist needs help, he or

she might look to a research facility." In the IT field, he says, it's certification that "layers the technical support." He says that layering is essential now because, just as in the medical field, a single person is no longer able to meet all of your needs.

Certification is an important indicator of skill, one of the most dependable indicators an IT professional could offer to demonstrate precisely which of the client's technical needs he or she is qualified to handle. Certifications are becoming more important indicators of technical skill than are technical degrees.

Ben Eckart feels that layering of skills is better indicated by certifications than by training provided in most trade and technical schools. He says, "I've been to trade schools and different places offering technical training, and you find that many of the people being sent to these schools are not technically inclined. The people sending the students for training are sending whomever is convenient." Eckart says that while certification might not work perfectly, it does help distinguish the capable ones.

Stana Steen, a manager at Laser Express in Houston, agrees. When looking for technicians to hire, she used to turn to the technical schools. "But the technical schools are churning out so many people. Many are unqualified. I don't know how they're going to get a job." Steen relies more on certifications these days, especially the A+ designation for technicians.

Shirley Nycum of the American Society for Association Executives believes that a key indicator in the growth in popularity of certification is that people increasingly see it as a better option than going back to school for another degree.

Certification benefits the nontechnical manager

While certification results can be helpful to any manager reviewing the skills of potential hires, it can offer particular help to the nontechnical manager when assessing technical skills. For example, where a human resources department has the responsibility for a hiring decision, the

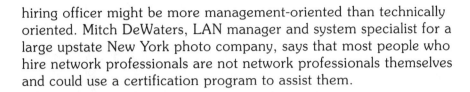

hiring officer might be more management-oriented than technically oriented. Mitch DeWaters, LAN manager and system specialist for a large upstate New York photo company, says that most people who hire network professionals are not network professionals themselves and could use a certification program to assist them.

Stanford VonMayhauser of Educational Testing Service says that the certification of computer skills is becoming increasingly important to HR departments. "Those responsible for HR," he says, "are becoming aware of certification as a way to understand the quality of applicants. It gives information that is job-related, useful, valid, and reliable."

HR departments also benefit from objective evaluation methods. Certification is often seen as providing accurate and consistent measures of skill—something that training programs alone rarely provide. Certification testing ensures candidates an equal and fair chance to demonstrate their skills. This minimizes the risk of litigation over issues of hiring, promotions, and layoffs.

Some people caution, however, that managers and HR people shouldn't depend on the certifying agency to do the screening for them. Relying too heavily on certifications without attention to experience could screen out desirable candidates.

Certification is another important piece of information to weigh in the total picture when making a hiring decision. For example, Jim Oleksiw, a telecommunications director with Travelers Insurance, says that he's helped by the CNX designation when hiring network management personnel. Oleksiw says he believes the exam is challenging and would help him decide if someone has the diverse experience he is looking for. "All things equal, I would lean toward the person with the CNX certification," he says.

 # Certification helps organizations purchasing IT repair services

Businesses, like individual computer owners, might need to call in outside help for repairs. When they do, they draw from a

marketplace of service providers, many of whom are unqualified for the tasks they are asked to perform.

For example, Clinton Watkis, a business computer user, called for service support and was told, after his computer was examined, "You're out of luck." The service provider told him they would need to replace his hard drive, after which he'd be "starting from scratch." Watkis did not follow the advice, but called for a second opinion. He learned that his hard drive was sticking, a minor repair was needed, and soon he was up and running again.

The difficulty in finding adequate service support has been documented by a number of consumer advocacy television programs. As one newscaster put it, "Once you call a computer repair person, your problems might just be starting."

One such program featured Don Doerr of the National Advancement Corporation and reported results of a "hidden camera" experiment. Before the station called in service technicians for help, Doerr loaded a virus on a computer. The virus had been rendered harmless but simulated the problem it would normally cause—erasure of data from the hard drive on power-up. According to Doerr, a trained technician should be able to spot the problem right away and correct it without any loss of data.

The station called in, one after the other, three apparently reputable technicians from nationally known service providers. "One by one," he said, "they gave us the bad news." None of them spotted the virus. The first eventually got the computer to work, but claimed that all of the data was lost. The bill was $250.00 for the office visit. The second said there were major problems that he couldn't fix, the data was lost, and the bill was $360.00. The third said the data was lost, he attempted no repair, but offered a bill of $350 for the office visit.

Doerr feels the level of service he encountered is common. He says, "If you've ever had anyone repair your computer, there's about a 40 percent chance that they replaced parts that didn't need replacing, and you paid for it." Of the people who lose data from their hard drive, 70 percent needn't have lost it permanently, he says. But few technicians are skilled in the simple methods of data retrieval.

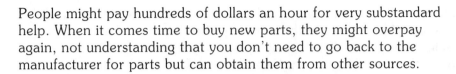
People might pay hundreds of dollars an hour for very substandard help. When it comes time to buy new parts, they might overpay again, not understanding that you don't need to go back to the manufacturer for parts but can obtain them from other sources.

Doerr and others are looking increasingly to certification of technicians as a protection to end users. Leon Ilanos, a Repair Depot manager, agrees. "Everybody has hundreds of field technicians and therefore there's just too many of them to have them all trained properly. But by being able to certify them and bring them up to a certain level, I think that's a tremendous plus."

A growing number of certification programs, such as National Advancement Corporation's Level II program, can protect end users from needless or substandard service repairs. The NAC program offers a certification exam that tests skills with the most commonly missed diagnostic problems in PC repair. Only a minority of candidates pass it. Doerr believes that programs like his will play an important role in protecting the consumer.

 # Certification helps end users make better use of human resources

Project planning becomes more realistic for both the short and long term when managers know the skill sets they have access to. Certifications help managers to inventory those skills.

Gary Monti, a certified networking professional for Aetna, experienced firsthand the contribution that certification can make to project planning in an emergency. Aetna's World Trade Center office was damaged in the terrorist bomb attack in February 1993. After the attack, Aetna immediately rented new office space in an old brokerage house on nearby Liberty Square. Monti was selected with a team of others to quickly reestablish the office network and information processing systems.

Certification helped Aetna managers select the team members, and Monti says that the training connected with his certifications made a difficult job possible. When he arrived to set up the new office

network, "There was nothing in the brokerage house except echo," he says, "About three in the morning when we started laying the first cable, I found myself digging deep into my knowledge of what to do. I found that to a large extent I was drawing from the certification programs I had gone through."

Monti says he benefited in particular from having prepared for tests that did not allow him to use reference books and other support materials—a requirement which he now feels can be very real-world. "In that room in the middle of the night, there were no books, no CD-ROMs, and there wasn't a telephone in sight."

"All that there was," he says, "was the cohesive knowledge of the individuals who were brought together for that task, and that knowledge, in many cases, was derived from certification training." Understanding clearly what knowledge individuals possess allows managers to create the cohesive team knowledge needed to complete tasks. Certification, by documenting specific knowledge and skill, is a powerful aid in project planning.

But beyond emergency project planning, certification creates a framework for determining job skills, job levels, and career paths. As Robert Wright did at Fort Leavenworth, the manager might design discreet levels of ongoing responsibility that correspond with various levels of certification.

Another technical manager configures his support operation to have four full-time CNEs working various shifts. This manager takes into account who is certified, who is close, and who should be on deck for training in order to ensure an adequate level of support to the operation around the clock.

Kevin L. Johnson says that Amtrak also has begun to redefine position requirements based on certifications. According to Johnson, "We're saying increasingly that for position A, you need to have credentials A, B, and C, and one of those credentials might well be a certification."

The information provided by certification helps managers to better fit employees to appropriate jobs and makes it easy to link reassignment

or compensation to competency. Once hired, an employee can be tested and recertified or attain new certifications at more advanced levels or in related disciplines to qualify for promotions. Certification also facilitates retraining to work effectively in other areas of the company as organization requirements change.

Certification can help lower operating costs and increase productivity by ensuring that the right person is in the right job. Placing an employee in the proper niche produces long-term job satisfaction and a lower turnover rate among incumbents as well as new hires.

These benefits to managers suggest that they would want to encourage their staff to become certified. Research shows they are in a strong position to influence the decision an employee might make to become certified. For example, the Dataquest study suggests that department heads and supervisors drive most decisions for certification.

Figure 4-6

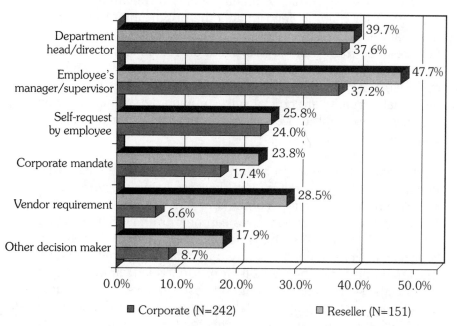

Decision-makers affecting certification

 # Certification supports end-user training and development

We are in the age of the learning organization, and much of the demand for new learning is caused by the technological revolution. IT professionals must continually learn new skills. As the demand for technical skills continues to increase, the importance of training will increase along with it.

While the promise and importance of training increases, pressures for greater productivity are forcing training departments to prove to upper management that they are producing results and to use their resources for greatest impact. Certification programs—both internal and external to the corporation—offer the modern training department significant advantages in doing both.

For demonstrating results to management, certification programs offer end-user training departments the opportunity to verify, through the quantifiable results of certification exams, that learning has, in fact, resulted from training. Certification scores can help determine if training programs are meeting their development goals and if candidates are learning information vital to their positions. Such quantifiable results are crucial since training departments are among the first to go in difficult economic times when their results are not quantified.

Certification does more to help training departments than just document with numbers that key skills are being mastered. It helps the training department become more efficient in a variety of ways. For example, certification scores can help training departments determine if further training is needed. Also, feedback from score reports can help students identify particular areas that remain to be mastered and focus their efforts appropriately. Training on demand, for specific skills, is an efficient and cost-effective way to meet the growth needs of employees. Determining if more training is needed and in what specific areas eliminates the travel, course costs, and downtime incurred by unnecessary training.

Training on demand is not only cost-effective but also more stimulating. Employees prefer programs directed very specifically at their individual needs rather than the needs of a department or other group to which they belong. Thus certification programs stimulate interest in training and help training departments build both interest in employee development and demand for training department programs.

Respondents to the Dataquest study believe that offering certification programs generally increases the overall demand for training, and that it also provides incentives to complete training.

Figure 4-7

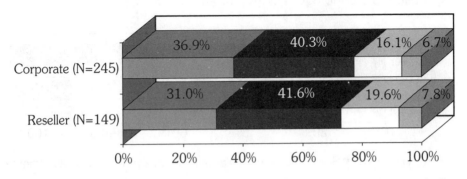

■ Strongly agree ■ Somewhat agree □ Somewhat disagree ■ Strongly disagree

Percent of survey respondents who believe that certification provides strong incentives to complete training (corporate vs. reseller)

External certification programs can help training department efficiency in another way: They might be testing and developing knowledge that is more useful for the end user than what their own internal training and testing programs could provide. One reason for this is that exams of external certification programs reflect a standard of performance on particular technologies held by the IT industry as a whole, rather than the narrower standards of a single company. In addition, certification exams are typically related to the particular knowledge, skill, and ability to perform a real-world job, rather than the knowledge to pass a single course of study. The former can have greater leverage in producing meaningful results than the latter.

Respondents to the Dataquest study indicated belief that certification results give a realistic feedback about the skills that matter. For

example, they said that certification testing is an important measure of educational effectiveness and a fair and accurate reflection of employee skills.

Certification also supports the efficiency of training departments by helping them to plan ahead for computer skills training. As Elliott Masie, president of The Masie Center, says, "Most companies do not link the acquisition of technology with the totally certain need for increased computer training and support. The majority of training requests are triggered by immediate needs, rather than a planned approach to technology skill investment."

Figure 4-8

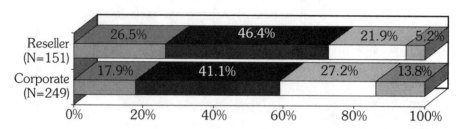

■ Strongly agree ■ Somewhat agree □ Somewhat disagree ■ Strongly disagree

Percent of survey respondents who agree that certification testing is an important measure of educational effectiveness.

Figure 4-9

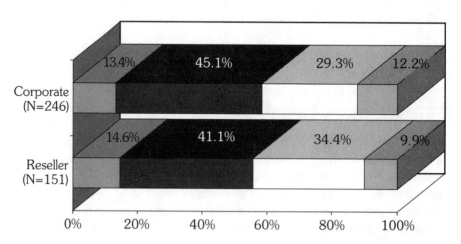

■ Strongly agree ■ Somewhat agree □ Somewhat disagree ■ Strongly disagree

Percent of survey respondents who agree that certification testing provides fair and accurate reflection of employee skills

An example is the release of Microsoft's upgrade to Windows, expected to be the largest single upgrade in the history of automation. The Masie Center reports that fewer than one percent of organizations surveyed in August 1994 had made any plans for training on or supporting this product.

Training departments need to identify not only the skills required to perform effectively today, but those that will be required in the future. They can gain that knowledge not only by studying the trends in their industries and in their organizations, but also by looking at the criteria of successful certification programs.

Certification naturally leads training, says Wayne Hodgins, technical director for customer learning, education, and training for Autodesk. First, standards are developed, and following that, testing and certifications are established. Then, he says, you train to those standards. "One of our biggest challenges," he says, "is that we don't know what we don't know and therefore, we have very inefficient training. Established standards and certification provide training departments with specific outcomes to define what their students need to know." Hodgins believes that certification is a great boon to training providers for that reason.

With cues from certification programs, training departments can target training efforts more effectively, recommending the right training to develop the right skills at the right time. Training departments can also sometimes improve their efficiency by outsourcing training to vendor-authorized education centers. For example, Novell and Microsoft have developed a network of authorized training centers to prepare candidates for their exams—the Novell Authorized Education Centers (NAECs) and the Microsoft Authorized Technical Education Centers (ATECs).

Such programs have the advantage of offering training materials that were developed in tandem with the certification exam by experts. For this reason, end-user training departments increasingly rely on the certifying agency to provide both the certification exam and the training leading to it.

The trend for end users to outsource training is further encouraged by the increasing variety and complexity of computer skills, combined

with the need for corporate downsizing. As a result, computer training departments are virtually disappearing from major corporations. According to Elliott Masie of The Masie Center, companies with 10,000 computer users can now be served by a computer training department of three or four, who primarily contract and schedule training with outside training firms. In this new environment, certification helps verify the results produced by these training firms and also helps an overworked training department handle its responsibilities for developing human resources.

Kevin L. Johnson says that Amtrak has eased its own training burden through use of the services of Learning Tree International. Amtrak offered certification training through Learning Tree to many of its technical employees nationwide.

Learning Tree training offered Amtrak the chance to train employees on a variety of technical skills that were not cost-effective for the company to teach in-house, particularly in the area of networking skills. Johnson occasionally teaches technical training courses himself, including OS/2. He says "It saves the company money when I do, but I can't teach everything."

Certification can also help training departments when the most efficient thing to do is to remove the training function altogether—that is, turn to outsourcing for technical help rather than relying on the skills of in-house trainers. Roseanne Cares, a Certified Banyan instructor working for Ameridata, says that she sees many companies choosing this approach "so they worry less about their internal training." She says that when they do, these companies expect certifications from their outside trainers to help ensure that the results of training will be as good as or better than what could be provided internally.

 # In-house certification programs can build specialized skill sets

When companies need to develop inventory skills that are not addressed by existing certification programs, they can choose to develop their own internal certification programs. Despite the downsizing of many training departments, some industry observers expect "customer-driven

certification" to increase. Companies that currently offer in-house certification programs include Texas Instruments, Kelly Services, Deloitte-Touche, American Airlines, and many others.

Companies can adopt internal certification as a way to formalize completion of company training programs. Graduates receive a certificate after passing a certification exam, and their new credential contributes to their pride and to their credibility within the organization. It can also boost confidence for people before beginning a new job. For example, it can give desk workers more confidence before handling their first customer support calls.

Test data can be used both to inventory skills and to meet prerequisites for higher levels of training offered by the organization, ensuring that trainees in each class are at skill levels similar to their classmates. This saves time for students and trainers alike. Test data can also be used to continually modify internal training courses and training materials.

Where the goals for the certification programs are well connected to training department and corporate objectives, results of the certification exams demonstrate progress in fulfilling the corporate mission. According to Wayne Hodgins of Autodesk, for training providers to really fulfill their mission, they need what he refers to as "diagnostics." These go beyond what most external certification programs can provide them. They need to know not just "yes or no— an employee can or cannot do a job," they need a more comprehensive inventory of the skills, knowledge, and experience an employee possesses. Internal certification programs can deliver more detailed and more appropriate information. With this inventory in hand, training providers can efficiently target "just in time and just enough" learning. Then companies will be in a position to mix and match employee skills to best advantage in forming project teams. Hodgins believes that virtual companies made up of self-directed project teams is where corporate America is headed.

As to how to get involved in internal certification, Tori Coward, president of Tangent Computer Resources, says that most companies begin by certifying their instructors. Support staff are usually next in line. Once the program is up and running, it can generally be

adapted with minor changes for different audiences, including end users, sales people, field support staff, and others.

Though certification programs can be expensive to begin and operate, a certification program can quickly become a revenue stream or development cost offset for the training department or company. Revenue can be generated from training courses and also from reference materials. Both could be marketed externally as well as internally.

Training departments need to decide for themselves what skills are crucial for the company to measure and to develop. Once this is decided, the means to develop the skills need not be created from scratch. Many off-the-shelf training and testing programs are available, and receiving such materials from outside vendors saves trainers the burden of developing them and keeping them up to date. Where training departments need to create their own exams, tailored to their unique needs, companies like Drake Prometric can provide expert help in test development.

Companies can also choose to create an internal certification program that uses external certifications as components. Aetna is one example. Its HITECH program has three elements: a Certified Novell Administrator (CNA), a Microsoft Certified Professional, and an industry certification, in this case the insurance industry's Associate in Automation Management (AAM). When an individual meets the requirements for all three modules, they become a certified HITECH employee. Approximately 700 people within Aetna hold the credential today. The new status carries a raise in pay and other employment benefits.

For in-house certification programs to succeed, Coward advises companies to make their programs fun. It's important, she says, to give the program a status and even to involve employees in certification and training development. A variety of positive incentives has been used. Coward knows of one company that makes attending training classes a prerequisite for new equipment.

Alan Hupp of Drake believes that we'll see more and more unique approaches to certification in the future. End-user organizations and all those using the services of IT professionals will continue to experiment, he believes, to find ways to use certifications to best advantage.

Certification as an integral business solution

Certification does more than benefit individual departments such as training and human resources. It is helping companies to restructure, to achieve synergy across departments, and to attain their corporate strategic objectives.

For example, Elaine Hamilton, HR director at International Network Services (INS), says her company benefits from certification in three areas. First is in the area of recruiting. INS is a network consulting company providing innovative networking solutions and consulting services. Its projected growth rate in 1995 is 100 percent.

INS competes with the manufacturers of network components to recruit the best networking professionals in the marketplace. Hamilton says that the professionals she recruits are impressed by INS's commitment to certification. INS currently employs 80 systems engineers; seven of these hold a designation of Cisco Certified Internetwork Expert. They also employ seven holders of the ECNE from Novell. INS is also considering alliances with vendors to develop their own in-house certification program. Hamilton says, "We recruit technical gurus, and we find that it's important to them that they have a group of expert colleagues they can draw from when they come on board."

The second area of benefit is in communications to the world. Hamilton says INS advertises its certifications through its newsletter and other marketing materials. The three-year-old company has been pursuing certifications intensively for the past six months. Hamilton believes certification helps INS develop credibility and name recognition. She says, too, "It validates our technical expertise to the internetworking community."

The third benefit of certification is that it encourages team building. Hamilton says that INS employees have formed study groups to prepare for certification exams and to exchange information about certifications through e-mail. Those who have passed explain to the new group coming up about the rigor and the intensity involved in

the certification process. They also tell them that it's okay to fail. She feels it has drawn employees closer together.

The company supports the camaraderie by removing any sense of onus from a failure. Hamilton will not release any information about individual failures with certification exams. Hamilton says that INS doesn't try to force certification on any employee, but they do pay for the certification exam and provide the time to take the training and the exam. INS has also rewarded employees with stock options for becoming certified—a further inducement to contribute to the company's certification goals.

Case Study: Using certification to strategic advantage at Lyondell Petrochemical

Information services at Lyondell are changing fast. The Houston-based petrochemical company decided in 1991 that it needed a competitive advantage based on a more successful information services organization.

Lyondell runs lean and needs to drive information for decision-making down to all levels of the organization. Doing that has required repeated revolutions in the way the company has used information over the past three years, and IS services is the change-agent trying to make it happen.

Before transforming the company, however, Lyondell's IS services has had to transform itself. In 1992, when the company began the transition from mainframe to networked PCs, the quality of service provided by IS was weak. They tried to support PCs without being properly trained on them. According to Ron Fovargue, manager of Lyondell's newly styled Workstation Services' group, their internal customers in 1992 were angry. "Our support was so bad that people quit calling; we even received cryptic notes saying 'You call this a help desk?'"

The IS group decided to develop their skill sets fast. Candace Marullo, the IS training coordinator, recommended that certification was the way to do it. Today, Fovargue and Marullo credit certification with opening three major opportunities for them. First, it was a way to quickly reestablish credibility with their internal customers. As a company, Lyondell is certified to ISO standards, so certifications in the support area carried a lot of weight.

Second, certification training developed the required expertise. Fovargue says, "It was a way for our support team to get smarter than our internal customers or at least to be on a par with the super-users and ahead of the curve with the majority of Lyondell's other employees."

Third, multiple certifications have provided a sufficiently broad base of skills to members of Lyondell's training and support groups that the two groups were able to merge into one unit called Workstation Services (WSS). Today, each of the 15 members of WSS rotates responsibilities for training, support, and help desk activities.

The advantage of that, Fovargue says, is that when you train customers, you identify what they need to do their jobs better. If you contract out your training, that knowledge goes out the door when the trainer leaves. But if your own group does the training, the knowledge they gain can be used to improve service. In the same way, when servicing your customers, you gain valuable knowledge that can be used for creating the next training course. Fovargue says that his group now knows Lyondell's 1200 employees well. He says, "What we learn from the 1200 by working with them in multiple roles on a day-to-day basis allows us to leverage our knowledge in creating new training and service solutions."

Training solutions are now flourishing in the "Lyondell University," which offers highly targeted one-hour courses to employees in each of Lyondell's three sites in Houston. In 1995, WSS will supplement instructor-led and video training with computer-based and network-available training. But Fovargue prefers not to use the word "training" at all. He says that combining support, consulting, and service roles allows WSS to create something still better than training: a knowledge transfer environment.

The success of WSS is hard to measure since it is still very young. In two years, WSS has formally trained 1800 students through Lyondell University. When they go network-wide, those numbers should dramatically increase. Positive comments from callers to the help desk have steadily increased over the last two years, as have the number of calls (they're up to 1600 to 1700 per week). Today's callers tend to ask for information that they can use to solve their own problems rather than complaining that "this thing's broke."

The knowledge transfer environment has supported Lyondell employees through a major technological transition and is preparing them for the transition to come. In 1993 Lyondell installed a

company-wide network, standardized the PC computing environment, and prepared for migration to client/server. In the near future Lyondell hopes to move "one year ahead of the rest of the world" by skipping the "Chicago" upgrade to their current network. Instead they will completely swap-out their network for a new system running NT 3.5 ("Daytona") on workstations and on the file server.

Fovargue says that the WSS role is to support employees through the changes. It's not for WSS, he says, to tell people how to do their job, but to listen to what they're trying to do and to help them be more productive. That role mainly involves teaching them how to use applications on the system. Users work in sales, marketing, accounting, and production. Fovargue says his users don't need to tweak configurations, they need to get information from the database to increase product quality and to beat the competition on sales.

Fovargue believes that WSS is succeeding and that certification has played a major role. He says, "Now all of a sudden, certification becomes a lot more than just a piece of paper. It becomes a strategy for successfully supporting this company."

The use of certification, however, has been complemented by another strategy: Lyondell simplified its information services technology by standardizing on Microsoft. In 1991, Fovargue says, Lyondell had 36 different machine name plate configurations and 1000 different configurations on those machines. It was not unusual, he says, to see four versions of the same spreadsheet application on a single machine.

The move to Microsoft in 1991 was a corporate decision. Microsoft was a major player, Lyondell could put its applications up for "an agreeable sum" and receive updates and support to their integrated system. Also, from a training standpoint, says Fovargue, once you teach Windows, you have a baseline for teaching other applications. This again helped WSS to leverage its efforts.

WSS staff have been pursuing Microsoft certifications to help the company through the transition. Nine staff members are now certified on one application; four are certified on two. The department goal is to be 100-percent certified on one with as many as possible certified on a second. When looking for new staff and for contractors, WSS certification criteria play an important role. Candace Marullo says that certification has worked so well for WSS product specialists that certification will also be used soon in the operations area. Five people are currently enrolled in a Microsoft Certified Systems Engineer fast track.

As Lyondell goes to a distributed enterprise database in the next few years, WSS will concentrate on teaching its users how to use that database. "They can learn everything they need to learn from us in fairly short courses," Fovargue says, "without themselves becoming certified."

In order to keep their staff as much "ahead of the curve" as possible, Lyondell arranges to get Microsoft product releases at the earliest possible date. It also receives early release beta versions of the certification exams. Lyondell cannot wait the normal time between product release and test development. "Our people need to be up on the new releases and certified," Fovargue says, "We just need to move right along."

Speed of training and certification is part of the competitive advantage. "Most support groups either get training after the fact or not at all," Fovargue says. "That's why, in my opinion, help desks and support teams are failing all over the country."

Fovargue and Marullo offer two cautions about their strategic use of certification. First, they believe that they could not have accomplished what they have without a staff strong in interpersonal skills. Their staff members carry degrees in such things as education and management as well as computer science. Microsoft certification, they say, does not develop people skills.

Second, they say that certification programs do not always teach exactly what their people need to know. For example, Microsoft certification programs have emphasized operating systems knowledge, while the WSS staff primarily needs applications knowledge. Where Microsoft stresses technical knowledge, WSS staff needs an equal emphasis on customer service and training skills. Marullo says that studying to pass exams that stress operating systems and technical support can give employees a false sense of what is important in their work.

Lyondell is trying to solve the problem by finding other certification programs to supplement those they currently use and by providing training themselves in interpersonal skills such as telephone customer service. But certification, despite those limitations, has been popular with the WSS staff and with Lyondell management. Each of Lyondell's locations has a "graduation wall" displaying graduation and certification information. Fovargue says that staff, managers, and vice presidents all take pride in the results.

Lyondell supports certification from the top down. WSS is a corporate service center, not a profit center. The company encourages certification candidates by paying for their exams and for any exam retakes; they also pay for certification training courses when they seem to be needed. Marullo says, "There won't be any problem in meeting candidate needs because we believe certification is so important; it makes a big difference."

Fovargue says that certification and other efforts at self-transformation undertaken by WSS have been a lot of work. "But," he says, "our people now understand their role for knowledge, productivity, and service. Certification has guaranteed a much higher level of success for ourselves and for the customer organization. Now we've got an organization that is really of value to this company."

5

Testing in the 1990s

CHAPTER 5

T ESTING in the 1990s offers test developers all of the traditional challenges in creating statistically valid, reliable, and legally defensible exams. But the pressures for developing effective tests are growing. As certification programs are increasingly relied upon for business and hiring decisions, test results need to stand the scrutiny of all interested parties. In an age that increasingly resolves its conflicts in the courtroom, test developers need to be aware that tests designed without rigor might be subject to legal challenges.

Other concerns in the 1990s are shaping test development in new ways. Today's market needs faster exam development, frequent exam updates, tighter security, greater accessibility, and more meaningful results.

This chapter examines the role of testing in the certification process and other topics in exam development. It also focuses on computer-based testing for its potential in creating better exams—exams that meet the new and emerging needs of the 1990s marketplace.

The certification test as gatekeeper

The main goal of certification testing is to determine candidate ability relative to a "cut score" or pass-fail point. Certifying agencies want candidates who pass to be more competent than those who fail. Above all, they want candidates who test above the cut point to be worthy of the certification credential, which means being capable of performing a job.

In their gatekeeper function, certification programs bear a heavy responsibility. Those who are certified must really prove their ability to perform a job or the value of certification will be questioned.

The rigor of certification testing can go a long way in determining how the public perceives the worth of a program. Mark Johnson, training manager at Apex, says, "The value and effectiveness of certification is going to be played out in the skills of the people we

say are certified. Certification has to be rigorous enough so that only the people who are getting certified truly have earned it."

Celeste Boyer of Microsoft says that certification testing has to provide a valid measurement tool if the industry is to have confidence in the results. She says some vendor programs support a marketing goal rather than a measurement goal, and customer perceptions of certification have been negatively colored as a result. But the trend, she says, is toward measuring factors for job performance. "Certification within the IT industry is evolving. I've seen the exams of our competitors, and they seem to be heading in the right direction."

At stake is not only the public perception of certification, but the government's perception as well. Certification, when well executed, protects the public interest adequately so that government regulation is not needed. One vendor comments that industry and government are both coming to recognize that certification is the best way to validate the competence of IT professionals. But meaningful standards and valid measurement tools are needed to win the confidence of the public and government alike.

For standards to be meaningful, they must be both rigorous and connected to real-world jobs. The market might hesitate to follow certification programs when certification requirements seem arbitrary and unconnected to the work actually required by professionals. Also, candidates resent training that doesn't help them in their work. Pat O'Connor, microcomputer analyst, says that "recertification may sometimes force you to study things that you don't really need in your job."

The connection of training to certification adds another level of responsibility to the work of test developers. Because testing influences the kind of instruction that will be used to prepare for the test, exam developers want to stimulate the development of real-world skills that lead candidates not only to test well but to succeed in their jobs.

Ben Eckart, an instructor at a technical school in Kansas, believes that a good certification exam should test knowledge in such a way that only those with prior experience can pass the exam. Valid

training for the certification exam would then include hands-on, real-life experience rather than merely prepping for test questions. Training that "teaches the test" rather than the job, Eckart believes, defeats the purpose of certification. Test developers bear responsibility for creating tests that cannot be passed after only a brief, book-oriented "rapid training program."

Drake's manager of psychometric services, Paul E. Jones, agrees. Drake, he says, wants to understand the effect of exams on the preparation process and to use that information in the design of future tests. He says, "We believe that an important but still largely ignored source of evidence for the effectiveness of a certification test or program is the change for the better that it initiates in the professional education community."

Connecting certification exams to real-world tasks is the fundamental aim of the test-development process. Test development begins with defining the particular skill and knowledge needed to perform the job adequately. Then questions are developed to assess whether a candidate has mastered these objectives.

The goal of a test-based certification program is to have the "indirect" process of testing yield the same results that the direct observation of the candidate on the job would give. Computerized testing in the 1990s is making the indirect assessment into an ever more powerful and realistic measure that deserves to be relied upon—by the public, by government, and by the test candidates themselves as they invest time to prepare for their exams.

But the job of the test developer today is complicated by another demand: the requirement for faster test development. Clients are in a hurry. They want their tests online before they are obsolete. Jones, says that "normally, if a test cannot be built within four months for between $10,000 and $30,000, it is too late and too expensive."

When exams are developed rapidly, test experts need many pieces of evidence to make them confident in the performance of the certification test. Jones says that there are at least nine things he'd want to know about an exam before having confidence in it to perform its gatekeeper function:

1 The exam's measurement objectives, taken together, reflect minimally acceptable levels of understanding and effectiveness for a certified person.

2 Test questions measure what the exam objectives say they should measure.

3 Candidates who perform well on independent measures of understanding and performance also tend to do well on the exam, while those who perform poorly on these measures also perform poorly on the exam.

4 The "cut score" is related, either by expert analysis or empirical observation, to an acceptable standard of competence.

5 Candidates who are thought to be sufficiently competent actually pass the exam, while those who are thought to be incompetent fail.

6 Candidates who pass one form of the exam tend to pass alternate forms as well, while those who fail one form tend to fail all forms.

7 Different test scores mean different levels of competence as defined by the exam, and scores are not influenced by other factors.

8 Each test question measures competencies that are generally important to success on the exam.

9 The certification exam stimulates instructional practices that lead to the kinds of understanding important for job success.

What kind of certification program are you testing?

The nature of the test is determined by the structure of the certification program. Certifications can be based on an existing training curriculum or they can be based on skill and knowledge requirements of a particular job.

Many of Drake's clients begin their test development with an existing training curriculum directed at employees, resellers, or end users. The

most straightforward approach in this case is often to define a series of certification tests, each covering the content of one or more training modules. The tests can then be grouped to create one or more certifications. A simple structure of five courses, two tests, and one certification might look like this figure:

Figure 5-1

A simple certification program structure

According to Drake psychometricians, beginning by defining the skills and knowledge required for one or more actual jobs is more complex but often more effective. From such a job/task analysis, specific instructional objectives can be defined. From these, testing can be developed in parallel. A simple example of the development process might look like the following figure. Drake assists clients with test development for both kinds of certification programs.

Figure 5-2

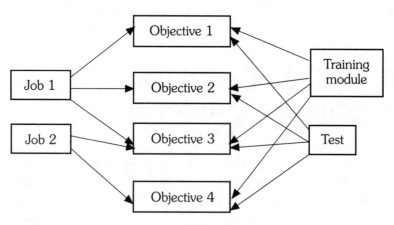

Defining objectives from a job/task analysis

Exam development: Some nuts and bolts

There are a variety of approaches to exam development. Standard practices are illustrated in Drake's own exam development process, described here.

1 *Job analysis.* This step identifies the specific knowledge the certified person should have acquired. That knowledge usually relates to tasks actually performed on the job, along with other less typical but potentially crucial responsibilities. At Drake, the job analysis is done by a "working group" of subject-matter experts led by Drake facilitators.

2 *Blueprint development.* Tasks and measurement objectives generated by the working group are sent out in survey form to a larger group of subject-matter experts. This larger group is asked to provide relative weights for each of the major job tasks; that is, to indicate what proportion of the exam should be devoted to each.

3 *Item development.* Drake brings together a group of test item writers for a three- to five-day item development conference. This writing panel can include members of the working group, the expert panelists who responded to the blueprint survey, and others. The group works to create test questions that accomplish the test objectives, while eliminating possible sources of error other than lack of knowledge. The item pool they create can be brought to additional technical reviewers if necessary. The items can also be reviewed by a cultural fairness panel composed of persons representing various cultural, minority, and ethnic groups.

4 *Pretesting.* The entire item pool is pretested or "beta tested" on a representative sample of examinees from the candidate population. The sample usually consists of 100 to 200 people. Pretesting serves a variety of purposes. For example, it can help to predict item performance, and also help determine the minimum test length. Pretest results can also be compared against the training and experience background of examinees to give additional evidence of validity. Further, pretests can help identify

subpools of questions with similar abilities to discriminate knowledge that can be used to create alternative forms of exams with the same difficulty. Finally, item difficulty information from the pretest can help to establish a realistic cut score.

5 *Item analysis.* The quality of individual test items is judged based on statistical characteristics, their importance as judged by the working group, and the comments made by the pretest examinees. Items should be neither too easy nor too difficult, and every item must also measure the competence for which candidates are being certified.

6 *Item selection.* Drake prefers to do item selection through a committee composed of Drake staff and members of the client's working group. Committee members have access to the text of the items, any associated graphics, the pretest item analysis statistics, and any comments from the pretest examinees. The committee then decides the fate of each of the proposed test items. It also identifies items that should not appear together on the same exam form (because of content overlap or cross-cueing) and also any items or item clusters that must be represented on every exam.

7 *Constructing alternate forms of the exam.* All forms of the exam must have the same relative weights given to content areas, as well as the same difficulty and reliability. In making the alternate forms, the total item test pool is divided into sections that represent the major job tasks or content areas. Each of these in turn is divided into groups of items selected to be as homogeneous as possible for content, difficulty, and discrimination. Items from each group are then distributed among the alternative forms, with equal numbers going into each form.

8 *Standard setting.* A number of means are available for determining the pass/fail standard or cut score for the exam. Drake prefers to involve the working group and expert panel in this decision. The entire group discusses the characteristics of a minimally competent candidate. Then the panel reads each item and estimates the proportion of minimally competent certification candidates that would answer the item correctly. Individual item judgments are summed across the exam for each panelist, and the mean (or median) of the panelists' ratings is taken to be the suggested number-correct cut score for the exam.

9 *Gaining evidence of reliability and validity.* Drake uses a variety of classical statistical means to quantify the consistency of exam results. Some of these methods look at the confidence level for individual exam scores, others at the consistency with which alternative forms of the test make the same pass/fail decisions.

Drake might also gather criterion-related evidence of the validity of the exam. That is, it might create a job-performance rating instrument and give it to peers or to supervisors of certification candidates. Ideally the results will demonstrate that people who do well at work do in fact get higher scores.

Jones describes one elaborate effort, currently underway at Drake, for achieving a high level of confidence in an exam. Drake is working with Novell to compare performance on two versions of Novell's service and support exam against ratings of job performance by the test candidate and candidate's supervisor.

Jones points out that the data related to job criteria give a different perspective on performance, and that this second view is extremely helpful in gauging the validity of an exam. But, he says, the data is costly to obtain. It's much easier to rely on an exam that has been well developed and appears correct based on its content.

10 *Maintaining the exam over time.* Drake periodically examines the performance of an exam throughout the exam's life. It continues, for example, to monitor score distributions, pass rates, reliability, and other indicators. If a test remains in service for more than a few months, Drake updates and refreshes its item pool.

Drake can manage test development for a client from start to finish following these 10 steps, or it can serve on a consulting basis for one or more phases of the project. The average time for test development when a client works with Drake is 14 to 18 weeks. The steps having the most effect on this time frame are the first four: job analysis, blueprint development, item writing, and item beta test.

Many organizations just beginning to think about developing exams want an idea of how their training courses might translate into

Figure 5-3

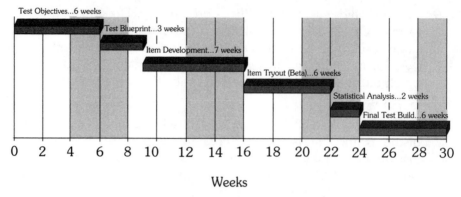

Weeks

Typical test development time line

candidate examinations. Here are some general rules of thumb for test development:

➤ A two- to three-day training course typically yields a single one- to one-and-a-half-hour examination, with a total of 60 to 80 questions in the test.

➤ Normally two forms of the exam are built out of the pool of valid test questions. To get the pool you need, you typically must write 180 to 225 valid test questions.

➤ To acquire 180 valid test questions, you typically must write 220 to 225 questions to be used in the beta test. Writing these test questions normally takes about 10 days, at 20 to 25 questions daily.

Even though tests can be developed quickly, given enough time, they will be refined and become better. New approaches to measuring a given kind of knowledge can be developed almost continuously.

Some of those new approaches might be suggested by customer feedback. Paul Jones says, "What drives us are the realities of the marketplace. A comment coming back from the certification population and those in charge of certification programs quickly give us a sense of what people are not satisfied with."

Despite the many steps involved in developing a good exam, the process can be practiced effectively within the budgets of most companies. Stanford Von Mayrhauser of Educational Testing Service (ETS) says that you needn't spend a fortune on test development. "It doesn't always have to be a Cadillac," he says. "It can be a darn good, professionally and legally defensible assessment tool without taking three or more years to develop and to validate."

The most important thing, he says, is to get the right group of people together at the start: job experts, industrial psychologists, test developers, HR people, statisticians, and legal support. "It needn't be a cast of thousands," he says. "With the right group, you can be off to a terrific start in developing a test in a cost-effective way."

The legally defensible exam

Certification exams are the keepers of the gate. Their pronouncements on abilities provide successful candidates an important competitive advantage: better job opportunities, increased pay, advancement, and respect. With so much riding on them, certification exams can be viewed as "high stakes" testing. Those who fail occasionally bring legal challenges against the certifying agency. When that happens, the issue most likely to be raised is the validity of the exam.

Building a test according to the steps described above is the best way to increase the likelihood that the test can withstand possible legal challenges from those who fail it. These steps build the cornerstones of an exam that accurately tests the particular knowledge, skills, and abilities that it intends to test. No test, however, is ever guaranteed to withstand any and all legal challenges that could be brought against it.

One of the ways in which an exam can fail to perform its gatekeeper function fairly and effectively is for it to screen out candidates not for the relevant technical ability, but for irrelevant factors of language or culture. An exam can do this if it hasn't been consciously constructed to avoid language or cultural biases.

The rights of minority groups to be free of unfair discrimination are protected by a variety of regulations. Guidelines specifically related to selection procedures, including testing, have been issued jointly by the Equal Employment Opportunity Commission (EEOC), the

Department of Labor, and the Department of Justice. But among antidiscrimination laws, the most important with regard to testing are Title VII of the Civil Rights Act of 1964, the 1991 Civil Rights Act, and the Americans with Disabilities Act (ADA).

Title VII is the most important of these laws for test takers. It prohibits discrimination on the basis of race, color, religion, gender, and national origin. Title VII protects minorities from both "disparate treatment" and "disparate impact."

Disparate treatment is conscious discrimination against one of the protected groups, for example, sexual harassment. Disparate impact means that discrimination has occurred against a member of the protected group with or without intent. A common example is height and weight requirements which, while neutral on the face of it, could be used to effectively screen out members of one sex or the other.

Once someone alleges that a test has had adverse impact, that individual needs to show that the test screens out disproportionate numbers of the protected group. Generally, "disproportionate" is interpreted to mean that the minority group is selected at a rate of less than 80 percent of the majority group. But just because a test has "adverse impact" doesn't mean it's illegal. The question then becomes, were the factors discriminating against the protected groups in the exam job-related and consistent with business purposes?

Since passage of the 1991 Civil Rights Act, questions such as this are no longer tried before a judge alone. The expert testimony of industrial psychologists and others must now be used to sway juries. The 1991 act also upped the ante for potential damages. Each claimant can now recover compensatory and punitive damages up to $300,000 in addition to back pay in a disparate treatment case. The same limit applies to those disparate impact cases where there was actual intent to screen out minorities.

Damages can also now be awarded when the employer has been shown to use the practice of "race norming," which rates a person in the context of his or her own race rather than with reference to the entire group tested.

The Americans with Disabilities Act extends protections to the disabled. This act has made the most serious new issues in the certification process, issues of accommodation. For example, has a person with back problems been allowed to stand up while taking the test or to have a different room in which to take the test? The purpose of the new protections is to give the disabled an opportunity to fairly demonstrate the skills that the test was designed to measure.

Tests built with these concerns in mind are more likely to serve the true interests of the testing agency: to distinguish those who have the knowledge and skills to perform a particular job from those who do not. Such tests are also more likely to be truly fair and equitable in the eyes of all of those with an interest in the results, including the courts.

Computerized testing

Test development in the 1990s has two great hopes: to make testing more accessible and to make it more meaningful. Computer technology is helping with both goals.

New technology and the accessible exam

The test development process previously described can be implemented with traditional paper-and-pencil-based testing. But the job market of the 1990s has created an additional set of demands on test developers, and computer-based testing offers important advantages in handling them. The net result is that computer-based testing is making certification exams more accessible to test takers.

The first of these advantages is rapid test development. With the influx of new technology and with repeated upgrades to those technologies, tests of ability in the technical arena need to be updated continually. A Novell spokesperson says that a test must sometimes be created within a matter of weeks, not months, "then, two months later, the test must be revised again." Computer-based

testing allows for "just-in-time" delivery of assessment instruments, designed to measure the skills currently in demand.

With distribution channels for IT products extending throughout the world, the audience for assessment of technical skills is now global as well. Computerized exams lend themselves to delivery worldwide because the number of personnel needed to deliver them is much less than with paper-and-pencil-based tests. One person now can oversee the delivery of many exams at once because the computer that delivers the test is also timing the test and aiding with test security. This logistical advantage has helped Drake develop a worldwide testing network, described in the next chapter.

Computerized testing is also more secure than paper-and-pencil tests. Questions on computerized exams are encrypted; only one question can be seen at a time, so theft or copying of the exam is extremely difficult. Computer-based exams can also be randomized easily and even individualized, further frustrating efforts to copy them.

Because they are less susceptible to theft, computerized exams need not be administered only at predetermined intervals as paper-based exams are. Instead, they can be offered continuously at many locations around the world. Computer-based exams then allow candidates the significant advantage of taking tests at times that fit their own schedules.

Vendors benefit from computer-based testing as well. For example, Novell, using Drake's worldwide testing network, can pilot-test an exam and make it available worldwide within about one week.

Organizations offering certification programs, as well as their testing agencies, enjoy another important convenience from computerized testing: The computer greatly reduces the administrative burden of dealing with large volumes of data from many locations.

Paul Jones points out that Drake downloads data every day to its clients. It filters out the information the client doesn't want while providing all the information the client does want. He says, "I can't imagine what it would require to do this in a paper-mediated world, especially when we're turning data around so quickly and gathering it from so many different sources." The need for quick handling of data from many sources is likely also to increase greatly in the coming years as interest in global testing and certification continues to expand.

New technology and the meaningful exam

Several important avenues to more meaningful tests are appearing now because of advances in basic computer capabilities: increased memory, CPU, and graphics-handling potential.

The new technologies allow for sophisticated question types delivered in more "real-world" contexts that better assess what a certification candidate really knows and can do.

Roy Hardy of ETS says that the earliest computer-based testing questions were paper test questions adapted to the computer format. Today's types of questions, however, cannot be replicated on paper. They require candidates, among other things, to move text, produce graphics, and perform other work with application packages. "This opens up a whole new area of possibilities," Hardy says. "We can test things that formerly could only be done and observed in a classroom."

Hardy says that much of the development of psychometric theory for use in computer-based testing occurred at ETS in the 1960s. ETS had to wait, however, for computer technology to develop enough to allow them to make use of the theory and for the public to become sufficiently comfortable with computer technology. ETS piloted its first computer-based exam in 1989.

Among recent computer-based testing advances are point-and-click technology, digitized images and sound, new question types, and multimedia. Point-and-click techniques often work with digitized images to test knowledge in a way that a paper test cannot. For example, one medical exam now presents digitized pictures of X-rays on the screen. The candidate uses a mouse to point and click on the separate areas of the X-ray to answer questions about a pathology. The same technique could be used by a test candidate to identify where on a computer to attach a 16-bit network board.

Similarly, multimedia technology—including integration of graphics and audio—is bringing test candidates more stimulation and a greater sense of operating in the real-world working environment.

Computer technology is also making practical the use of new types of questions. Short-answer questions are being added, and the traditional multiple-choice, single-answer question is supplemented with "multiple rating" questions—questions for which every choice on the screen is more or less desirable and the test taker must rate them in terms of their adequacy.

The possibility for quick feedback in a computer-based test presents another advantage to test takers: an opportunity to combine learning with assessment. For example, the Equitas software program tests users on their skills with many of the most common software offerings in the marketplace. Equitas tracks the order of steps that candidates use while performing the test. Then it instructs test takers on shorter routines with fewer keystrokes to arrive at the same results. Learning while taking the exam is another way in which the testing experience is becoming more meaningful.

Adaptive testing

Among the most sophisticated new potentials of computer-based testing is the adapting of the exam to the abilities of the test taker while the test is in progress. In adaptive tests, if the candidate answers the first question correctly, the exam presents a more difficult question. If the candidate answers the first question incorrectly, the exam presents an easier question. This process continues until the candidate's competency is determined.

Questions used in adaptive tests have been developed through many trial examinations. They have proved their worth in discriminating the knowledge of candidates.

Adaptive testing offers advantages to the candidate. One is efficiency. Adaptive tests more quickly assess the test taker's knowledge. Fewer questions are needed, and the test can be taken much more quickly—something that test takers enjoy. A spokesperson from Novell says,

"People taking our adaptive tests love the fact that it might take them only 20 minutes to measure their expertise rather than an hour."

Candidates also like the fact that questions on adaptive tests are pitched to their ability to answer them and won't be excessively easy or difficult. The candidate will be neither bored nor overwhelmed while taking an adaptive test.

Adaptive testing also benefits the organization giving the examination: It adds a higher level of security to the exam since the candidate views a limited number of test questions.

Working with Novell, Drake Prometric pioneered the first large-scale commercial application of adaptive testing in 1991. The popularity of the technique has been growing since. The Educational Testing Service, for one, now offers adaptive testing along with standard "linear testing" (i.e., every test question is given in the same sequence to everyone). They also offer questions in a hybrid model called "computerized mastery testing" in which a decision on the level of difficulty to present next is not made with every question, but after a group of questions.

Performance-based testing

Performance-based testing measures a candidate's ability to define and solve authentic problems they would typically encounter at work. A performance-based test differs from a conventional exam because it presents work scenarios and data in the way that the job might actually present them.

The computer offers the potential for simulating actual job situations and assessing the ability of the candidate to apply knowledge and solve problems. As performance-based testing techniques develop, they will improve the fidelity of testing—the degree to which the "indirect" process of assessment mirrors the "direct" process.

A test given by ETS to architects offers one example of performance-based testing possibilities. Most of what architects do today is on computer using a computer-aided design (CAD) system. During the

test, architects sit at a computer, just as they would in a work situation; the only difference is that both their process and their product are being evaluated as they do it.

Collaborating with Novell and other clients, Drake is pioneering the use of performance-based testing methodology. Through Windows-based software and use of CD-ROM technology, test candidates are accessing graphics, documentation, and soon other software programs to solve problems.

Novell's new exam for service and support technicians is the first such exam administered by Drake. During the exam, candidates must navigate through a variety of CD-ROM-based information sources that they would normally use on the job. Drake's preliminary study of the data suggest that these kinds of questions are among the strongest at predicting actual job performance.

Drake is working on the technology to launch applications from within exams. Applications can include spreadsheets, word-processing programs, or other application packages. Candidates taking such tests are given a problem to solve and go into the application to solve it. The testing system receives information from the application. Scoring could be done by looking at an operation performed in the application program, or the application might have been used only to get information to bring back into the test.

Other Novell exams released in early 1995 simulate NetWare utilities. For example, one test delivers candidates into a simulation of the 4.1 NetWare Administrator, the Windows-based interface of the 4.1 product. After performing tasks there, the candidate presses a "done" button and returns to the test item where he or she left off. The variables from the simulation that are relevant to the problem are transferred to the test driver, and the test driver does the scoring.

Delivering an exam of this sophistication to its 700 testing sites presents practical challenges that Drake is aggressively addressing. Drake's motivation, a spokesperson says, is that "both Drake and our clients know that this is the right way to go."

Simulations of the work environment might be continuous, or they might be represented in a series of separate test items linked together as snapshots of a common solution pathway. Candidates are asked to solve problems at each snapshot.

Paul Jones says that the "static simulations" are less costly and more quickly developed than continuous simulations. They are also likely, he says, to provide valuable views of problem-solving ability in the real-world job environment, but more research needs to be done on them before experts can be certain.

Performance-based testing gives test takers a chance to show what they can do in an environment as close as possible to their normal working environment. When test takers are disabled, their normal working environment might include a number of physical aids for sight, hearing, or movement. Performance-based tests need to provide candidates with disabilities similar aids in order to give a fair and accurate assessment of their skills.

Computer-based testing increasingly comes equipped with means for accommodating test takers who are disabled. ETS, for example, now has a program that allows candidates with hearing disabilities to receive an American Sign Language translation of the test. They are continually looking for ways to adapt the test to paralell the working situations of candidates with disabilities.

 # Test design and the knowledge it captures

Exams are designed differently depending upon what one wants to measure and to certify. Jones, Bryan Bradley, Kim Thayn, and Jerry Griph of Drake Prometric identify three basic kinds of "competent performance" that one might wish to certify and the kinds of exam approaches one would use for each. Their discussion illustrates the role of computer-based testing in improved assessment of knowledge and skill.

The Drake group's "competent performances" include:

> ➤ *Knowing the right things.* This means demonstrating that one knows information about a subject; for example, in a written driver's test.

> ➤ *Understanding sufficiently.* This requires demonstrating that you understand a subject well enough to solve typical problems, as, for example, in a computer programming test or a written medical board exam.

> ➤ *Performing effectively.* Here, candidates must demonstrate that they are able to perform effectively in the work environment, as in a word-processing test or a flight-simulator assessment.

Knowing the right things

When people are new to a technical area, they usually need to learn something about it before they even begin to acquire skills. This means acquiring what cognitive psychologists call "declarative knowledge"—what we can talk or write about, as opposed to "procedural knowledge," which is what we can do.

Novices need declarative knowledge to understand instructions, read manuals, and interpret the actions of teachers. Even in a computerized environment, this kind of knowledge is usually tested with multiple-choice items. Multiple-choice items have gotten a bad reputation, the Drake team says, because they're so often written poorly. There are guidelines, however, for writing effective multiple-choice exams; some of those guidelines have a research base to support them.

Two other design strategies help when testing for declarative knowledge. One is to be sure that the test doesn't require the candidate to know something that is unimportant. (An expert review panel should rate items for appropriateness and frequency of real-world application.) The other is to be sure that the questions test only the knowledge that the exam is designed to test.

Understanding sufficiently

Understanding is more than just knowing information. It involves procedure—knowing how to do something and recognizing when to do it. It is the product not just of book learning, but also of real-life experience. Understanding does not, however, necessarily imply the ability to manipulate tools and controls, which is more related to performance effectiveness.

The Drake team suggests eight strategies for gathering evidence about understanding:

1 Require multiple cognitive steps on the way to a response. Even the multiple-choice test item can play a role in this. For example, on a medical exam, the multiple-choice question might be about alternative treatment regimens. To arrive at the answer, the candidate must review a clinical case history, a transcript of medical records, and reports of previous treatment and lab results, then make a diagnosis.

2 Present better and worse answer options, not just right and wrong ones. Tests can present answers on a quality continuum and weigh them appropriately. Candidates who evaluate the given options for their degree of suitability have a better opportunity to show what they really know.

3 Differentially weight items according to their difficulty. Giving the same weight to both easy and difficult questions leaves out important information about competency.

4 Require the candidate to use real online resources on the way to a response. One weakness of test items in general is that they usually spoon-feed all of the necessary information to the candidate. This is markedly different from typical real-life problem solving where one has to seek out the needed information. Multimedia offers vast potential here by making available during the exam information sources that would normally be available to the candidate on the job. For example, Novell's exam for service and support technicians is a good test of the candidate's ability to use two different CD-ROM-based research tools.

5 Require the candidate to process dirty data rather than sanitized data. In real life you get what's there—the confusing details of a surgery or of a computer's mechanical breakdown. The information for solving the problem is not neatly separated out and presented to you. Similarly, in a test situation, problems should be presented with salient but irrelevant features of the situation as well as relevant features. Again, multimedia has enormous potential here. If problem data normally come over the phone, digitized audio can be used to simulate the situation during the exam. If the candidate has to be able to locate anomalies in a detailed data display, he or she can be required on the test to point to a trouble spot with a mouse.

6 See if the candidate's knowledge base is densely articulated. That is, are the elements in the candidate's knowledge base richly interconnected with one another? For example, a novice history student would see World War I, the Great Depression, and World War II as separate chapters in a textbook. An advanced student would see the causal fibers linking the three events together.

One way to determine the extent of the candidate's "knowledge network" is to have the candidate build one. The candidate can be provided with the names of a few concepts and a menu of conceptual links and be asked to construct a network, almost as if it were a Tinkertoy structure. How such a representation should be scored is still a research question.

7 Require evaluations and point-and-click designations as responses. Evaluations can be worked into multiple rating questions in which candidates rate the given answers for their worth in solving the problem. For example, the question might describe a call into the Microsoft Word 6.0 Help Line. In the scenario, the caller wishes to interchange two rows of a table constructed in Microsoft Word.

The candidate is asked to rate each of the following sets of instructions given by the Help Line using this scale: A for best possible answer, B for good answer, C for workable but clumsy, D for unclear instruction, F for will fail. The various strategies presented by the Help Line might be presented in text, images, video or sound clips. Microsoft is currently conducting research with Drake into the effectiveness of evaluations as compared to the more usual multiple-choice questions.

Evaluations do require a more real-life response to complex situations. Similarly, pointing and clicking on a hidden hot area on a complex image of a graphic requires true understanding; it would be difficult in such a situation to hit upon the correct answer by chance or by elimination.

8 Require the candidate to integrate information from multiple sources and accumulate information over time. In real-life problem solving, people gather information from many sources and learn something during the early stages of solving a problem that comes in handy later on. The exam can provide multiple information sources and mimic the accumulation of problem information over time by presenting multiframe problems or "testlets."

The set of frames proceeds in chronological fashion, each frame representing a snapshot of the solution process as it traverses a particular solution pathway. Candidates respond in each frame, sometimes analyzing the current problem state, sometimes choosing an appropriate next action, sometimes searching for a key piece of information.

Each response might or might not be followed by feedback. In any case, the candidate is forced to stay on the correct pathway. The goal is not to provide a simulation, but to test understanding within a temporal, problem-solving context.

⇨ **Performing effectively**

"It's one thing to understand a domain," Jones says, "it's another to meet the 'bottom-line' performance requirements of a job." To test a candidate's ability to perform, a test must evaluate not only understanding, but also certain psychomotor and self-management abilities. Candidates must not only solve problems, they must solve them appropriately and efficiently.

Testing for effective performance requires that we remove constraints from those parts of the performance that matter to us in order to make the test as life-like as possible. The Drake team recommends several design strategies to help with this.

First, allow as much freedom to act in the test environment as possible, and provide immediate feedback on the consequences of each action. A good example that Jones cites is the Clinical Competency Test (CCT) of the American Veterinary Medical Association. While the test is paper-and-pencil-based, Jones feels that it would lend itself beautifully to multimedia presentation.

The exam presents 14 problems. Each begins with a written case scenario, including a description of the time, place, species, initial complaint, the client's desires, etc. Following this scene are a series of frames, each presenting a menu of alternative actions. When the candidate chooses an action, it is followed by immediate written feedback describing the results of the action. Some actions will be helpful to the resolution of the case. Some will be neutral. Some will be harmful.

Second, measure appropriateness of response by counting errors of commission and errors of omission. The candidate's performance on a CCT problem is scored by summing the number of errors of commission and the number of errors of omission (not choosing actions that are clearly indicated) and subtracting this sum from the maximum total score.

Appropriate action, according to the CCT, means choosing all the essential actions while not choosing any that are harmful or detrimental. Candidates are not penalized for choosing neutral actions, although one can imagine situations where any response that is not required would be considered inappropriate.

Third, measure efficiency of response when it is important to effective performance. Speed is not crucial to the performance of all real-world tasks, but there is pressure in many office environments for quick performance of duties. Testing of one's ability to use software, for example, would typically involve measuring the efficiency of performance.

One strategy for testing how efficiently the candidate uses software would be to launch the application from the test and to have the candidate perform specific manipulations while the test keeps track of elapsed time and counts keystrokes and mouse clicks (as in the

Equitas exam). At the end of the procedure the candidate simply points out the answer or deposits it in the appropriate location or submits the file for evaluation. The scoring program evaluates the product and produces an accuracy score based on the product and an efficiency score based on time and keyboard events.

Of course, all of the computer-based and performance-based items recommended have a cost. The Drake team points out that bitmap images can be big and slow—slow to build on substandard equipment and slow to disseminate electronically. Redrawing bitmaps as sleeker, faster vector graphics is expensive. Good photography and video require a major production effort. Digital audio and video files of nontrivial length take huge amounts of storage space.

The trick, they say, is to represent complexity only as it serves specific objectives in testing. The goal, as always, is to make an exam that predicts who will function well in the real-world demands of a particular job and who won't.

The future of test taking

Computer-based testing is developing rapidly and opening new possibilities for assessing knowledge and performance. For example, important improvements in the simulation of the work environment are just around the corner. According to Paul Jones, the marketplace is soon likely to see the creation of "problem-solving environments" or "micro-worlds" in the place of test items of the usual variety.

A test, for example, might simulate a service-support help desk. A video phone would let candidates see and hear a "client" calling in with a difficulty. Menu items on the exam would allow the candidate to select questions to ask the caller about the problem, some of which would be appropriate, some not.

Documentation and online research tools would be available to the test taker, just as they would on the job. The exam would also let the candidate actually solve the problem physically by, for example, modifying a configuration file, or by working on a graphic of a piece

of hardware to change a jumper setting. When the problem is solved, the candidate would click on a "done" button and be scored.

Encouraged by its clients, Drake is currently developing a sample test incorporating these features. Jones says, "Everyone who sees our demonstration of these concepts believes that that's what testing should be." Exactly how long it will be before it's available is uncertain. According to Jones, "There are problems to work out between here and there, but the idea has been laid out and we are working toward that. Within the next couple of years that kind of testing will be a reality."

Many of the pieces of the "micro-world" already exist. For example, color, animation, and sound-based questions in music and language are already appearing in new item types. Satellite links are being created to feed digital information and also live audio to test takers.

What the longer-term future might be for the technology of testing is hard to predict. One industry observer speculates that test takers might one day don virtual reality helmets and grab a joy stick to enter a world that replicates their work world to the finest details.

Exams of the near future will use new technology not only to simulate the real world, but also to present new item types to better gauge understanding. For example, Paul Jones predicts that exam questions will increasingly test procedural rather than merely declarative knowledge. That is, correct responses will depend on the particulars of a situation, rather than being merely abstract answers to abstract questions.

Jones also predicts that as technology allows, exams will increasingly evaluate the pathways that the candidate takes to a solution rather than just the solution itself. In that way, the richness of information about candidate performance deepens.

The richness of information will also soon increase with a major development in the allowed complexity of candidate responses. According to Roy Hardy of ETS, computer scoring of natural language responses is currently being developed to allow test takers to type out a paragraph and have that paragraph scored electronically. A number of technical challenges need to be overcome along the way.

As Hardy says, "It sounds easy to have a person respond to a question in their own words. But if they don't give certain words in a certain order, you've got a problem." At that point he says, you have to actually analyze that response. ETS is looking at options to do that, including artificial intelligence.

The increased density of test information might soon deliver a clear picture that goes beyond what Paul Jones calls declarative or procedural knowledge. It might also yield a picture of what he calls the "metacognitive level" or ability to manage cognitive processes in order to set problem-solving goals and to achieve them.

This kind of deep understanding on the part of the candidate goes beyond what's required to perform realistic diagnostic tasks appearing in most job descriptions. But gauging a candidate's ability at the metacognitive level might play an increasingly important role in certification testing, particularly where the testing is part of systems whose goals are not just assessment but also improvement.

To test that level of understanding, candidates need a good deal of free play within the exam context. "If there's no degree of freedom," Jones says, "there's nothing to manage." Technology increasingly gives test takers freedom to behave in complex ways and test makers the power to make sense of their behavior.

Technology might also affect the way we access testing in the future. Some industry observers predict that one day people might take tests on their TV at home or in their company's training center or on the Internet. Registration might also be accomplished through these media. All of this will make testing more accessible to candidates. Test-taking in the 1990s and beyond will be more accessible and more meaningful than ever before.

The Drake Worldwide Testing Network

CHAPTER 6

DRAKE Prometric currently delivers tests through more than 700 authorized testing centers worldwide, and that number is growing rapidly. The number of exams delivered is also growing rapidly. Drake is now delivering tens of thousands of certification exams each month and recently celebrated delivery of its millionth test.

Figure 6-1

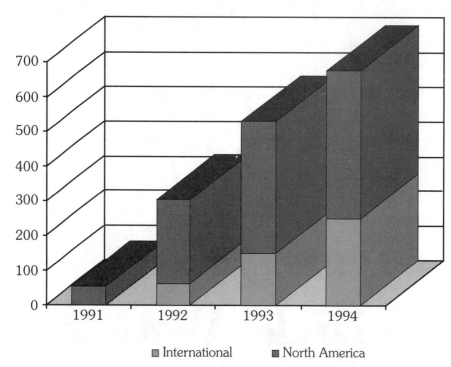

■ International   ■ North America

Test-center network expansion, 1991 to 1994

The global testing network provides convenience to test takers, allowing them to choose facilities located close by and offering hours that are convenient. It serves their employers by reducing travel costs and time away from the job. It also benefits Drake's clients—the organizations whose certification exams Drake administers.

Most of these clients are global companies. They need certified professionals everywhere around the world to support end users. Only a global network of testing centers can meet that global demand for certified support. But Drake's clients, along with exam candidates and their employers, need more from testing centers than worldwide

proliferation and accessibility. They need test centers to safeguard the integrity of the exam process and ensure that exam results can be relied upon. Drake has developed an elaborate system of requirements to ensure that exams delivered through its testing network meet needs for convenience, comfort, and dependable results.

The Drake Authorized Testing Centers

Drake works with training and testing centers worldwide to deliver its exams through their facilities. This system gives Drake access to a wide-ranging network of high-quality testing facilities, and gives the centers a broader customer base, more revenue, and an enhanced image as a total solution provider.

Drake helps ensure the centers' success by providing the administrative support the centers need to deliver exams. For example, Drake registers and schedules exams for the candidates and reports results to candidates and to the certifying agency. Drake also provides technical support for installing Drake software and provides other ongoing technical support.

Once the center is qualified as a Drake Authorized Testing Center (DATC), it is tied electronically to Drake's hub of operations in Minneapolis. Each evening, every DATC worldwide electronically connects to the hub to send a file containing the day's test results and to receive its testing schedule for the next day.

Before a center can become a Drake Authorized Testing Center, however, it must meet a variety of criteria for its facility, scheduling, staff, equipment, and security.

Facility

Testing candidates are under considerable pressure to perform well on their tests, so each candidate has the right to expect a professional testing atmosphere. Drake safeguards that right by setting a number of conditions for the DATC.

The testing room must be quiet and free from distractions such as printers, copiers, telephones, and conversations. It must also be pleasantly furnished, well lighted, and well ventilated, with a comfortable temperature. The working space and chairs are ergonomically designed for comfort.

The room where tests are administered must be dedicated to testing, reducing the risk that the equipment might be unavailable for any reason. It contains at least three testing workstations, each of which is separated from the others by an acoustical partition. The room also allows constant visual monitoring of candidates by a Certified DATC Administrator.

Sherry Reid, Drake's vice president of operations, says that Drake wants consistent, high-quality, secure testing centers. "Not that all the walls have to be gray," she says, "but that we have quiet testing rooms conducive to taking a test."

Facilities also need to avoid overcrowding. Diane Helling, Drake's manager of testing center services for North and South America, monitors testing volumes to be sure centers are not overcrowded and that candidates have adequate access to the facility. She says that once a testing center reaches about 85 percent of capacity, "It's time to expand with more seats or more testing hours, or it may be time to open another center in the area."

Test centers in the United States have an additional group of concerns: They must satisfy the requirements of the Americans with Disabilities Act. According to Reid, Drake works hard to make exams accessible to those with special needs. For the physical environment, this means the DATCs have wheelchair access, no testing happens on upper floors reachable only by stairs, and levers on restroom doors allow easy entry.

Drake also accommodates the visually impaired by providing them with readers, and, when necessary, provides sign language interpreters for the hearing-impaired. Drake also follows ADA guidelines to provide time extensions for those with dyslexia or other learning disabilities. According to Reid, "We have yet to run across an individual who has registered with us whom we haven't been able to accommodate."

Scheduling

Requirements for test center scheduling are designed to give reasonable access to the centers and reasonable notice to test takers if schedules change. The minimum time that a DATC can be open for testing is six consecutive hours per day, five days per week. Once the hours have been established, Drake will schedule candidates for tests accordingly. The DATC is notified each morning which candidates to expect, when to expect them, and for which exams.

Since many candidates schedule their tests weeks in advance, they have a right to adequate notice should a DATC change its hours and their exam need to be rescheduled. Drake requires 30 days notice from the DATC for any change in its hours of operation.

Staff

Every DATC designates at least two people to be trained as Certified DATC Administrators. These people need much more than a basic understanding of hardware and software; they also need strong customer-relations skills. Reid says, "Candidates should be treated well, so we lessen their test anxiety. The way in which an administrator greets and helps them can make a big difference."

To ensure that test administrators are well trained, Drake provides a complete training package for them. Following their training, they must pass a series of online certification tests; after that, Drake provides them ongoing telephone support. Administrators might have other responsibilities in the center organization, but they must be dedicated to the tasks of managing daily communications with Drake and administering tests as they are scheduled.

Equipment

Authorized testing centers must meet a long list of requirements for both hardware and software. Helling says, "Basically, we're using IBM equipment—pretty much industry standard, which makes it

easier for the testing center to acquire and easier for Drake to support technically."

Drake requires its testing centers to have a file server with a minimum of 486-level equipment, 33 megahertz, with 16MB of RAM. The file server must be secure; that is, it cannot be used for delivering both testing and training. At least one workstation must have a CD-ROM.

A variety of requirements also apply to the administrator's workstation, which cannot be used as a testing workstation. Helling says that Drake is starting to use digitized photography, and room must be available to connect a camera at the administrator workstation.

Software requirements include, among other things, Windows software, and, of course, any applications software that is part of the exam being administered.

Security

Dependable exam results require high security. The costs of test development, the proprietary content of the tests, and the integrity of the whole testing system are at stake. Drake uses proven methods and procedures to ensure security. It sets high standards for monitoring candidates in the Drake Authorized Testing Centers, for securely transferring candidate tests and records, and for maintaining the central hub of operations in Minneapolis.

At the testing center, candidates are required to show two forms of identification (both must have a signature, and one must have a photo) before they can even enter the testing room. They also sign in and out of a log book, and leave all papers and books outside the room for closed-book tests. After the exam, proctors collect and destroy any scratch paper used.

During the test, a Certified DATC Administrator must continually monitor activities in the test room and be alert for any misconduct. In practice, this means that the administrator watches the room continuously on closed-circuit video or remains at his or her workstation to view the candidates through a viewing window. The

test room is never left unattended. But cheating is unlikely for another reason: Individual tests are generated on a custom basis out of the total pool of questions created for a particular certification exam. Every candidate always has a test that is different from the test of every other candidate in the room.

Candidates will also find that the people around them in the exam room are very often taking tests on topics completely unrelated to their own. As Helling says, "You might be taking a Banyan exam, the person to the left of you is taking a real estate exam, and the person to the right is taking an insurance test."

Communications between the Minneapolis hub and the Drake Authorized Testing Center are also designed with security in mind. For example, tests are sent from the Minneapolis hub to Drake Authorized Testing Centers in encrypted form. Test items are only unencrypted when they appear on the computer screen for the candidate to answer. After they appear on the screen, test items, along with the candidate's answer, are automatically encrypted again. The encrypted candidate test records are automatically and electronically relayed to the hub daily.

Minneapolis is the center of operations for Drake Prometric. The facility has been designed to meet rigorous government standards for high-level security. In addition, the area of the facility devoted to processing test data and communicating with the DATCs is off-limits to all but a handful of employees with the proper security clearance.

The facility is well protected, not only against intruders, but also against electronic error. For example, the hub computer system uses continual disk mirroring to provide real-time backup for all data. An uninterruptible power supply (UPS) maintains operation and protects data in the event of a power outage. Drake's real-time disaster recovery, located in a separate facility, also ensures that operations can continue in the event of a catastrophic event or natural disaster.

Ensuring quality

To ensure that Drake Authorized Testing Centers comply with all that's asked of them, Drake incorporates a "secret shopper"

program. Professional observers register as test candidates and observe operations at the testing center. Observers might be from an independent company or they might be Drake employees.

The observers provide Drake an exhaustive report, and Drake communicates the findings back to the DATC with recommendations for improvement or for quick remedial action. A breach in test security would lead to immediate suspension of testing at the center while the situation was investigated.

Sherry Reid says that results of secret shopper investigations have been very encouraging. She says, "The results have been excellent. About 90 percent of the test centers continually operate at a satisfactory or excellent rating." But, she adds, "We keep raising the bar and making our standards higher all the time."

Drake also works to keep communication lines wide open with the DATCs and provide them all the support they need to succeed. Drake staff regularly visit them to strengthen the relationship and to improve customer service. The DATCs also have the opportunity, through regular surveys, to evaluate the service and support provided them by Drake.

A worldwide system for uniformity and access

According to Helling, the Drake testing network procedures, though uniform, also allow for some differences from one region of the world to another. The differences keep the Drake testing network in line with regional business realities and help increase candidate access to the system worldwide.

For example, she points out that in Latin America the cost of a phone call can be prohibitive. For that reason candidates usually register, schedule, and pay for their exams through their local testing center, rather than through a centralized 800 number as they would in North America. Registration information is batched and sent electronically to Drake, and Drake itself enters the information into the centralized registration system.

Gary L. Alley, Drake's director of operational standards for Europe, says that registrations in Europe also tend to be collected and sent in groups to Drake by the testing centers, though for a different reason. In Europe, he says, Drake Authorized Testing Centers are often training institutes offering Drake certification exams as a value-added service.

Candidates taking the certification exams are often closely associated with those training centers and might have paid for their training and their exam as a package. As a result, some 60 percent or more of registrations in Europe are submitted in bulk to Drake by the Drake Authorized Testing Centers.

Alley says that there are no major differences in the operation of the Drake testing system anywhere in the world. He says that the same computer system is used worldwide to handle registrations; it is only how those registrations are generated—in bulk or individually—that differs.

The rules for taking tests are the same everywhere, and the hardware and software requirements are virtually equivalent. Alley says, for example, that it can be more difficult for a training center to be approved by telecommunications firms for use of a modem in Europe, but the particular type of modem required by Drake and the requirements for the CD-ROM do not vary.

Alley says that while Europe has only three test facilities completely owned by Drake (in London, Paris, and Dusseldorf), the DATCs understand that their work with Drake is independent of other work done at their sites and must be in strict compliance with DATC requirements.

"We do adapt as needed for cultural and geographic differences," Alley says, "but we don't make fundamental changes." Alley says that most of Drake's clients are large international firms who require quality and consistency in exam administration. "They need the assurance," he says, "that what Drake does for them in Hong Kong is the same as what we do for them in London and in Dallas." Alley says that has to be true because "the client's tests don't vary, and their standards of performance don't vary. So the delivery mechanisms and the standards of service can't vary either."

 # Drake's Regional Service Centers

One important means to handle the unique service requirements of individual regions is the Regional Service Center. Regional Service Centers guarantee that candidates receive support in their local language, local currency, and local time while serving as the focal point for registration and scheduling functions. In that way they support individual candidates and also the DATCs worldwide.

Each Regional Service Center has a list of testing sites in their region along with testing schedules, directions to the site, and site contacts. The centers arrange for the candidate to take exams at the most convenient sites and times.

The centers also arrange for a test in the appropriate language. Currently, Drake can deliver exams in most languages, including Japanese. Drake's clients are responsible for translating their exams.

Following is a list of the six Regional Service Centers and the regions they serve.

Minneapolis	North, South, and Central America
London	Northern Europe, UK, South Africa, and the Middle East
Paris	France, Spain, Portugal, and North Africa
Dusseldorf	Germany, Italy, Eastern Europe, Russia
Tokyo	Japan
Sydney	All Pacific Rim countries (except Japan)

The decentralized registration and scheduling made possible through the Regional Service Centers allows candidates to enjoy better customer support. At the same time, centralized data collection through the Minneapolis hub allows the certifying organization to receive their data back promptly (within 48 hours of the exam).

Drake is careful in opening and staffing the Regional Service Centers just as it is with the DATCs. Where sufficient business volume exists, a new center will open to serve clients and candidates in that region.

Figure 6-2

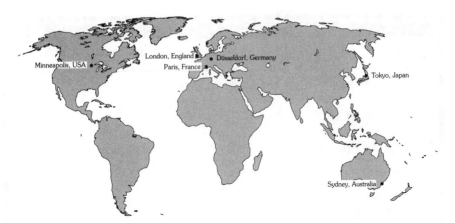

Locations of Drake Regional Service Centers

Recently, new Regional Service Centers opened in Australia and Tokyo. Reid says that China might be next.

Selection of staff, particularly the center manager, is handled with care. Reid says that the manager of the Japanese Regional Service Center was chosen not only for experience and skill, but also for an appearance of politeness, gentleness, and discretion, qualities so important to Japanese culture.

Reid says that staff "have to wear so many hats" to handle the needs of a variety of cultures from the Regional Service Center. But, she says, the staff handle their responsibilities beautifully. "So far," she says, "we've been very lucky. We've been able to staff our Regional Service Centers with extraordinary people."

The Drake test delivery system

Drake delivers tests through its network of worldwide DATCs using a sophisticated yet easy-to-use Windows-based computerized testing system. The screen in Fig. 6-3 shows a typical format.

Drake's system offers a variety of possible question types, including multiple choice, single answer; multiple choice, multiple answer;

Figure 6-3

Item 3 of 14 ▲

☐ **Mark**   **Current Time: 10:50:27 AM**

What is the official language of Ivory Coast?

○ a. Akan

◉ b. French

○ c. Kiswahili

○ d. Kikuyu

Select the best answer.

| Next | Previous | Help |

Sample test question

true/false; point-and-click; and short answer. Online graphics and exhibits also sometimes appear within questions.

To allow candidates to get familiar with the various question types and how to answer them, an online tutorial is available to use before the test. All testing appointments include an extra 15 minutes to sign in and use the tutorial.

Each tutorial is specific to the test to be taken and clearly shows how to answer the kinds of questions that appear in that test. For example, the tutorial connected with a conventional exam shows candidates how they can scroll and mark and review questions, returning to them as desired to change answers. The tutorial connected with adaptive tests explains that in that kind of exam, the candidate cannot return to a question after it is answered.

The center administrator is also available to help with the tutorial and ensure that candidates understand how to answer questions. In addition, online help is always available during the exam.

Other features have been built into the testing system for ease of use:

➤ Answers can be selected with keyboard or mouse.

➤ The software keeps a record of questions not fully answered and prompts the candidate to review them.

➤ An onscreen clock reminds candidates of time remaining.

➤ Every answer is immediately and automatically backed up by the system in case power is lost or the system is interrupted.

➤ Results of the exam appear on the screen immediately after the candidate completes the exam.

Test result displays can be customized to various formats. A typical one appears in the following illustration.

Section scores can also be shown on another customizable screen illustrated on the following page.

Figure 6-4

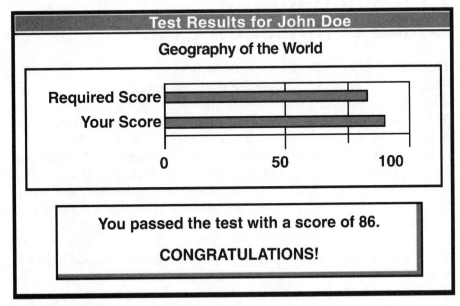

Sample test results

Figure 6-5

Section Scores for JOHN DOE			
Geography of the World			
Section Title	0	100	**Score**
Flags of the World			100
Geography of Europe			100
Geography of the Americas			50
Continental Geography			100
Animals of the World			0
Capitals of the World			50
Languages of the World			100
Rivers and Lakes of the World			50

OK   Help

Sample test results by sections

 # Procedure for the Drake certification exam

✳ Decide what certification exam to take

Chapter 7 contains descriptions of the certification programs administered by Drake Prometric for the information technology field. This collection includes most of the certifications that are offered anywhere in the IT field today. These write-ups can be helpful in determining if a particular certification program can be of use to you. You'll quickly discover in reading them if you are a part of the audience for whom the certification program was designed and what benefits you might enjoy by holding the certification or employing others with that certification.

You'll also be able to quickly identify what is required of you before you take the exam and how best to prepare. Specific testing information, including exam fees, is provided along with phone numbers for additional information about the exam and to register. The toll-free (800) registration numbers listed in these program descriptions are administered by Drake. Drake customer service

representatives are trained in the specifics of each certification program and can answer your questions about the programs and about training opportunities or refer you elsewhere for more detailed information.

❋ Contact the regional service center to register

In North America, call the toll-free registration numbers listed for each program description in Chapter 7. Elsewhere in the world, contact the Regional Service Center. For up-to-date phone numbers for contacting Regional Service Centers outside of North America, or for any general questions about registering for exams administered by Drake Prometric, call Drake in Minneapolis, Minnesota, at 612-896-7000.

The first time you call Drake to register, an electronic file of information is built with your name, address, phone, fax number, and social security number. This eliminates the need to gather redundant data with every registration. Over time, the complete record of your testing history is kept for you as well.

Once the customer service representative has you on file, you need only tell him or her the exam you are registering for. Payment for the exam can be made by Visa, Master Card, American Express, or by check. Often the candidate's employer pays for the exam in advance by purchasing vouchers from Drake. In that case, the candidate needs only to supply the voucher number to complete payment. Cancellations are refundable if made more than 24 hours before the exam.

Once guaranteed payment is made, the test can be scheduled. Those paying with credit card or voucher can schedule immediately; those paying with check can call back to schedule three days after mailing the check.

Candidates have access to all of the Drake Authorized Testing Centers around the world. Customer service representatives work with each candidate to find the most convenient location and to schedule the exam for the most convenient time. Many centers are open after normal business hours and on weekends. As Diane Helling says, "Our testing centers recognize that people don't always want to take their tests between 8:00 a.m. and 5:00 p.m., Monday through Friday, so they offer extended hours."

Convenience also means little or no wait. Some of Drake's clients permit the candidate to take the exam on the same day they register. It might be possible to register with Drake at 9:00 a.m. and take the exam at 2:00 the same afternoon.

According to Helling, "Once the exam is scheduled, all the candidate has to do is to show up." But don't forget two forms of identification, both with signatures and one with a photo. Some certifying agencies might also require candidates to bring additional authorization forms with them to the exam. If other forms are required, the customer service representative always reminds candidates about this, as well as about the rules for closed book exams.

Those taking their exam more than four days after they register can also expect to receive in the mail a confirmation of their test location and time. Candidates who have requested information about any of the certification programs or about training or self-study guides to prepare for the exam will receive other printed materials on these subjects from the Drake customer service representative.

✳ Show up for the test

Expect to receive all the help you need both from your online tutorial and from your center administrator. The test delivery system and the testing environment have been designed to make the testing experience as comfortable and pleasant as possible.

✳ Receive your exam results

Your exam results are shown to you onscreen immediately after you complete the test, and a score report is printed and embossed for you at the testing center to indicate that it's an official score report. No other printed report of exam results is made; the certifying agency receives results electronically from Drake. No one else sees the report except the testing center administrator.

The certification itself is a separate document from the score report. That certificate will be sent to you from Drake or directly from the certifying agency.

If a candidate fails, he or she can register to take the test again. Some of Drake's clients require waiting periods before the candidate

may retest, others do not. Most of the score reports that candidates receive at the end of the test tell them the specific areas in which they did well or poorly. That information is very helpful in preparing for a retest.

Drake's customer service representatives not only give information out to candidates about exams but also receive information back from them. Candidates with complaints or concerns about their exam are invited to call the Drake customer service representative.

The registration process for Drake's exams is easy and getting easier. According to Reid, Drake's customer service and registration system is growing rapidly and also improving. Drake receives more than 60,000 calls per month from people asking about or registering for certification exams—double the rate in 1994. Reid says that in February 1994, Drake customer service employed a staff of 12; by January 1995, the number of staff had grown to 85. Beyond adding new staff, Reid says that the Drake Call Center is working to improve customer service by investing in a state-of-the-art telephone system and developing an improved registration and scheduling system.

Drake is committed to making effective certification testing accessible throughout the world. That means making registration easy and offering candidates even greater options in scheduling and location for their exams. It also means making test centers comfortable, free of distractions, accommodating to those with special needs, and secure. This guarantees that the needs of all those who depend on certification results are best served. Candidates have a pleasant testing experience in an environment that allows them to prove what they know. Employers review certification results that are not influenced by extraneous circumstances of noise, improper equipment, or confusion about the testing process. The certifying agency has a test delivery system worthy of its significant investment in the exam and its certification program. Finally, the information technology industry has a dependable mechanism to grow certification and, with it, the industry's credibility, strength, and vitality in the years to come.

Individual programs

CHAPTER 7

➡️ Apricot Computers

apricot

➡️ Company background

Apricot Computers is part of Mitsubishi Electric, itself part of one of the world's largest group of companies. Acquired in May 1990, Apricot was Mitsubishi's first-ever acquisition of a fully operational company. Its decision was strongly influenced by two factors—the importance of the Open Systems market and Apricot's international reputation as an innovative force in network computing. Apricot is now responsible for the worldwide development of all Mitsubishi Electric's work-group PC and server products, and all Mitsubishi Open Systems products are branded with the Apricot name.

➡️ The Apricot Certified Engineer program

Every network system is a fusion of hardware and software technology. To achieve minimum downtime and maximum performance, it is important to ensure that your support staff understand the way that server platforms interact with network operating systems.

The Apricot Certified Engineer program was developed specifically to provide support staff with this vital understanding. It is designed for all staff who are directly involved in the installation and field support of Apricot network servers—from hardware engineers and in-house support personnel to network managers.

The program covers the main configuration issues associated with Apricot servers and shows engineers how to optimize Apricot servers for use with the main network operating systems. Apricot Certified

Engineers have the knowledge to identify the exact cause of system problems and provide a better understanding of how to put them right the first time.

This certification program, via the appropriate combination of tests, provides the objective measurement necessary to ensure that the training has achieved the desired results.

✳ Preparation

All Apricot Certified Engineers attend a minimum of two intensive, one-day courses. The first day is a detailed introduction to Apricot server hardware. Engineers then go on to a further course on the operating system of their choice. The first day covers all of the factors liable to influence network configuration on the Apricot servers, including hardware and firmware revisions, reliability testing and SCSI devices. The operating system courses cover the relationship between Apricot hardware and the network software, including hard disk types, LAN adapters, Apricot Server Environment Packs, memory requirements, disk duplexing, tape backup, workstations, and upgrading Apricot VX-Net.

✳ Examination details

Topics The topics are based on the materials covered in the courses described.

Length The time limit for each exam is 60 minutes. Each exam consists of 60 multiple-choice questions delivered in random order from a pool of questions typically twice this number.

Fees Each exam costs £65.

Registration To register to take the test at a Drake Authorised Testing Centre, call Drake at 0800 592873 (UK).

Benefits and deliverables

For anyone involved in the maintenance and configuration of Apricot networks in the field, the Apricot Certified Engineer certification provides the assurance that the investment involved in undertaking the

program is quickly repaid in faster repairs, fewer call outs, and improved system performance.

 # Contact information

For more information about Apricot courses and certification programs, call 0121 717 7171 (Birmingham, England).

 # AST Computer

 # Company background

AST Computer designs, manufactures, and markets desktop, server, and notebook computers. The company's computer products are sold worldwide at more than 10,000 dealer and retailer locations.

AST's goal is to be the easiest company to do business with, in every way. To meet this goal, the company is focused on providing total customer satisfaction with PCs that are easy to use, easy to obtain, and easy to afford.

 # Guardian Care certification program

The Guardian Care testing program certifies a candidate's ability to perform field diagnosis and repair on AST Server products. AST authorizes service centers to participate in this on-site repair program if they have at least one Guardian Care Certified Technician on staff.

With Guardian Care, AST Servers and the AST options they contain can be upgraded to four-hour on-site response. Depending on the service center's needs, coverage can either be during normal business hours (Monday through Friday, 8 a.m. to 5 p.m.) or 24 hours a day, 7 days a week, 365 days a year.

✳ Audience

The Guardian Care certification program is for field repair service technicians in AST Authorized Service Centers who perform configuration and repair tasks on a wide range of AST Servers.

✳ Requirements

The successful candidate will pass both the AST Guardian Care server hardware exam and one of five Guardian Care Advanced Operating System (AOS) exams. AST plans to have the following exams available; Novell NetWare, Windows NT, IBM OS/2, SCO UNIX, and Banyan Vines. Contact the AST Service Training Department at 714-727-8232 for further details on available training classes.

The hardware exam measures the technician's ability to perform configuration and repair tasks on a wide range of AST Server systems. The AOS-specific exams test the ability of the candidate to work competently within a given environment and to perform AST-specific configuration tasks. Once the technician is Guardian Care certified on the hardware and one operating system, as many additional AOS certifications as desired may be added.

✳ Preparation

Guardian Care certification classes are conducted by AST Service Training. The AST server hardware and support class covers all pertinent systems and related components/peripherals.

Video training is available for AST-specific configuration issues on all certifiable advanced operating systems. To order, contact the AST Service Training Department at 714-727-8232.

Basic AOS training should be obtained from the operating system software vendor or other approved source. For example, CNE-level

knowledge allows the candidate to answer the questions related to Novell NetWare on the Guardian Care NetWare AOS exam.

Computer-based self-assessment exams are available at no charge from AST Service Training to help the prospective Guardian Care Technician determine readiness or areas for further training prior to taking the certification exam.

✳ Examination details

Topics The Guardian Care hardware exam is divided into two major sections: Prerequisites and Server Systems. The Prerequisites section measures the candidate's ability to operate in a DOS environment, manage PC resources (processors, IRQs, memory), configure EISA and SCSI hardware, and define RAID hard drive subsystems (levels 0, 1, and 5). The Server Systems section measures the candidate's general knowledge of system installation, configuration, capabilities, and troubleshooting tasks.

The Guardian AOS exams are divided into two major sections: Prerequisites and AST Configuration. The Prerequisites section measures the candidate's basic competency in the AOS, including theory, configuration, common issues, and troubleshooting. The AST Configuration section measures the candidate's ability to integrate AST hardware into the specific AOS.

Length All AST exams are one hour and consist of 40 to 50 multiple-choice questions.

Fees Each exam costs $120 U.S. Fees might vary outside of the United States and Canada.

Registration At the time this book went to print, exams were being developed. Contact the AST Service Training Department at 714-727-8232 for further details.

✳ Recertification requirements

Certified individuals must renew their certification status each year by passing both the AST Guardian Care hardware exam and one of five Guardian Care AOS exams.

Benefits and deliverables

AST resellers are invited to join the Guardian Care program in order to provide the highest level of on-site support to their customers. Guardian Care certification is available to AST Authorized Service and Support Centers (ASSCs). After completing the requirements necessary to become Guardian Care certified, the ASSC qualifies as an ASSC+, a designation that represents enhanced service.

Only Guardian Care Certified Technicians, trained to deal with AST Server hardware as well as advanced operating systems (AOS) such as Novell NetWare, Microsoft Windows NT, and IBM OS/2, will be dispatched by AST for on-site service needs.

Certified Guardian Technicians receive a certificate of completion that allows them to perform warranty on-site repair on all AST server systems for one year. Certification also allows the technician free use of the AST Technical Support Hotline.

 # Contact information

For additional information, contact the AST Service Training Department at 714-727-8232.

 # AT&T Microelectronics

 # Company background

AT&T Microelectronics is a leading manufacturer of metal oxide semiconductors (MOS) and high-performance integrated circuits (HPIC), power supplies, connectors, printed circuit boards, advanced integrated modules, and lightwave transmitters and receivers. The AT&T Microelectronics mission is "to become vendor of choice through excellence in customer satisfaction, technology, design, production, and applications."

AT&T Certified Sales Advantage (CSA) program

This program ensures that the AT&T Microelectronics global sales force has the requisite knowledge to properly represent AT&T Microelectronics. The program has three primary objectives: to define the knowledge requirements for sales personnel to properly represent AT&T Microelectronics; to provide the needed education and training to acquire this knowledge; and to provide a means to measure and recognize each individual's mastery of the required knowledge.

✶ Audience

The Certified Sales Advantage (CSA) program is intended for the AT&T Microelectronics global sales force.

✶ Requirements

The CSA program is an individualized program. Each salesperson works with his or her manager to develop a program consisting of CBT modules and certification tests.

The CBT modules and certification tests available are:

- ➢ Product Selection Guide
- ➢ AT&T Overview
- ➢ Overview of ME
- ➢ RAMDAC Products
- ➢ Digital Signal Processors Products
- ➢ Field Programmable Gate Arrays Products
- ➢ LAN-ICs Products
- ➢ Application Specific Integrated Circuits Products
- ➢ Lightwave Products
- ➢ Power Systems Products
- ➢ AT&T Annual Report

✳ **Preparation**

Prior to taking exams, candidates are required to complete computer-based training (CBT) courses for each of the subject matters to be tested.

✳ **Examination details**

Topics The exam topics are covered in the CBT courses.

Length Most exams are 60 minutes long and vary in number of questions.

Fees Each exam costs $50.

Registration To register for an exam, call Drake at 800-487-EXAM (800-487-3926).

⇨ Benefits and deliverables

The CSA program provides the needed education and training for the AT&T sales personnel to properly represent AT&T. The program provides an objective means to measure and recognize each individual's knowledge level.

⇨ Contact information

For additional information on the Certified Sales Advantage program, write to Pat Durning, AT&T Microelectronics Sales Education Organization, 555 Union Boulevard, Room 20E-137 BB, Allentown, Pennsylvania 18103, or call 610-712-5297.

⇨ Comments

"The knowledge I gained from the CBT has helped me increase sales. Volumes are up to about 122 per month, and they are looking into our next generation of RAMDACs. The Certified Sales Advantage really is an advantage—thanks for the great support!"

Prime components salesperson, AT&T Microelectronics

 # Autodesk

 ## Autodesk

 ## Company background

Autodesk is the world's leading supplier of computer-aided design (CAD) automation software and the fifth-largest PC software company in the world. The company develops, markets, and supports a family of design automation and professional multimedia software and component technologies for use on personal computers and workstations. Since its founding in 1982, Autodesk has revolutionized the design and drafting process for engineers, architects, facilities managers, and many other professionals.

AutoCAD certification program

The AutoCAD certification program offers a fair, comprehensive measure of AutoCAD skills for professionals. These standardized exams, offered worldwide, test general AutoCAD knowledge and AutoCAD drawing skills. The exams are a fact-based way for CAD managers to evaluate and allocate their CAD professionals and administer a comprehensive CAD pre-employment test.

✳ Audience

AutoCAD Level I or Level II certification exams are intended for AutoCAD professionals who want to demonstrate a measurable level of accomplishment to their employers or prospective employers.

Companies bidding on projects—commercial or public sector—can use AutoCAD certification of their employees to differentiate their company from the competition.

✳ Requirements

There are two levels of exams, Level I and Level II, from which the candidate can choose to become certified. Candidates should choose the level that is right for them.

The Level I certification is recommended for candidates who have training and experience equivalent to an intensive 32-hour AutoCAD Level I course and 300 hours of production time using AutoCAD software.

The Level II certification exam is recommended for candidates who have training and experience equivalent to an intensive Level II course with on-the-job experience and 600 hours of production time using AutoCAD.

✳ Preparation

Candidates should review the exam format charts in the Autodesk Certified Testing program brochure to choose the certification level that is right for them. Brochures are available from Drake Prometric by calling 800-995-EXAM.

Local Authorized Autodesk Training Centers (ATC) offer top-quality AutoCAD instruction, including an eight-hour "Exam Prep" course. For the location of the nearest ATC, call 800-964-6432.

Candidates can also buy the *AutoCAD Certification Exam Prep Manual* that offers several sample tests to guide the candidate through the certification process. A pretest is included to assess current skill levels and point toward areas for improvement. Sample exams give the candidate some preliminary experience in handling test problems and questions. Two post-tests are offered to help the candidate measure progress in both Level I and Level II skill areas. Packaged with the manual is the EXAMiner for AutoCAD, a disk-based tool developed to simulate the electronic testing environment. The disk tests your general AutoCAD knowledge and provides an online report with results. The *AutoCad Certification Exam Prep Manual* is available from Delmar Publishers. To order, call 800-347-7707.

The "AutoCAD Level I Training Guide" by Autodesk comes with a hands-on exercise disk for quickly learning basic AutoCAD commands. The guide covers 2D drawing and editing commands, drawing tools and object snap, inquiry and display commands, basic blocks and layers, color, linetypes and cross-hatching, and beginning grips. The training guide is available for purchase through Autodesk at 800-435-7771.

The AutoCAD Level I Professional Training Kit from Autodesk is packed with valuable training tools. The kit contains an AutoCAD demo disk, a two-hour AutoCAD training video, AutoCAD Simulator, "AutoCAD Training Guide," *AutoCAD Certification Exam Prep Manual*, EXAMiner for AutoCAD, a 30-percent discount coupon from participating Authorized Autodesk Training providers, and more. The kit is available from AutoCAD dealers. For the location of the nearest dealer call 800-964-6432.

✳ Examination details

Both Level I and Level II exams are scored on a scale of 200 to 800. Candidates must achieve a minimum score of 620 to become certified.

Topics For a list of test objectives, call 800-995-EXAM and request a program brochure.

Length The Level I and Level II exams have both general knowledge questions as well as drawing or performance-based sections, and each is two hours in length. General knowledge questions are multiple choice, multiple answer; multiple choice, single answer; and fill-in-the-blank.

The drawing portions for both AutoCAD Level I and Level II require candidates to create or edit various AutoCAD drawings and then answer questions about those drawings. At the time of registration, candidates are given a choice of disciplines, either mechanical or architectural/engineering/construction.

Fees The Level I and Level II certification exams are $150 each.

Registration To register for exams, call Drake at 800-995-EXAM. Outside the United States or Canada, registration requests may be faxed to 612-820-5050.

Benefits and deliverables

When candidates successfully complete the exam, they receive a Certificate of Achievement from Autodesk. Candidates also receive a detailed diagnostic report that gives them a wealth of analytical information on how their skill set can be improved.

Contact information

Additional information about the AutoCAD Level I or Level II certification exams are listed in the program brochure. To receive a brochure, dial 800-995-EXAM.

For information not included in the brochure, contact the Autodesk Certified Testing Program Manager at 415-507-6407 or write Autodesk Customer Education & Training, 111 McInnis Parkway, San Rafael, California 94903.

 # Comments

"The certification exam was so thorough in analyzing my skills that I was able to improve my own weaknesses almost immediately. This resulted in a positive review and annual salary increase and the possibility to move into new opportunities within the company that I otherwise would not have been qualified for. If you want to advance your career or keep up with your competition, I recommend the AutoCAD exam. It looks great on a resume or in your portfolio!"

Designer/drafter, El Dorado Hills, California

Banyan Systems, Inc.

BANYAN

 # Company background

Banyan Systems, Inc. is a pioneer and leader in enterprise-wide networking and messaging software products. These products enable

customers to integrate multiple heterogeneous computer platforms into a unified global network that is easy and economical to use and manage. Founded in 1983 and headquartered in Westboro, Massachusetts, the company markets products worldwide through Authorized Network Integrators, Resellers, and International Distributors.

Banyan certification programs

At the time this publication went to print, Banyan was finalizing the 1995 certification programs for VINES and BeyondMail. Contact Banyan Customer Communications at 800-2BANYAN for the most up-to-date information on these programs.

Banyan VINES technical certification program

Banyan currently offers two levels of certification, Certified Banyan Specialist (CBS) and Certified Banyan Engineer (CBE). The intention of Banyan's certification program is to set a standard of excellence for technical professionals in end-user and reseller environments who are responsible for administering or supporting networks based on Banyan technology.

Certified Banyan Specialist (CBS)

❋ **Audience**
This certification targets systems and network administrators and support staff.

❋ **Requirements**
Individuals who want to become a CBS must complete the series of certified Banyan courses and exams outlined:

Course number	Course name	Certification test number
EDU120	VINES Administration	020-120*
EDU201	Advanced VINES Administration	020-201*
EDU212	VINES Gateways	020-212
OR		
EDU610	Problem Solving for VINES Networks	020-610

* The VINES Administration and Advanced VINES Administration courses can be waived by passing the corresponding certification tests. Individuals who enroll in the courses must pass the certification tests in order to receive CBS certification or advance to the CBE level.

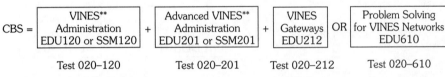

Figure 7-1

** Test out option available

Certification tracks for CBS

An individual is first enrolled as a candidate in the CBS program. Upon fulfillment of the CBS requirements, he or she is automatically enrolled as a candidate in the CBE program and may continue taking courses toward the CBE level.

⇨ Certified Banyan Engineer (CBE)

✳ Audience
The CBE program targets Banyan network and systems engineers who provide backup support or who are involved in network design and performance tuning.

✳ Requirements

Individuals who want to become a CBE must complete the following series of certified Banyan courses and exams after completing CBS certification requirements:

Course number	Course title	Certification test number
EDU801	Technical Support I	020-280
EDU901	Technical Support II	020-290

Note: Candidates must complete the CBS certification requirements prior to enrolling in the CBE program.

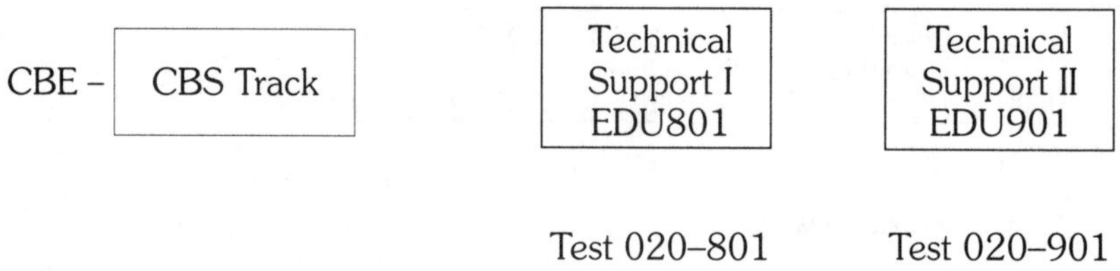

Figure 7-2

```
CBE –   CBS Track        Technical        Technical
                         Support I        Support II
                         EDU801           EDU901

                      Test 020–801     Test 020–901
```

Certification tracks (subject to recertification)

Banyan BeyondMail certification program

This program is intended to set a level of excellence among technical professionals who use BeyondMail. Banyan currently offers one level of BeyondMail certification, BeyondMail Certified Consultant (BCC).

✳ Audience

This certification targets technical professionals in end-user and reseller environments who use BeyondMail.

✳ Requirements

The four courses listed are available to those wishing to attend BeyondMail training at Recognized BeyondMail Education Centers (RBECs) or through Banyan, but they are not a prerequisite to

becoming a BCC. In order to become a BCC, the candidate must first complete a BCC enrollment form, which can be obtained by contacting the technical certification coordinator at 508-898-1795, and then pass all corresponding tests.

Course number	Course title	Certification test number
BND101	Basic Concepts	202-101
BND102	BeyondRules	020-102
BND103	System Administration	020-103
BND104	Workflow Applications Design	020-104

✳ Preparation

Training for Banyan's technical certification program is available from Banyan Training Centers and more than 100 Banyan Certified Education Centers and Recognized BeyondMail Education Centers around the world. To locate the Certified Education Center nearest you, call 800-2BANYAN in the United States and 905-855-2971 in Canada, or call 508-898-1000 and ask for teleservices.

Candidates can prepare for VINES certification tests by using the Banyan Study Guides for each course. Study guides are provided with certification enrollment packages, upon request from the technical certification coordinator at 508-898-1795.

✳ Examination details

Topics Topics on the exams are covered in the course study guides.

Length VINES exams range from 45 to 120 minutes and have 40 to 85 questions. BeyondMail exams are 30 minutes.

Fees Each Banyan VINES certification test is $125 U.S. and each BeyondMail test is $75 U.S. Pricing might vary outside of the United States and Canada.

Registration To register for exams, call 800-736-EXAM (800-736-3926).

✳ Recertification requirements

On an annual basis, Banyan publishes an updated list of requirements for certification. Previously certified individuals have a specified period of time to successfully complete the new requirements in order to retain their certification status.

 # Benefits and deliverables

The technical certification program provides the individual with the opportunity to be formally recognized by the networking industry and VINES users as a qualified support provider. Employment of a CBS or CBE enables an organization to provide high-quality technical support for Banyan networks. Authorized Network Integrators with two or more Certified Banyan Engineers on staff can become eligible for the Banyan Premier Network Integrator program.

Upon becoming certified, a CBS receives a plaque and a logo sheet for personal use of the CBS logo. A CBE receives a certificate, plaque, CBE pin, and logo sheet for personal use of the CBE logo.

Through continuing requirements, certified individuals remain current with Banyan technology and are included in special programs, events, and mailings sponsored by Banyan.

 # Contact information

For additional information on the Banyan technical certification program, contact the technical certification coordinator at 508-898-1795.

 # Comments

"The Certified Banyan Specialist [certification] has helped me better understand how system network architecture works going from client station into mainframe. I've gained a lot of new knowledge and confidence working with Banyan technologies. My peers are starting to look at me differently also. I'm even starting to run into task contracts that require the use of Certified Banyan Specialists."

Microcomputer analyst, Federal Government

"Certified Banyan Engineers are a step ahead of other certified networking professionals because of the difficulty of the test. It is very demanding. I know that I'm more employable having gone through this."
Product manager, Ameridata

Cisco Systems, Inc.

Company background

Cisco Systems, Inc. is a leading global supplier of internetworking products, including multifunction, multiprotocol routers; LAN and ATM switches; dial-up access servers; and network management software. These products, integrated by the Cisco Internetwork Operating System (Cisco IOS), link geographically dispersed LANs, WANs, and IBM networks. Cisco is headquartered in San Jose, California, and in the United States is traded under the NASDAQ symbol CSCO.

Cisco Certified Internetwork Expert (CCIE) program

To remain competitive in today's complex and dynamic internetworking environment, organizations are placing ever-increasing demands on their internetworking professionals. Key among these demands are the following:

➢ Expanded network functionality

➢ Rock-solid network stability

➢ Greater network capacity

Because of Cisco Systems' position as the worldwide leader in internetworking technology, these organizations look to it for guidance and support in meeting these challenging demands. Cisco has responded to this challenge by introducing the Cisco Certified Internetwork Expert program (CCIE), a high-level certification program designed to identify and serve the best internetworking experts.

The Cisco Certified Internetwork Expert program provides:

> ➤ A definition of expert-level technical knowledge and skill

> ➤ State-of-the-art methods to evaluate this knowledge and skill

> ➤ Enhanced services targeting the needs of these best-in-class engineers

✳ Audience

The Cisco Certified Internetwork Expert program targets network and system engineers who support diverse internetworks that use routing and bridging technologies.

✳ Requirements

A candidate must satisfactorily complete all requirements to earn the title of Cisco Certified Internetwork Expert. Requirements include passing a qualification test and completing a two-day hands-on lab exam.

✳ CCIE Qualification Test

The CCIE Qualification Test is used as a primary means of evaluating a candidate's knowledge. Each candidate must complete the Qualification Test before attempting the CCIE Certification Lab Test.

✳ Certification Laboratory

Internetworking experts agree that written evaluations alone cannot adequately measure the ability to design, implement, and solve problems in a dynamic internetwork. Proper evaluation of these skills must include hands-on, under-pressure execution that is observed and quantified by an internetworking expert.

Figure 7-3

Internetworking Background	CISCO Training Classes
• Two + years internetwork administration • Solid understanding of TCP/IP • Solid understanding OSI/RM and client/server architecture • Experience with packet-level diagnosis • Extensive experience with CISCO products in a production environment	• Internetwork basics self-study • Introduction to router software • Installation and maintenance of CISCO routers • Advanced router configuration • SNA configuration for multi-protocol administrators • CISCO internetwork design • CISCO internetwork trouble-shooting class

Merge your internetworking background with CISCO systems' product training to become the ideal CCIE candidate

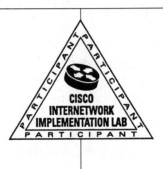

Required Evaluations

• CCIE Qualification test
• CCIE Certification Lab.

CCIE recommended and required steps and prerequisites

Cisco has taken this concept to heart by creating the CCIE Certification Lab. This final step to achieving CCIE status pits the candidate against difficult build-break-restore scenarios.

✳ Preparation

CCIE certification requires a solid background in internetworking. Cisco Systems recognizes the wide variety of training, education, and self-study material available in core technology areas, including TCP/IP, client/server and OSI architecture, and network media, and encourages candidates to take advantage of them. Cisco-developed training continues its product focus, and with the addition of the Network Troubleshooting class, fills in key elements absent from the marketplace in general.

Cisco training classes are recommended but not required for completion of the CCIE program.

✳ Recommended classes

Cisco recommends that CCIE candidates complete the following Cisco product and technology training classes or have the prerequisite knowledge before seeking certification:

- ➤ Internetworking Basics Self-Study
- ➤ Introduction to Cisco Router Configuration
- ➤ Installation and Maintenance of Cisco Routers
- ➤ Advanced Cisco Router Configuration
- ➤ SNA Configuration for Multiprotocol Administrators
- ➤ Cisco Internetwork Design
- ➤ Cisco Internetwork Troubleshooting
- ➤ Cisco Internetwork Implementation Lab (CIIL)*

* Only available in the San Jose, California, CCIE lab. This lab is designed for intermediate-level CCIE candidates who want to prepare for certification through participation in a CCIE-like lab. No certification is awarded in this "participation only" lab. This lab is ideal for candidates who have little to no access to internetwork devices and resources on which to develop their skills in preparation for certification.

✳ **Recommended Internetworking Background**

Expertise in the following areas is also recommended:

➤ Two or more years experience in internetwork administration

➤ Solid understanding of TCP/IP

➤ Solid understanding of the OSI Reference Model and client/server architecture

➤ Experience with packet-level diagnosis

➤ Experience with Cisco products in a production environment

✳ **Examination details**

The CCIE Qualification test is a closed book exam. The minimum passing score is 65 percent.

Topics The CCIE Qualification Test covers the following areas:

➤ General knowledge

➤ Data encapsulation, layering, and protocol demultiplexing

➤ LAN/WAN media characteristics and access control methods

➤ Common service discovery, name and address binding

➤ Virtual circuit services in contrast with datagram services

➤ Windowing, flow control, and relation to delay

➤ Error detection and recovery

➤ Buffering, queuing, and their impact on load conditions

➤ Link-state and distance-vector algorithms

➤ Switching algorithms and implications

➤ Network access control and security

➤ Management, monitoring, and fault isolation

➤ Corporate technologies

➤ Identifying major services provided by desktop, WAN, and Internet groups:
  - Desktop includes AppleTalk, Banyan VINES, Novell IPX, XNS, NetBIOS/NETBEUI/LAN Manager, IEEE 802.3 and 802.5 MAC layers, and IEEE 802.2 LLC1/LLC2 layer
  - WAN includes baseband ISDN, frame relay, SMDS, X.25, and synchronous point-to-point serial lines.
  - Internet includes TCP/IP, OSI with TP4/CLNS, DECnet Phase IV, Phase IV+ and Phase V, and SNA/APPC

➤ Identifying major protocols and their functions and addressing structures

➤ Identifying routing and bridging implications of each

➤ Cisco technology
  - Cisco router platforms, their architectures, and applications
  - Cisco communication servers, their architectures, and applications
  - Cisco protocol translation and applications
  - Common configuration commands and system/network impact
  - Built-in diagnostic capabilities, usage, and impacts
  - Configuration and management features and usage
  - LAN/WAN interfaces, capabilities, and applications

Currently the test is divided into the following five major areas covering all of the previously mentioned topics:

➤ Network Fundamentals

➤ Bridge/Router Technology

➤ Internetwork Protocols

➤ Cisco Specific Technology

➤ Network Scenarios

The CCIE Lab Candidates work to achieve the following exercise goals in a diverse lab environment:

➤ Build, configure, and test complex internetworks to provided specifications

➤ Diagnose and resolve media, transport, and session problems

> ➤ Isolate application-layer problems

> ➤ Use packet/frame analysis and Cisco debugging tools

> ➤ Document and report the problem-solving processes used

Candidates are evaluated individually by the lab administrator, who is a senior internetworking engineer. Cisco's intent is to make the CCIE Certification Lab as close to a realistic environment as possible. The CCIE Certification Lab lasts two full days and includes homework.

CCIE candidates are presented with complex designs to implement from the physical layer through logical configuration. Candidates are not required to configure any end-user systems but are responsible for any devices residing in the internetwork, including hubs, MAUs, DSUs/CSUs, etc. Candidates are provided with network-specific point values and testing criteria used to assess correctness of the individual configurations.

Upon completion of the implementation, the administrator inserts faults in the candidates' internetworks. The candidates must recognize, isolate, document, and resolve each fault. Additionally, candidates are required to outline the proper reporting procedures when dealing with the Cisco Technical Assistance Center (TAC).

Each configuration scenario and problem has preassigned point values. Candidates must attain minimum scores of 80 percent to pass.

The CCIE Certification Lab is available in San Jose, California; Raleigh, North Carolina; and Brussels, Belgium.

Length The CCIE Qualification Test lasts two hours and has 97 questions. The CCIE Lab is two days long.

Fees The CCIE Lab fee is $1000 U.S. and the CCIE Qualification Test is $100 U.S. Fees might vary outside of the United States and Canada.

Registration To inquire about training class and lab schedules, to enroll in the CCIE Certification Lab, or to request additional information, contact your account representative/distributor or call

Cisco Systems directly at 800-553-NETS in the United States and Canada or 408-526-7209.

 # Benefits and deliverables

CCIE status denotes proficiency in supporting diverse internetworks that use routing and bridging technologies. A CCIE's organization or customers know that he or she has passed strict testing and hands-on skill evaluations. They also benefit from the CCIE's privileged partner relationships with Cisco Systems support organizations, which enable the CCIE to more effectively deploy and manage internetworks. Organizations supported by CCIEs will benefit from reduced overall cost of ownership and accelerated deployment capability.

Specific benefits of CCIE status include:

➤ *Industry recognition.* CCIEs are recognized throughout the internetworking industry as highly qualified technical professionals.

➤ *Privileged technical support.* CCIEs may elect to have their cases queued immediately to second-level support engineers in Cisco's Technical Assistance Centers (TACs). This election, optional on a per-case basis, allows access to senior expertise when the Internetwork Expert has ruled out known problems.

The Cisco Certified Internetwork Expert program certifies individuals, not companies. Even if CCIEs move to other companies, their status remains with them as long as they adhere to the program requirements and maintain their certification. However, access to enhanced services requires a Cisco maintenance contract or partner support agreement.

Because Cisco Systems' partner companies have CCIEs on staff, they achieve higher levels of partner certification and special support contract considerations not available to other companies.

 # Contact information

For more information on the Cisco Certified Internetwork Expert program, contact your account representative/distributor or call Cisco Systems at 800-553-NETS, 408-526-7209, or cs-rep@cisco.com.

Comments

"CCIE certification and being a Cisco Gold-certified partner are extremely important to us. We believe that the bar for internetworking skills acquisition not only has to be set high but needs to be continually recalibrated in order to keep up with technology changes. Our customers rely on us to be two steps ahead of them in knowing hardware and operating system functionality, protocols, interoperability, new product changes, and how to implement them effectively.

"Our drive to build additional expertise in Cisco solutions is amply demonstrated by the fact that we committed early on to support the Cisco channel certification program as an integral part of our service strategy. Additionally, our data applications consultants (similar to sales engineers) have committed to be every bit as strong as the Cisco Technical Assistance Center (TAC) and Cisco's own sales force, and we're dedicated to maintaining that standard."

Senior engineer, !NTERPRISE Networking Services from US West

"You have to know quite a bit to get the Cisco Certified Internetwork Expert (CCIE) certification. You need to pass two exams: a written exam and a lab exam. The written exam weeds out people who aren't ready. It also gives people an idea of what they need to go back to study. The certification lab is a tough test of debugging skills; can you find the problem within the time constraints? If a person is qualified by Cisco, you can feel much more confident about them. That person has put their career where their mouth is."

Systems engineer, Networking Consultant

"The CCIE is a big confidence builder for engineers to make it through. It's a tough test, and it can be intimidating. But it carries weight. It's a prestige thing, and people feel better about themselves for having done it. The CCIE program is doing a great job. They're really keeping standards high."

Regional systems engineering manager, International Network Services

 # CNX—Certified Network Expert

 # Company background

Azure Technologies, Hewlett-Packard, IBM-Field Service Support, Network General, Microtest, The AG Group, and Wandel & Goltermann sponsor this program to give organizations a yardstick for assessing and hiring network management personnel. The cooperation between network analysis vendors assures that the CNX program does not favor one network analysis technology over another and that it addresses the broad spectrum of technologies that confront managers.

 # CNX certification program

The CNX program is designed to identify individuals who are experienced and knowledgeable in managing, designing, troubleshooting, and maintaining sophisticated multivendor networks.

Network professionals who successfully complete the examination are awarded the CNX certification.

✳ Audience
The CNX program is designed for network engineers, managers, administrators, and technicians with two or more years of experience troubleshooting with a network analyzer.

✳ Requirements
Candidates must pass either the CNX token-ring exam or the CNX Ethernet exam to receive their CNX certification. Additional certification for other technologies is currently under development.

✳ Preparation

Prerequisites for the CNX certification do not consist of a predetermined number of classes; instead the exam is designed to certify an individual based on a culmination of academic and practical experience. The vendors participating in the CNX program recognize that many excellent training programs exist in the marketplace today.

Classroom training may be obtained from CNX vendors or outside sources. However, the CNX certification does not simply test on classroom knowledge alone; one must have practical experience as well in order to pass the exam.

"CNX Pre-test Guides" are available to help prepare candidates for testing. The guides provide a detailed description of the test, a technical outline of the key issues included on the exam, self-study questions, and some sample questions. The "CNX Pre-test Guide" costs $50 and is available for purchase by calling Drake at 800-CNX-EXAM.

✳ Examination details

Topics The CNX exam requires significant understanding of the organization and interpretation of elements in a layered, interprocess communications system.

Initial testing covers either Ethernet or token ring data link topologies. Additional certification for other technologies is currently under development. CNX exams test proficiency in the following areas:

- ➢ Fundamental network technologies and engineering
- ➢ Open Systems Interconnect (OSI) model
- ➢ IEEE 802 architecture
- ➢ Repeater, bridge, and router technologies
- ➢ Signal transmission technologies
- ➢ Baseline, benchmark, and performance analysis
- ➢ Printed tract file analysis

CNX Token-Ring Exam

Candidates should be well versed in current IEEE specifications relating to 802.5 engineering standards. The token-ring exam requires in-depth knowledge of ring operation, including:

> ➤ Use of control bits such as priority, monitor count, ARI/FCI, error-detected, functional address, and source-routing-present

> ➤ Ring poll/neighbor notification, station insertion and removal, soft error reporting, contention, and fault domain isolation

CNX Ethernet Exam

Candidates should be well-versed in current IEEE specifications relating to Ethernet/802.3 engineering. The Ethernet exam requires in-depth knowledge of CSMA/CD, including:

> ➤ Similarities, differences, and areas of incompatibility between Ethernet implementations using Version 2, 802.3, SNAP, and Novell

> ➤ Bit patterns associated with frame corruption, including propagation delay problems, reflection problems, environmental noise, and fault hardware

> ➤ Media access technology, such as preamble generation, bit jam, exponential back-off algorithm, SQE heartbeat, and jabbering

Length The CNX exam is four hours long and consists of 60 questions chosen randomly by computer from a pool of more than 300 possibilities. The questions consist of the following:

> ➤ Approximately 40 multiple-choice questions on either Ethernet or token-ring technology

> ➤ Approximately 20 multiple-choice questions that require interpretation of trace file printouts obtained from the network analyzer of your choice (Network General's Expert SnifferR, Network Analyzer or Foundation Manager, Hewlett-Packard's Network Advisor, Wandel & Goltermann's DA-30, or others)

Fees The testing fee for each CNX exam is $250 U.S. worldwide.

Registration To register for a CNX exam, call 800-CNX-EXAM (800-269-3926).

⇨ Benefits and deliverables

CNX certification shows employers and other industry professionals that you are a cut above the rest. Successfully complete the CNX exam to differentiate your technical knowledge and real-world troubleshooting skills. Use it to advance your career and contribute to the continued success of your company.

✳ Features

- ➤ Study at your own pace
- ➤ Use your choice of network analyzer
- ➤ Test on multiple platforms and protocols
- ➤ Receive test results online
- ➤ Supported by multiple network industry vendors

✳ Individual benefits

- ➤ Gain industry recognition of your knowledge and expertise
- ➤ Improve your salary potential
- ➤ Enhance your image as a network professional
- ➤ Advance your career

✳ Corporate benefits

- ➤ Document return on investment for network training
- ➤ Establish a hiring standard
- ➤ Demonstrate employee expertise to customers
- ➤ Motivate employees
- ➤ Improve employee morale

 # Contact information

For additional program information, candidates should contact their vendor affiliate representative.

Azure Technologies
Axel Tillmann
63 South St.
Hopkinton, MA 01748
508-435-3800

Network General Corp.
Monica Sarmiento-Alesse
4200 Bohannon Dr.
Menlo Park, CA 94025
415-473-2837

Hewlett-Packard Corp.
Mike Young
5070 Centennial Blvd.
Colorado Springs, CO 80919
800-851-7898

The AG Group, Inc.
Janice Juda
2540 Camino Diablo, Ste. 202
Walnut Creek, CA 94596
510-937-7900

IBM Corp.
Bob DeCuircio
1500 Riveredge Pkwy.
Atlanta, GA 30358
404-858-8240

Wandel & Goltermann
Mike Stelzer
1030 Swabia Ct.
RTP, NC 27709
919-460-3333

Microtest
Mark Johnston
4747 N 22nd St.
Phoenix, AZ 85015-4708
800-LANWORK

 # Comments

"I wanted networking skills without being too vendor-specific. I got that from the CNX. The program has helped me cover all the bases in learning networking skills. I did it more as a personal thing for myself, but I know it's benefited my company also."
Software analyst, Saskatchewan Government Insurance

"CNX is an excellent program. It really shows one's abilities with protocol analysis and with networking troubleshooting. Few people have the certification today, but Network General is a well-recognized name, so the certification gives a competitive edge."
Network administrator, Brown & Root

Compaq Computer Corporation

 ## Company background

Compaq Computer Corporation is a world leader in the manufacture of server, desktop, portable, and notebook computers. Compaq products are sold and supported in more than 100 countries. To ensure the successful sales, service, and support of products, Compaq offers programs such as technical hotline support, the Accredited Systems Engineer program, and CompaqCare System Partner program.

 ## Compaq Accredited Systems Engineer (ASE) certification program

The Compaq Accredited Systems Engineer, or ASE, program is targeted toward systems engineers who work with networks and Compaq computers. Compaq ASE designations are based on the industry accreditation of leading operating system vendors in combination with required Compaq expertise. By meeting ASE requirements, these professionals demonstrate Compaq product knowledge and integration proficiency with Microsoft, Novell, SCO, or Banyan products.

Through rigorous testing, the Compaq Accredited Systems Engineer program accepts and certifies only qualified individuals. Additionally, because Compaq regularly evaluates the appropriateness of the training, modifies it as necessary, and requires annual recertification, Compaq ASEs are up to speed with the latest technology from Compaq. ASE certification also means that the certified individual has access to a network of other Compaq certified ASEs as well as information and support resources that are not generally available to non-ASEs.

Figure 7-4

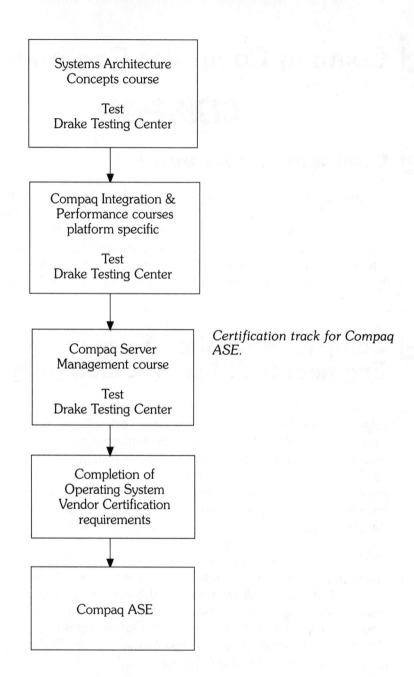

Certification track for Compaq ASE.

Compaq ASE—NetWare

✳ **Audience**

This certification is intended for systems engineers who work with personal computers and NetWare, Novell's networking software.

✳ **Requirements**

For Compaq ASE—NetWare certification, a candidate must first be certified as a Certified Novell Engineer (CNE) or Enterprise Certified Novell Engineer (ECNE).

Once the prerequisites are met, the candidate must pass the following proficiency exams to become ASE certified:

➤ Compaq Systems Architecture Concepts

➤ Compaq/NetWare Integration and Performance

➤ Compaq Server Management

 # Compaq ASE—SCO UNIX

✳ **Audience**

This certification is intended for systems engineers who work with personal computers and SCO UNIX networking software.

✳ **Requirements**

To earn Compaq ASE SCO UNIX certification, a candidate must first be certified as an SCO ACE or SCO ACE+.

Once the prerequisite is met, the candidate must pass the following proficiency exams to become ASE certified:

➤ Compaq Systems Architecture Concepts

➤ Compaq/SCO UNIX Integration and Performance

➤ Compaq Server Management

Compaq ASE—Microsoft Windows NT

�֍ Audience

This certification is intended for systems engineers who work with personal computers and Microsoft Windows NT networking software.

✶ Requirements

For Compaq ASE Microsoft Windows NT certification, a candidate must first be a Microsoft Certified System Engineer for Windows NT.

Once the prerequisite is met, the candidate must pass the following proficiency exams to become ASE certified:

➢ Compaq Systems Architecture Concepts

➢ Compaq/Windows NT Integration and Performance

➢ Compaq Server Management

Compaq ASE—Banyan VINES

✶ Audience

This certification is intended for systems engineers who work with personal computers and Banyan VINES networking software.

✶ Requirements

To earn Compaq ASE Banyan VINES certification, a candidate must be a Certified Banyan Specialist or Certified Banyan Engineer.

Once the prerequisite is met, the candidate must pass the following proficiency exams to become certified:

➢ Compaq Systems Architecture Concepts

➢ Compaq/Banyan VINES Integration and Performance

➢ Compaq Server Management

✶ Preparation

While training is not a requirement, Compaq strongly recommends that ASE candidates complete pertinent training courses before taking ASE certification exams. Compaq recommends the following courses:

> ➤ Compaq Systems Architecture Concepts Course

> ➤ Compaq Integration and Performance Course

> ➤ Compaq Server Management Course

Candidates may also review "Self-Assessment Guides" for each ASE Accreditation exam to help determine if they have the requisite knowledge to pass the tests without training. These guides are available through Compaq PaqFax, an automated fax back system at 800-345-1518.

✳ **Examination details**

Topics ASE Accreditation exams cover platform-specific topics related to integrating and managing Compaq networks. Specific topic information is listed in the Compaq "Self-Assessment Guides."

Length ASE exams are one hour and have 50 questions.

Fees Each test is $100 U.S. Fees might vary outside of the United States and Canada.

Registration To register for Compaq certification exams, call 800-366-EXAM (800-366-3926).

Contact information

To speak to someone directly about the ASE program, call the Compaq ASE program administrator at 713-374-2266.

To receive the latest information about the ASE program, Compaq Training, and Self-Assessment Guides, call Compaq PaqFax at 800-345-1518 and choose the FAX option.

To register for ASE training classes, call 800-732-5741.

Benefits and deliverables

Certification provides a benchmark, or reference point, that indicates the certified individual has acquired a certain level of expertise or knowledge. Compaq recognizes the hard work that accompanies certification by providing ASEs with a level of support and tools that

are not available to non-ASEs. ASEs have access to worldwide Compaq support resources as well as the ability to network with other ASEs around the world.

ASEs receive a certificate and business logo sheets to promote their status. In addition, ASEs receive subscriptions to tools and information that non-ASEs must pay for.

❋ **Recertification Requirements**

ASEs are required to renew their certification annually. This includes training on new Compaq products. These renewal requirements are specified by Compaq on an as-needed basis and might require further testing.

 # Comments

"Non-ASEs are almost at a disadvantage at keeping up with changing technology. I think it [being an ASE] is well worth the investment."

ASE, Alphanumeric Systems Inc.

"The training, timely information, and support that I've received from Compaq since I've become an ASE has definitely made a difference for me."

ASE, ComputerLand, Southern California

 # CompTIA

Company background

The Computing Technology Industry Association (CompTIA) is a not-for-profit trade association serving all segments of the computer industry. Members of the association, located in all 50 states of the

United States and Canada, represent major companies that manufacture, distribute, publish, or resell computer-related products and services. The association was formed to encourage professionalism, sound business practices, and fair and honest treatment of vendors, resellers, and customers. CompTIA committees deal with issues affecting the computer industry and act as a representative voice for resellers, distributors, and manufacturers.

CompTIA certification programs

A+ certification is a CompTIA-sponsored testing program designed to certify the competency of individuals in the computer industry. By passing the A+ exam, service technicians demonstrate their competency, as defined by computer service experts from companies across the industry. Successful candidates earn a nationally recognized credential as competent service professionals. Program development and marketing was funded by more than 62 leading computer industry companies committed to service excellence.

The Certified Document Imaging Architect program will be available in the fall of 1995. It was designed to ensure the competency of individuals who work with document imaging. By passing the certification examination, candidates demonstrate a mastery of basic knowledge and customer relations skills essential for the successful imaging solution provider.

A+ Certified Service Technician

✻ **Audience**
This program is designed to certify the competency of computer service technicians who work in reseller and end-user environments.

❋ Requirements

To become certified, the candidate must pass a proficiency test that covers basic knowledge of configuring, installing, diagnosing, repairing, upgrading, and maintaining microcomputers and associated technologies.

 # Certified Document Imaging Architect Program

❋ Audience

This program is designed to certify the competency of document imaging professionals.

❋ Requirements

The successful candidate must pass a proficiency test that covers the basic knowledge required for baseline competency with imaging systems. Specific topics covered include input/capture; display; storage; records management, retrieval, and indexing; communications and networking; output; and imaging business issues.

❋ Examination details

Topics The A+ computer service technician exam is based on recognized and approved job tasks for technicians who service microcomputer and related equipment. The tasks and required knowledge covered on the exam do not include manufacturer-specific procedures or product information. Instead, the exam tests for a command of the fundamental knowledge required for tasks related to a set of core technologies, without regard for brand.

The CDIA exam has been designed to demonstrate the fundamental knowledge related to tasks around developing a document imaging system, without regard for brand. Therefore, it covers a set of core competencies related to procedures and information about imaging technologies that are not related to specific products.

The exam is divided into sections that correspond to the imaging architect's areas of responsibility. Technologies emphasized in the test include input/capture; display; storage; records management, retrieval,

and indexing; communications and networking; output; and imaging business issues. Paper handling, preprocessing, and the standard office computing environment are also covered.

Length The A+ certification program consists of three modular exams. Candidates must take the core exam and have the choice of either of two specialty exams: A+ Microsoft Windows and DOS Environments or A+ MAC OS Specialty. The core exam is one hour in length and consists of approximately 72 questions. The optional exams are each 45 minutes long and consist of 52 questions.

Fees A+ exams are $100 each, or $165 for both tests if taken at the same sitting. Candidates employed by CompTIA member companies receive promotional discounts.

Registration Call Drake at 800-77-MICRO to register for the A+ certification exam.

Benefits and deliverables

Everyone benefits from A+ certification. Service technicians gain recognition for a set of skills that are essential to performing well. If they are independent, they gain immediate credibility, which can give them a much-needed competitive edge.

Owners of systems benefit because they can have a much higher level of confidence in the work an A+ Certified technician does and in the advice he or she might give. Employers of technicians benefit because they have a selling and marketing edge. Less obviously, these employers also have a highly useful tool in evaluating prospective new hires.

Vendors of hardware benefit because they can dispense with repetitive basic training, as many already have. Explaining laser printers or color displays, for example, is unnecessary with a class of technical trainees who are already A+ Certified. Instead, vendors can focus training on what differentiates their products. The result is that technicians are better prepared to help users get the product functionality and connectivity they paid for. In turn, this makes for happier customers and builds repeat business.

Upon successful completion of the A+ proficiency test, individuals receive an A+ certification certificate, lapel pin, and an ID card. Service organizations that have 50 percent or more of their technicians certified are designated as Authorized A+ Service Centers.

Candidates who successfully complete the CDIA certification exam will receive a valuable credential that provides benefits in enhanced job opportunities, recognized proof of professional achievement, and opportunities for advancement. The industry benefits, too, through lower training costs and greater customer satisfaction. Successful candidates will receive a CDIA certificate by mail within a few days of passing the exam.

 # Contact information

For more information about the A+ certification program, call Drake at 800-77-MICRO.

The CDIA exam is scheduled to be available in the fall of 1995. Until then, for more information or advance notice of test availability dates, call CompTIA at 708-268-1818, extension 301.

 # Comments

"It's an excellent test—it measures service technician skills in every aspect of the industry."
Technician, CompUSA, Dallas, Texas

"Being A+ Certified gives these students an extra edge that could help them get a job. It helps them land jobs more quickly. For example, Xerox was hiring and having local interviews for two positions. Three of my students went to interview in Kansas City. The interviews and testing took an entire day; when the interviews were over, my students landed both positions!"
Computer repair instructor, Manhattan Area Technical Center, Manhattan, Kansas

"A+ is an industrywide standard; that's a strong thing. It's a powerful statement that so many vendors have gotten together to support this. The demands on service trainers have increased incredibly over the years. It used to be that you were called in to replace a chip. Now we work with CPUs, monitors, and give software and network support and consulting services. Those are the kinds of things that we can't address through our own service training. The A+ certification serves that role."

Service technician supervisor

Computer Associates

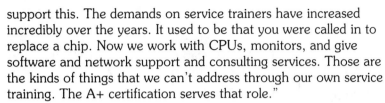

Software superior by design.

Company background

Computer Associates is a leading independent software company for multiplatform computing, serving most of the world's major business, government, research, and educational organizations. CA designs, develops, markets, and supports a broad range of software products for mainframe, midrange, and desktop computers. CA products address the areas of systems management, information management, business application, and application development.

CA-Unicenter certification program

✳ Audience

The CA-Unicenter Authorized Reseller program is designed for VARs, systems integrators (SIs), and independent software vendors (ISVs) who are working with client organizations that are moving to client/server systems. The certification program is designed to ensure CA Authorized Resellers have a base of knowledge in CA-Unicenter sales and marketing, technical product knowledge, and product support. The goal of the program is to ensure that the mutual clients of the reseller and Computer Associates receive the highest caliber of support and service.

Figure 7-5

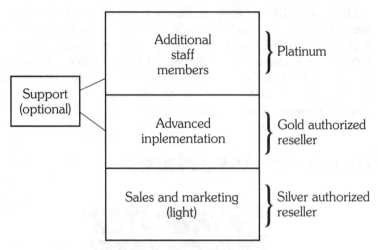

CA-Unicenter support and service levels

❋ Requirements

Sales and marketing certification is the initial required level of training in order to participate as a CA-Unicenter Authorized Reseller. The cost of participating in this two-day course is included in the initial fee that is required to join the program. Following acceptance of the Business Partner application, resellers have 30 days to schedule an employee to attend the sales and marketing training. The sales and marketing training covers the product positioning challenges facing new users of client/server technology, the market opportunity, prospect identification and qualification, using the sales materials effectively, and the basic sales presentation and product demonstration. The certification examination must be scheduled within 30 days of completion of the training. Successful completion qualifies resellers as Silver Authorized Resellers.

CA-Unicenter for UNIX Implementation is a five-day hands-on course designed to prepare the student to install and implement CA-Unicenter for UNIX. The course is based on implementation of a "company" running autonomous divisions with mixed environments in all divisions. Presentations of the topics are integrated into the case studies. The implementation course and the advanced course (described in the following paragraph) are the prerequisites for Gold certification.

CA-Unicenter for UNIX Advanced Topics and Techniques is a four-day hands-on course designed to provide detailed information on more advanced technical topics relating to systems management in a homogeneous or heterogeneous client/server environment. In the course, students learn to perform multinode installation, customization of the GUI, and the basics of implementing CA-Unicenter for UNIX. Reseller organizations who pass the certification exams on implementation and on advanced topics become Gold Authorized Resellers. To qualify as a Gold-level reseller, the partner organization must certify two technical resources as CA-Unicenter for UNIX consultants and one technician as CA-Unicenter/STAR consultant.

Product Support Training is a two-day hands-on course that is optional (but recommended) for all Gold-level resellers. Completion of the product support training qualifies the reseller organization to provide (and charge for) direct front-line support for their clients.

Resellers can advance to CA's highest level program designation (Platinum Authorized Reseller) by certifying additional sales and technical resources on CA-Unicenter and CA-Unicenter/STAR. To become a Platinum-level reseller, two additional certified UNIX consultants (CUCs) for Unicenter and two additional CUCs for Unicenter/STAR must be trained. (Reseller firms with more than one location must have at least one CUC per location.)

✳ Preparation

Courses are available at CA Authorized Education Centers (AECs) or at a Computer Associates Learning Center.

✳ Examination details

Topics The topics on the exams are covered in the Computer Associates training.

Length The certification exams are one to two hours long with 55 to 120 questions.

Fees The exams are $75 to $100 U.S.

Registration To register for exams, call Drake at 800-859-EXAM (800-859-3926).

 ## Contact information

For more information on the CA-Unicenter Authorized Reseller program, call 800-225-5224.

 ## Benefits and deliverables

The CA-Unicenter Authorized Reseller program ensures CA Authorized Resellers have a base of knowledge in CA-Unicenter sales and marketing, technical product knowledge, and product support. The program ensures that mutual clients of the reseller and Computer Associates receive the highest caliber of support and service.

 # Digital Equipment Corporation

 ## Company background

Digital Equipment Corporation is a world leader in the development of network platforms for client/server computing. Digital's products and services for open computing environments help customers simplify business processes and enhance organizational productivity. The company does business in more than 100 countries and develops and manufactures products in the Americas, Europe, Asia, and the Pacific Rim. Building on its core competencies in software, systems, networks, and services, Digital provides a complete range of information-processing solutions—from personal computers to integrated worldwide networks.

 # Digital Business Partner University training and certification program

Digital Business Partner University consists of three schools: Basic School, Specialty School, and the Update School. Certification supports both the Basic and Specialty Schools, while the Update School supports recertification.

The program provides business partners the opportunity to increase their product knowledge on Digital products, ensure readiness to sell and support the sale of Digital products, and assess acquired knowledge by means of certification testing.

Digital uses certification programs for its resellers because certification helps determine an individual's knowledge level. Through certifying individuals, the business partner is better able to deploy resources appropriately, thus ensuring the proper sales and support coverage in each area. Digital's customers benefit from the program because they have the assurance and confidence they are buying from a certified expert who has the credentials to prove it.

Figure 7-6

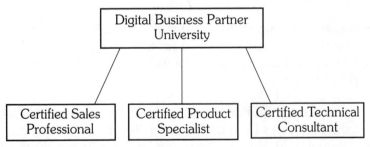

Digital's certification options

✱ Digital Systems certification

This certification is designed to test the basic product knowledge of Digital systems, software, networks, and services for the sales professional as well as the technical support professional.

✳ **Alpha Systems certification**

Two certification tests on Alpha systems are available. One is designed for the sales professional and the other for technical support. They are based on product knowledge and the level of difficulty differs based on the candidate. They include knowledge of the following:

➤ Alpha architecture concepts and benefits

➤ Computing styles

➤ Open System standards, compatibility, and migration

➤ Alpha operating systems

➤ Open VMS and OSF/1 clustering concepts

➤ Storage works concepts

➤ Digital's warranty and service options

➤ Basic knowledge of Alpha sales support tools

➤ Alpha configuration guidelines

✳ **Pathworks certification**

Pathworks certification offers multiple tests with different levels of difficulty depending on the individual's needs. All tests are based on product knowledge.

Understanding the Pathworks Advantage and Selling Pathworks Solutions certifications are designed for the sales professional, and the tests are based on basic product knowledge needed for selling Pathworks products.

Other Pathworks certification tests have been designed to meet the needs of the Pathworks Product Specialist, Technical Consultant, Product Integrator, Middleware Specialist, and the Pathworks Developer.

Tests include the following Pathworks product knowledge certifications:

➤ Open VMS/LM Server

➤ Open VMS/NetWare Server

➤ Windows and DOS Client

➤ OSF.LM Server

➤ Windows NT

➤ Open VMS/Macintosh Server

➤ Macintosh Client

➤ Open VMS Integrator

➤ OSF Integrator

✳ Audience

This program is for sales and technical support professionals who work for Digital business partners.

✳ Requirements

To become certified, an individual must pass a written exam administered by Drake Prometric.

✳ Preparation

Candidates can prepare for certification tests by attending the appropriate Digital Business Partner University training course.

If a candidate feels they have all the knowledge they need to pass the certification exam, they are encouraged to register to take the test without attending the training courses.

✳ Examination details

Topics Exam topics vary and are based on subject matter. Examples are Alpha Systems, Software, Networks, and Services. Tests are developed by Digital subject-matter experts and consultants. If the candidate fails, he or she is encouraged to attend the appropriate training or review specific modules and re-take the test.

Length Tests vary in length, but an average test has approximately 100 questions and requires two hours to complete.

Fees Test fees vary depending on which country it is administered in. To receive information on test prices by location, call Drake Prometric at 800-207-EXAM.

Registration To register for exams, call Drake at 800-207-EXAM.

 # Benefits and deliverables

Through certification, customers can be assured that their Digital business partners are prepared to sell and support the sale of the products.

The certified candidate receives:

- ➤ Certificate mounted on a walnut plaque
- ➤ Certification ID card
- ➤ Name listed in the certification directory, which is distributed to Digital salespeople and potential customers
- ➤ Subscription to the Digital Business Partner University catalog and newsletter

 # Contact information

For additional training and registration information, call Digital Business Partner registration at 800-332-5656, or Bruce Betz at 508-467-9242.

 # Comments

"The new certification venture is one of the most aggressive moves Digital has made in years. Certifying their Business Partners shows the customer base how serious this company is about the professionalism of their Business Partners. Digital certification is not just good training—it's good business. Potential customers will turn to Digital Business Partners who are certified, as will the Digital salespeople themselves. Any Digital salesperson, after all, wants to be represented by well-educated Business Partners they can rely on."
Director of sales, Pioneer Technology Groups

"Given the kind of company we aim to be—the most technically capable distributor—it behooves us to be smarter than the average bear. That means making sure our salespeople are trained beyond the norm. The better trained an employee is, whether sales or technical, the more successful he or she will be."

Executive vice president, Computer Products for Wyle

"One of the values of the certification process is that it represents a clear and measurable benchmark. Because Avnet is concerned with providing our customers the best service possible, we have adopted a Total Quality Management, or TQM, approach to our business. With TQM, the only way to improve quality is to measure it, and certification helps us measure the technical ability of our people and how it improves over time."

Vice president of systems marketing, AVNET

"The Digital training is terrific. It certainly isn't easy, but the skills and knowledge it provides are well worth the time, expense, and effort. One thing I know for sure—it will pay off in better service for our customers and, therefore, greater sales for us."

President, McBride & Associates

 # Epson America Inc.

EPSON

 # Company background

Epson America, Inc. markets a wide range of computer products through all distribution channels in the United States and is a major original equipment manufacturer (OEM) supplier to the information technology industry. Founded in Torrance, California, in 1975, the company is the sales and marketing arm of Seiko Epson Corporation in North, South, and Central America. Although Epson is best known as the world's leading supplier of impact printers, the company also designs, builds, and sells a complete line of ink-jet and laser printers; notebook, handheld, and desktop computers; magnetic and optical disk drives; PC-POS systems; LCD displays; PCMCIA cards; gate arrays; and OEM printer mechanisms.

 # Epson TechKnow CBT certification program

The Epson TechKnow CBT certification program is designed to qualify authorized Epson Customer Care Center technicians for entry into Epson service training seminars.

Technicians complete the Epson TechKnow Training CBT courses that are part of the Epson TechKnow CD-ROM Product Support Library and then confirm their knowledge of basic Epson printer diagnosis and repair techniques by completing the TechKnow CBT certification test.

Passing the Epson TechKnow CBT certification test is required before students may attend Epson seminar service training. Each Epson Customer Care Center must have one Epson-trained technician on staff at each servicing location. Seminar certification is valid for two years.

✳ Audience

This program targets authorized Epson Customer Care Center technicians planning to enter into Epson service training seminars.

✳ Requirements

Candidates must pass the Epson TechKnow training certification.

✳ Preparation

Candidates for TechKnow CBT certification should carefully work through the entire Epson TechKnow Training CBT course library and complete all sample study questions presented in the course. Students who are comfortable with the scope of questions presented in the CBT

should have no difficulty passing the Epson TechKnow CBT certification test.

❊ **Examination details**

Topics The Epson TechKnow CBT certification test covers all topics presented in the Epson TechKnow training CBT course: theory of operation, basic electronics, electromechanical devices, logic electronics, troubleshooting, adjustments, and maintenance.

Length The Epson TechKnow CBT certification test contains 100 questions and takes approximately one hour to complete.

Fees The regular cost of the test is $149 U.S. Fees might vary outside of the United States and Canada.

Registration Candidates should call 800-35-EPSON to register for the Epson TechKnow CBT certification test.

⇨ Benefits and deliverables

Successful candidates are awarded a certificate and a TechKnow certification medallion.

⇨ Contact information

For additional information on Epson training seminars, call Epson training at 800-765-2885. To have a current Epson service training seminar schedule sent to you by fax, call Epson's FaxBack system at 800-234-1445, extension 4214, and request document number 2910.

⇨ Comments

"Our technicians have become more capable and more confident when working on the Epson products. We plan on sending more people to be certified. Another benefit: Epson is sending a lot of new business to us, so it's paying off well."

Technical services manager

 # Hewlett-Packard

 # Company background

Hewlett-Packard Company is an international manufacturer of measurement and computation products and systems. The company's products and services are used in industry, business, engineering, science, medicine, and education in approximately 110 countries. HP has 98,400 employees and had revenue of $25 billion in the 1994 fiscal year.

 # HP certification and training programs

Hewlett-Packard's certification program is designed for HP's Computer Systems Organization (CSO) resellers. "HP Certified Channel Partner Sales Professional" certification is recognition by Hewlett-Packard that these computer resellers have the necessary level of knowledge to effectively sell and support HP products.

 # HP Channel Partner Sales Professional

✳ **Audience**

This program is for HP Channel Partner Sales Professionals within HP's Computer Systems Organizations (CSO) resellers.

❊ Requirements

Certification is obtained by passing the required HP product line exam(s). HP requires HP Channel Partner resellers (VARs, DARs, OEMs, System Integrators, and Distributors) to have one HP Certified Sales Professional in each geographic area in which the Channel partner is authorized. Distributors must follow the requirements stated in their contracts regarding technical professional certification.

Existing Channel Partner organizations need to comply on contractual renewal beginning March 1, 1995. New Channel Partner organizations signing reseller contracts after March 1, 1995, have six months to reach the required certification level. If the designated HP Certified Sales Professional leaves the company, an organization has six months to replace its HP Certified representative.

The following exams are available for the HP Certified Sales Professional:

➤ 580-001, HP 9000 Series 700 Sales Professional Certification Exam

➤ 580-002, HP 9000 Series 800 Sales Professional Certification Exam

➤ 580-003, HP 9000 Series 700 & 800 Sales Professional Certification Exam

➤ 580-004, HP 3000 Series 900 Sales Professional Certification Exam

Certification is by product line. For example, if you are a sales professional whose company resells both the HP 9000 Series 700 and Series 800, you should request exam #580-003, not exams #580-001 and #580-002.

❊ Preparation

Self-assessment tests are available to candidates to help determine areas where additional training might be necessary. To order self-assessment tests, call Drake at 800-HP4-EXAM.

✳ **Training for HP Channel Partner Sales Professionals**

Participation in the Power On with HP training provides sales professionals with the knowledge and tools necessary to pass the HP Product Certification exam. If the individual seeking certification is an eligible Channel Partner enrolled in the Impact program, all costs are fully reimbursable through co-op funds. VARs need to apply for reimbursement from their distributor.

✳ **Self-study courses**

Optional self-study courses are available to help sales professionals increase their general knowledge of technology basics and HP products. To order these self-study workbooks, call 408-447-1000. To order a certification exam self-assessment guide, call Drake at 800-HP4-EXAM in the United States and Canada.

✳ **Examination details**

Topics To receive information about topics covered on the exams, call Drake at 800-HP4-EXAM.

Length Exams range from 60 to 90 minutes and consist of 45 to 70 questions.

Fees The cost of exams range from $75 to $125 U.S. Fees might vary outside of the United States and Canada.

Registration To register for the product-knowledge exam at a Drake Authorized Testing Center near you, simply call 800-HP4-EXAM (800-474-3926) in the United States and Canada. Be sure to have the following information ready when you call:

➤ Your HP Channel sales rep's or HP contact's name

➤ Exam number (see page 213)

➤ Method of payment (prepaid by credit card, personal check, or company check)

✳ **Recertification requirements**

Certified individuals are required to pass an annual exam to maintain their HP Certified Sales Professional status.

Benefits and deliverables

By presenting themselves as well-informed about Hewlett-Packard's products and services, HP Channel Partner Sales Professionals have a definite advantage that translates into added value for their customers. HP's Power On with HP certification and training programs provide Channel Partners with the tools and skills they need to move onto the fast track with complete confidence. This training features product-knowledge certification programs as well as high-quality self-study and classroom courses. Certification is recognition from HP that they can demonstrate their knowledge of the HP products they represent. Whether they are most interested in new product positioning, learning more about the technical aspects of networking, or gaining a better understanding of the competition, Channel Partners find that HP offers a variety of programs designed to accelerate their success.

 # Contact information

To register for the Power On with HP Sales Professional classroom training, call 800-TRAIN-YU or 408-447-1000. For additional information, call 408-447-1000 and ask for the program registrar.

 # Comments

"We've worked with HP for 14 years as a small systems integrator. We're currently working hard to develop migration strategies. Certification has been tremendous for managing a team of salespeople. It gives you as a manager a baseline for your sales reps. It shows that they have the basics required. It's also been a tremendous sales tool. For example, everyone's claiming to be a UNIX guru today. In our case, HP has actually certified our folks on their UNIX skills. That gives us a real competitive edge. It also gives a baseline to be sure your salespeople are keeping up with latest and greatest in the technical area."

Manager of sales and marketing, Independent Computer Consulting Services, Inc. (ICCS)

"I took a good two-day hands-on training course through HP. The course has made me more familiar with the HP 3000 minicomputer. It clarified for me the ordering process; which components work with which units. It's really helped me understand how many resources are required for the client based on their size and their particular work requirements. That is a reasonably complex process, since we need to meet the client's requirements not only for now but for a year or more into the future. I feel more competent and comfortable working with customers as a result."
Sales representative, ICCS

⇨ IBM

⇨ Company background

IBM develops, manufactures, and sells advanced information-processing products, including computers and microelectronic technology, software, networking systems, information consulting services, and information technology-related services. IBM offers value worldwide—through business units in the United States, Canada, Europe/Middle East/Africa, Latin America, and Asia Pacific—by providing comprehensive and competitive products and services.

⇨ Professional Certification program

The Professional Certification program from IBM provides worldwide industry recognition for technical software professionals who service and support IBM software programs for workstations and networks. The program today acknowledges the professional competence and ability to provide solid, capable technical support in candidates who support AIX, OS/2, and OS/2 LAN Server. In 1995, the program will expand to include other information systems professionals in the areas of database, networking, work-group applications, and systems management.

Individuals, rather than organizations, are certified for a specific role by passing a test or series of tests designed to measure their knowledge of the tasks of that role.

The Professional Certification program from IBM provides the certifications needed to complete the IBM Business Enterprise Solutions Team (BESTeam) program membership requirements. The BESTeam program is designed to meet the needs of systems integrators, network integrators, value-added resellers, and consultants. The program provides multiple levels of membership and offers sales, marketing, and technical tools necessary to excel in the information systems marketplace. For more information, contact the IBM BESTeam Project Office at 800-627-8363.

IBM offers certification programs targeted toward technical professionals who support, administer, and use IBM products in end-user and reseller companies. These programs include AIX, OS/2, and LAN Server.

⇨ AIXpertise certification program

This program is designed for computer professionals who use, install, administer, support, or develop applications for the AIX environment. Each exam tests the proficiency of the computer professional's application of the AIX skills and knowledge required to perform these tasks. The following three certifications are available under this program:

➤ Certified AIX User (AU)

➤ Certified AIX System Administrator (ASA)

➤ Certified AIX Support Professional (ASP)

Certification is earned by passing one or more certification tests to demonstrate the participant has the knowledge and skill required for each level. Once certification is achieved in the first level (Certified AIX User) the candidate may progressively advance to the next level of certification.

 # Certified AIX User (AU)

✳ Audience

The Certified AIX User program is geared toward individuals who use AIX systems. The Certified AIX User has demonstrated knowledge and skill in working with AIX applications that do not have a Common User Interface. This exam evaluates the participant's foundation for more technical roles, such as system administrator or programmer.

✳ Requirements

Participants are required to pass the AIX User exam to become recognized as a Certified AIX User.

 # Certified AIX System Administrator (ASA)

✳ Audience

The Certified AIX System Administrator program is designed for the AIX Systems Administrator who requires a deeper level of knowledge beyond the AIX User designation. Passing this certification level demonstrates proficiency in the application of AIX skills and knowledge required to install AIX and perform basic system administration.

✳ Requirements

Participants are required to pass the AIX System Administrator exam. Areas of expertise examined are maintenance, managing devices, basic problem determination, Logical Volume Manager, managing AIX users, data preservation, fundamentals of TCP/IP and commands, simple shell scripts, and system administration tools.

 # Certified AIX Support Professional (ASP)

✳ Audience

The Certified AIX Support Professional designation is the next level of achievement for professionals who require a deeper level of knowledge beyond the AIX Systems Administrator level. Passing this certification

level demonstrates the ability of AIX system administrators to perform routine operations and maintenance of the AIX system to support users.

* **Requirements**

Participants are required to pass the AIX System Administrator exam as a prerequisite to this program. Once certification as an AIX Systems Administrator is achieved, the participant must also pass an additional exam to become an AIX Certified Support Professional (ASP). Emphasis is in the areas of problem determination, installation and selective fix of the AIX operating system, performance, and system administration.

OS/2 and OS/2 LAN Server Professional Certification

This program is designed for individuals who support IBM OS/2 and OS/2 LAN Server. IBM Professional Certification candidates include people working in technical roles such as network administrators, consultants, remarketers, technical coordinators, sales support representatives, and trainers who work with OS/2 or OS/2 LAN Server. The following certifications are available under this program:

➤ Certified OS/2 Engineer

➤ Certified LAN Server Administrator

➤ Certified LAN Server Engineer

Certification is earned by passing a series of proficiency tests and returning a signed agreement.

Certified OS/2 Engineer

* **Audience**

The Certified OS/2 Engineer program is geared toward individuals who support OS/2 installations. The certified OS/2 Engineer has demonstrated proficiency and expertise in fine-tuning and customizing OS/2 systems.

※ **Requirements**

Prerequisite knowledge of PC fundamentals with DOS 5.0 or equivalent DOS knowledge is recommended. The candidate must pass four tests to earn the Certified OS/2 Engineer designation.

 # Certified LAN Server Administrator

※ **Audience**

The LAN Server Administrator certification program is designed for people who are responsible for supporting day-to-day network operations. LAN Server Administrator certification underscores the candidate's proficiency at managing OS/2 LAN Server resources and tasks, including backing up the server, maintaining security, and loading applications.

※ **Requirements**

LAN Server Administrator certification requires an understanding of PC fundamentals, experience with DOS 5.0, and basic knowledge in the use and customization of OS/2. The candidate must pass one exam to become certified.

Certified LAN Server Engineer

※ **Audience**

This certification program is intended for individuals who have primary responsibility for providing services and support for OS/2 LAN Server networks. The certified LAN Server Engineer designation enables candidates to provide expertise in network design, performance tuning, and installation.

※ **Requirements**

LAN Server Engineer certification requires an understanding of PC fundamentals, experience with DOS 5.0, and basic knowledge in the use and customization of OS/2. The candidate must pass six tests to earn the certification. Individuals who are Certified Novell Engineers receive credit for one test toward the certified LAN Server Engineer.

Figure 7-7

Certification	Audience	Requirement
AS/400	Designed for AS/400 system operators	One proficiency test Signed agreement
Certified AIX system administrator	AIX users & technical professionals	Two proficiency tests Signed agreement
Certified AIX user	Individuals who use AIX systems	One proficiency test Signed agreement
AIX Support	AIX users who require a deeper knowledge beyond the AIX user designation	ASA Certification one proficiency test Signed agreement
Certified OS/2 engineer	Professionals who support OS/2 installation	Four proficiency tests Signed agreement
Certified LAN server administator	Professionals who support day-to-day networks operations	One proficiency test Signed agreement
Certified LAN server engineer	Professionals who provide services & service for LAN server network	Six proficiency tests Signed agreement
Certified LAN server engineer	Professionals who provide services & service for LAN server network	Six proficiency tests Signed agreement

IBM's certification options

✳ Preparation

IBM authorized training is not required prior to taking certification exams. Previous education, experience, or current job skills might

enable a certification candidate to successfully complete a certification designation.

For the candidate who wants formal classroom instruction, instructor-led courses are available through IBM Education and Training. Independent training companies might also offer education to prepare the candidate for Professional Certification from IBM.

Self-study handbooks, test objectives, and sample tests are available from Drake Prometric at 800-959-EXAM (800-959-3926). Call 800-IBM-TEACH (800-426-8322, extension 1600) in the United States or 800-661-2131 in Canada for a listing of current course schedules, locations, and prices.

✳ Examination details

Topics A list of test objectives covered on each exam is available for interested candidates. Call 800-959-EXAM (800-959-3926) from anywhere in the United States or Canada to have the list sent to you.

Length Exams range from 60 to 90 minutes and consist of 50 to 100 questions.

Fees Exam prices range from $100 to $170 U.S. Fees might vary outside of the United States and Canada.

Registration To register for any IBM certification exam, call 800-959-EXAM (800- 959-3926).

✳ Recertification requirements

Each program has continuing recertification requirements from time to time to ensure that certified professionals stay up-to-date with current technologies. IBM contacts certified candidates by mail to notify them of recertification requirements.

⇨ Benefits and deliverables

After meeting all requirements, certified individuals receive a number of benefits:

➤ Option for certified professionals to be named in IBM's *Professional Certification Directory*

➤ Priority technical support

➤ One free issue of two CD-ROMS—the *Technical Connection Personal Software* and the *OS/2 Online Book Collection*

➤ Personalized certificate and lapel pin

➤ Authorization to use the designated IBM certification mark

➤ A variety of free subscriptions to IBM technical publications

⇨ Contact information

For program details, call Drake Prometric at 800-959-EXAM (800-959-3926) or IBM at 800-IBM-TEACh (800-426-8322).

⇨ Comments

"IBM certification really opened doors for me. I found that a lot of companies use certification as a benchmark to find qualified professionals, so my IBM certification was instrumental in helping me land a good technical position."
Student

"Because certification recognizes knowledge in a measurable way, I felt a real sense of professional achievement when I became IBM certified."
IT professional

"IBM certification sets you apart from other technical professionals. I found certification to be a good marketing tool for my business."
Consultant

 # Learning Tree International

 # Company background

Learning Tree International is a multinational organization devoted to helping information professionals keep their technical knowledge and skills up-to-date through intensive education. As one of the world's leading providers of instructor-led advanced technology education, Learning Tree offers hands-on, intensive short courses in networks, operating systems, programming languages, software development, and client/server systems. Every Learning Tree course reflects more than 20 years experience in implementing a high-performance system of course development, instructor training, and course delivery.

 # Learning Tree certification programs

As technology changes at an ever-increasing pace, a gap is formed between the foundation provided by an academic education and the technical competency that is required in today's business environment. Learning Tree Professional certification programs were established to bridge this technical education gap. Professional certification provides

participants with the technical knowledge, skills, and hands-on experience required to stay up-to-date in the advanced areas of information technology that are key to productivity and competitiveness.

Learning Tree's vendor-independent, technology-based certification programs differ significantly from product-based certification programs. Product-based certification provides a measurement of how well an individual can use the features of a particular version of a product. Learning Tree's programs are developed to measure knowledge and skills required for an individual to successfully master a job function. Each of the programs provides breadth and depth in the full range of technology needed to excel in a job function. In addition to real-world "how-to" skills, Learning Tree certification covers the spectrum of knowledge that provides insight, understanding, and the "why" that is required for successful decision-making in complex, multivendor, multiplatform environments. Learning Tree certification programs provide the knowledge to make key decisions and trade-offs about when, where, and how to apply advanced information technology as both business goals and technologies evolve.

 # Certified Local Area Network Professional

✳ Audience

The Local Area Network certification program is designed for communications specialists, network managers, systems analysts, engineers, planners, information systems (IS) and IT professionals, support technicians, and other personnel involved with the day-to-day operation and management of local area networks (LANs).

✳ Requirements

Participants in this program take the following four core courses as well as one elective course and the associated exams:

> ➤ Introduction to Datacomm and Networks

> ➤ Local Area Networks: Implementation and Configuration

> ➤ Hands-on PC Networking

> ➤ Hands-on LAN Troubleshooting

 # Certified Wide Area Network Professional

❋ Audience

The Wide Area Network certification program is designed for communications specialists, network managers, systems analysts, engineers, planners, telecommunications staff, IS and IT professionals, support technicians, and other personnel involved with the day-to-day operation and management of wide area networks (WANs).

❋ Requirements

Participants in this program take the following four core courses as well as one elective course and the associated exams:

- ➤ Introduction to Datacomm and Networks
- ➤ Telecommunications and Wide Area Networking
- ➤ Hands-on Datacomm and WAN Troubleshooting
- ➤ Hands-on X.25

 # Certified Internetworking Professional

❋ Audience

The Internetworking certification program is designed for communications specialists, network managers, systems analysts, engineers, planners, IS and IT professionals, support technicians, and other personnel involved with the day-to-day operation and management of networks and their interconnections.

❋ Requirements

Participants in this program take the following four core courses as well as one elective course and the associated exams:

- ➤ Local Area Networks: Implementation and Configuration
- ➤ Multivendor Networking
- ➤ Internetworking: Bridges, Routers and Gateways
- ➤ Hands-on Introduction to TCP/IP

 # Certified Open Systems Professional

✳ Audience

The Open Systems certification program is designed for IS, IT, and data-processing managers, technical managers, system and network analysts, systems development staff, strategic planners, marketing support staff, and all personnel involved with planning, implementing, and managing open systems.

✳ Requirements

Participants in this program take the following four core courses as well as one elective course and the associated exams:

> ➤ Introduction to Open Systems

> ➤ Introduction to Datacomm and Networks

> ➤ Introduction to Client/Server Computing

> ➤ Multivendor Networking

Certified Client/Server Systems Professional

✳ Audience

The Client/Server Systems certification program is designed for IS professionals and managers, system planners and architects, system integrators, application development staff and managers, programmers, network managers, database administrators, and all those involved in the design, development, implementation, and support of client/server systems.

✳ Requirements

Participants in this program take the following four core courses as well as one elective course and the associated exams:

> ➤ Introduction to Client/Server Computing

> ➤ Client/Server System Design & Configuration

> ➤ Data Management for Client/Server Systems

> ➤ Building Client/Server Applications: A Hands-on Workshop

 # Certified Oracle7 DBA Professional

✳ Audience

The Oracle7 DBA Professional certification program is designed for database administrators who are or will be working in the Oracle7 environment. Certified graduates of this program have a solid foundation in relational database concepts as well as an in-depth understanding of the architecture and processes of the Oracle7 server. They are able to create and manage databases in both centralized and client/server environments.

✳ Requirements

Participants in this program take the following three core courses as well as two elective courses and the associated exams:

➤ Relational Databases: Design, Tools, and Techniques

➤ Oracle 7: A Comprehensive Hands-on Introduction

➤ Oracle 7 for Database Administrators: Hands-on

 # Certified Oracle7 Application Development Professional

The Oracle7 Application Development certification program is designed for application developers who are or will be working in the Oracle7 environment. Certified graduates of this program have mastered a wide range of skills in the effective use of SQL, SQL*Plus, and PL/SQL. They are able to quickly generate complex queries, develop effective database applications, and tune applications for optimal performance.

Participants in this program take the following four core courses, one elective course, and the associated exams:

➤ Oracle 7: A Comprehensive Hands-on Introduction

➤ Oracle 7 for Application Developers: Hands-on

➤ Tuning Oracle 7 Applications: Hands-on

➤ Complex SQL Queries: Hands-on

Certified C and C++ Programming Professional

Audience

The C and C++ Programming certification program is valuable for software engineers, system and application programmers, systems analysts, technical managers, and other personnel who want to benefit from advanced programming techniques in C and C++.

Requirements

Participants in this program take the following four core courses as well as one elective course and the associated exams:

- C Programming Hands-on Workshop
- Hands-on C++ Libraries, Tools, and Advanced Programming
- C++ Hands-on Object-Oriented Programming
- C Advanced Programming: Techniques and Data Structures

Certified UNIX Programming Professional

Audience

The UNIX Programming certification program is designed for application and system programmers, system analysts, network managers, technical managers, and other personnel involved in developing and maintaining programs for UNIX-based systems.

Requirements

Participants in this program take the following four core courses as well as one elective course and the associated exams:

- UNIX Hands-on Workshop
- C Programming Hands-on Workshop
- Hands-on UNIX Programming: Exploiting the UNIX API
- Hands-on UNIX Network Programming

 # Certified UNIX Systems Professional

❋ Audience

This UNIX Systems certification program is designed for users, system administrators, network managers, software support specialists, system analysts, system and application programmers, technical managers, and other personnel involved in the day-to-day operation of UNIX-based systems and networks.

❋ Requirements

Participants in this program take the following four core courses as well as one elective course and the associated exams:

- ➤ UNIX Hands-on Workshop
- ➤ Hands-on UNIX System and Network Administration
- ➤ Hands-on Introduction to TCP/IP
- ➤ UNIX Tools and Utilities: Hands-on Workshop

 # Certified Software Development Professional

❋ Audience

The Software Development certification program is designed for software development staff and managers, programmers, system and business analysts, project managers, quality assurance professionals, and all those involved in managing, implementing, or supporting software development projects.

❋ Requirements

Participants in this program take the following four core courses as well as one elective course and the associated exams:

- ➤ Software Project Planning and Management
- ➤ Identifying & Confirming User Requirements
- ➤ Software Quality Assurance
- ➤ Software Configuration Management

⇨ Certified PC Service and Support Professional

✳ Audience

The PC Service and Support program is designed for PC support staff, service technicians, engineers, system and network administrators, information center/help desk staff, and other personnel involved with the daily operation, maintenance, and support of PC hardware, software, networks, and applications.

✳ Requirements

Participants in this program take the following four core courses as well as one elective course and the associated exams:

- ➤ Hands-on PC Configuration and Troubleshooting
- ➤ Advanced PC Configuration, Troubleshooting, and Data Recovery
- ➤ Hands-on Windows
- ➤ Hands-on PC Networking

✳ Preparation

Each Learning Tree Professional certification program is composed of five courses—typically four required core courses and one elective course selected by the participant. To become certified, participants must attend all five courses and pass the examination associated with each course.

Some participants might be qualified to take an exam without first taking the associated course. Either through extensive on-the-job experience or from attendance at other courses, these participants might already possess the knowledge and skills provided by a particular course. Learning Tree offers these participants the opportunity to apply for "transfer credit" for up to two courses. Transfer credit applicants complete a form on which they describe the educational and professional experiences that have provided them with the knowledge and skills equivalent to those provided by the course. Once the application is approved, the participant can take the

associated certification exam. (Note: There is a $180 processing fee for "transfer credit" examinations.)

※ **Examination details**

Topics Exam topics are based on materials covered in each of the training courses outlined above. All exams are "closed book," which means that examinees cannot refer to notes or reference materials during the exam.

Length The maximum time limit for the exam is 60 minutes, although most candidates finish in 40 minutes. Each exam consists of 40 multiple-choice questions chosen randomly by computer from a pool of 120 possibilities.

Fees Each exam is $85 U.S. Fees might vary outside of the United States and Canada.

Registration In addition to taking exams at Drake Authorized Testing Centers, participants have the option of taking exams at the course site on the last course day. To register to take the test at a Drake Authorized Testing Center, call Drake at 800-LRN-EXAM.

Benefits and deliverables

Each Learning Tree Professional certification program is a structured, multicourse, professional development plan that prepares participants to succeed in today's technical and business environment. A Learning Tree Professional certification enables participants to acquire a breadth of knowledge and in-depth skills in the technical area of their choice; to be more productive and achieve more on the job as a result of their enhanced knowledge and skills; to gain credentials that document and validate their expertise; and to enjoy the professional recognition and career advancement that results from their on-the-job accomplishments and hard-earned credentials. Diplomas of Professional Certification are awarded to program graduates as tangible recognition of technical achievement.

The American Council on Education recommends each Learning Tree Professional certification program for nine or more semester hours of college credit to more than 1500 colleges and universities in North America.

Figure 7-8

Learning Tree certification programs offer college credit.

 # Contact information

For more information about Learning Tree courses or certification programs, or for a free Learning Tree catalog, call:

United States	800-THE-TREE or 703-709-9019
Canada	800-267-1696 or 613-748-7741
United Kingdom	0800 282 353 or 0372 364610

Comments

"When I got to Learning Tree for training I was really surprised at the quality of the instructors. The two were Ph.Ds in computer science. They were both involved in creating international standards for the IT industry and related what they were doing in their careers to what we were studying in class. As I've gone through the seven classes, I've found the same high level of instructors in all of them. The founder of the company even came to class one day to explain the company vision. The training really reflects where the industry is going. They also steer away from vendor-specific information, which was good for me, and they don't teach to the test. The test is really challenging."

Computer specialist, U.S. Navy

 # Lotus Development Corporation

 ## Company background

Lotus Development Corporation provides software products and services that meet the needs of individuals, work groups, and enterprises. Lotus' extensive range of products form the foundation for the company's "Working Together" strategy, which focuses on integrating applications, platforms, and people.

 ## Certified Lotus Professional (CLP) program

The Certified Lotus Professional program has been developed by Lotus Education to help provide a quantitative measure of product knowledge, experience, and expertise while enabling an individual to earn industry recognition as a skilled technical professional. Lotus certification sets a standard for technical professionals with a recognized and proven skill set. Lotus currently offers eight different certification designations for Lotus Notes, Lotus cc:Mail, and SmartSuite.

* **Audience**
  The CLP candidate is typically a Service Provider or an IT professional supporting internal operations in the corporate sector.

 # Certified Lotus Professional (CLP) for Lotus Notes

The certification program for Lotus Notes is divided into four specific functional designations. Differentiating these programs allows individuals to specialize skills in areas where they can best impact their individual job performance as well as their company's profitability. The following four designations are available.

✳ Lotus Certified Notes Application Developer (LCNAD)

This program certifies application developers responsible for designing and creating sophisticated workflow applications. These developers typically perform tasks such as designing applications, creating forms and views, controlling database security, writing help and policy documents, and testing the database.

✳ Lotus Certified Notes System Administrator (LCNSA)

This designation applies to individuals responsible for the organization-wide deployment of Lotus Notes. Notes System Administrators install and maintain complex Notes networks utilizing multidomain, multi-Notes named network and multiprotocol environments. Some of their tasks include workstation and server installation and setup, managing interdomain security, replication, routing mail, monitoring servers, and creating program documents.

✳ Lotus Certified Notes Consultant (LCNC)

This certification program is directed toward individuals responsible for both installing and rolling out Notes client-server technology and creating databases. This certification denotes mastery of setting up, operating, and maintaining Notes servers and client workstations and a solid foundation in designing databases.

✳ Lotus Certified Notes Specialist (LCNS)

This designation is for individuals responsible for the organization-wide deployment of Notes and designing and creating sophisticated workflow applications. It denotes a mastery of both high-level system administration and application development. Individuals seeking this

certification are typically responsible for tasks such as Notes rollout and maintenance in large, multidomain, multi-Notes named networks and multiprotocol environments, and the planning, designing and implementation of workflow applications.

Certified Lotus Professional (CLP) for Lotus cc:Mail

The Lotus Certified cc:Mail Specialist certification designation is the most recent addition to the Certified Lotus Professional program. As the cc:Mail communication tool becomes more widely implemented, the demand for a clearly recognized pool of experts to implement and maintain vital communication networks will increase. The Certified Lotus Professional for Lotus cc:Mail provides cc:Mail installations with the recognized skill set required for successful implementation and deployment.

Lotus Certified cc:Mail Specialist

The LCCS designation is intended for individuals responsible for maintaining and administering cc:Mail in an organization. The designation denotes mastery of skills in the organization-wide deployment, installation, and configuration of cc:Mail across multiple networks and platforms.

Certified Lotus Professional (CLP)

The CLP designation Lotus Desktop for Windows encompasses technical competency for Lotus 1-2-3, Lotus AmiPro, Lotus Freelance Graphics, and Lotus Approach. This certification is currently available in select European countries, with plans for expansion to other regions.

Lotus Desktop for Windows

This certification program is designed for users who need to understand the basic technical issues and the more complex support

issues for the Lotus Desktop for Windows products, including networking and connectivity, Notes integration, and Notes F/X.

✳ Requirements

To earn certification under any of these programs, an individual must demonstrate a command of Lotus product subject matter by passing a series of examinations. The exam content is designed to recognize individuals with specific product knowledge, experience, and expertise. Candidates may take the exams in any order, but it is highly recommended that the requisite amount of product experience (usually 3 to 6 months) is achieved before beginning the certification process.

✳ Preparation

The technical competency that is tested in each of the CLP exams is best achieved through a combination of training and real-life experience. Lotus Education offers a full range of classroom and self-paced training courses to help an individual achieve certification. Lotus Education courses are highly recommended, but are not required, to help an individual prepare for certification. Candidates are free to choose any method available to gain the requisite knowledge.

Lotus-authorized courses Classroom training is available from Lotus and provides individuals with an opportunity for hands-on learning with opportunities to address specific student needs and questions. Training can be delivered through the Lotus Authorized Education Center channel or training classes can be brought in-house to support an organization's specific needs.

Courses are taught by Certified Lotus Instructors using courseware developed by the Lotus educational curriculum team. The Lotus Authorized Education Center (LAEC) program is a worldwide alliance of training organizations devoted to the ongoing delivery of high-quality education. LAECs are fully qualified and authorized by Lotus to ensure consistent course delivery for all Lotus Notes and cc:Mail product training.

Computer-based training (CBT) Lotus Education and CBT Systems have developed a library of computer-based training (CBT) courses for Notes. These courses are designed to enable learners to work on their own desktops at a pace that suits their particular

needs. Using a simulated Notes environment, these courses are highly interactive, engaging the student in a constant dialogue with the course. These courses run in a Windows environment, allowing the user to switch between the CBT and Notes. They also offer review questions and record the student's progress.

Exam guide The exam guide is a tool for certification candidates who have mastered the requisite knowledge and are ready to begin taking the certification exams. The guide is designed to help candidates understand the content and structure of the tests, so that they can study more effectively to achieve their certification goals. Included is a complete list of question objectives for each examination.

Assessment diskettes Assessment diskettes provide certification candidates an opportunity to familiarize themselves with the actual exam experience. The diskettes simulate the Drake testing environment and provide sample test questions for the various exams. Candidates are able to practice and evaluate their knowledge in preparation for taking a Lotus certification exam.

✳ Examination details

All exams are closed book. Candidates may not have any printed material, computers, or calculators with them during the exam. All of the exams are administered on a computer and are made up of multiple-choice and multiple-answer questions.

A set percentage of the questions must be answered correctly to pass the exam. The percentage of correct answers required to pass an exam is provided at the beginning of each exam. If a candidate does not pass the exam, he or she must re-register for the exam and pay the exam fee again.

Topics Exam topics are published in the "Lotus Education Certification Guide" with complete certification path information. The Certification Guide and study tools such as the exam guide and assessment diskettes are available through the Lotus Education Helpline:

North America:
Lotus Education Helpline
800-346-6409 or 617-693-4436
(Monday-Friday, 8:30-5:30 p.m. EST)

Europe:
Lotus UK/Nordic
44 784 445692 or
44 784 455445

Central Europe:
Lotus Central Europe
01 80 5 323220 or
49 89 785 09 398

Australia/New Zealand:
Lotus Australia
1800-627-608 or 61-2-350-7751

Singapore:
Lotus Singapore
65 444 0035

Length Each exam is between 60 and 90 minutes long.

Fees Each exam is $90 U.S. Fees might vary outside of the United States and Canada.

Registration To register for exams, call 800-74-LOTUS.

✳ Recertification requirements

CLPs are obligated to recertify based on product upgrades. Certification expires six months following a major product revision. Lotus notifies all certified professionals of recertification requirements as early as possible.

 # Benefits and deliverables

✳ Publications

All Certified Lotus Professionals receive regular mailings from Lotus, including a newsletter that specifically addresses their issues, along with Technical Bulletins and White Papers.

✳ Special privileges

As a CLP, individuals are invited to participate in beta programs for course and certification exam development and delivery, which allows them a first look at new Lotus Education product releases. Also, CLPs receive special limited opportunities to increase their knowledge of Lotus Software, Lotus companion products, and Lotus Education programs and products. These special offers might include education product discounts and Lotus product trials and are subject to availability.

✳ Logo usage

CLPs are authorized to display the appropriate mark in advertisement, company literature, and business cards. Camera-ready logos, along with a usage guide, are included in the Welcome Kit individuals receive when they achieve CLP status.

✳ Discounts

Certified status also entitles individuals to discounts at select Lotus-sponsored events.

✳ Additional benefits

Certification provides a benchmark for recruiting, ensuring industry-recognized professionals are part of your team. It provides a method for assessing in-house training needs and training successes. Individuals attaining certification enjoy the personal satisfaction of increased knowledge and job performance. Certified individuals maintain a strong link to Lotus and stay current with new technology.

When working with outsourced vendors, managers in an organization can be assured of quality when vendors have Certified Lotus Professionals on staff.

 # Contact information

For more information, contact the Lotus Education Helpline at the previously listed phone numbers.

 # Comments

"Notes is a dynamic product that is going to be around for years to come. Certification helped me to understand the 'behind-the-scenes' product issues. My knowledge and confidence improved tenfold."
Network administrator, Filenet

"The greatest value of certification is in the process. Our CLP study group gained excitement and enthusiasm for the product and our knowledge. By creating and troubleshooting real-life situations, we learned from each other and renewed our commitment to certification."
LCNS, programmer/analyst for a major health care company

"It wasn't until I was speaking with a peer that I learned of the value certification carried outside of my organization. As the demand for this type of knowledge grows, certification will play a key role in the success of our organization's Notes rollout and administration."
Staff programmer analyst, Seagate

"When I first became certified several years ago, I had to explain what certified meant, but today my customers not only understand certification, they typically require it of the consultants and instructors they contract."
Certified Network Solutions

 # Microsoft Corporation

 ## Company background

Microsoft Corporation develops, markets, and supports a wide range of software for business and professional use, including operating systems, network products, languages, and applications, as well as books, hardware, and CD-ROM products for the microcomputer marketplace.

 ## Microsoft Certified Professional program

The Microsoft Certified Professional (MCP) program is designed for professional developers, systems engineers, network administrators, support engineers, value-added resellers, integrators, consultants, trainers, and others who must gain and display technical expertise in Microsoft products.

The Microsoft Certified Professional program provides the best method to prove one's command of current Microsoft products and technologies. Microsoft, an industry leader in certification, is on the forefront of testing methodology. The exams and corresponding certifications are developed to validate an individual's mastery of crucial competencies as they design and develop or implement and support solutions with Microsoft products and technologies. Computer professionals who become Microsoft Certified are recognized as experts and are sought after throughout the industry.

⇨ Microsoft Certified Systems Engineer

✳ Audience

This certification is designed for professionals who plan, implement, maintain, and support information systems with Microsoft Windows NT and the Microsoft BackOffice integrated family of server software.

Figure 7-9

Microsoft Certified Systems Engineers	
Microsoft Certified Systems Engineers are required to pass four system exams and two elective exams.	
Operating Systems Requirements	Electives (choose two)
Microsoft Windows™ OR Microsoft Windows™ for Workgroups	Microsoft Mail-Enterprise
	Microsoft TCP/IP on Windows NTTM
	Microsoft Systems Management Server
Microsoft Windows NT™ Workstation	Microsoft SNA Server
	Microsoft SQL Implementation
Microsoft Windows NT™ Server	Microsoft SQL Administration for Windows NT OR Microsoft SQL Administration for OS/2®
Network with Microsoft Windows OR Network with Microsoft Windows for Workgroups	Microsoft LAN Manager Network Administration
	Microsoft LAN Manager Advanced Network Administration

Microsoft Certified Systems Engineer requirements

✳ **Requirements**

To become certified, the candidate is required to pass four operating
system exams and two elective exams. The four required operating
systems exams include:

➤ Microsoft Windows or Microsoft Windows for Workgroups

➤ Microsoft Windows NT Workstation

➤ Microsoft Windows NT Server

➤ Networking with Microsoft Windows or Networking with
   Microsoft Windows for Workgroups

The electives exams offered are:

➤ Microsoft Mail Enterprise

➤ Microsoft TCP/IP on Windows NT

➤ Microsoft Systems Management Server

➤ Microsoft SNA Server

➤ Microsoft SQL Server Database Implementation

➤ Microsoft SQL Server Database Administration for Windows NT
   or Microsoft SQL Server Database Administration for OS/2

➤ Microsoft LAN Manager Network Administration

➤ Microsoft LAN Manager Advanced Network Administration

⇨ Microsoft Certified Solution Developer

✳ **Audience**

This certification is designed for individuals who are qualified to design
and develop custom business solutions with Microsoft development
tools, technologies, and platforms, including Microsoft Office and
Microsoft BackOffice.

Figure 7-10

Microsoft Certified Solution Developer	
Microsoft Certified Solution Developers are required to pass two core technology exams and two elective exams.	
Core technology requirements	Electives (choose two)
	Microsoft Visual Basic®
Microsoft® Windows Operating Systems and Services Architecture I	Microsoft Excel and Visual Basic for Applications
Microsoft Windows Operating Systems and Services Architecture II	Microsoft Access
	Microsoft SQL Implementation

Microsoft Certified Solution Developer requirements

✳ Requirements

To become certified, the candidate is required to pass two core technology exams and two elective exams. The two core technology exams are

➤ Microsoft Windows Operating Systems and Services Architecture I

➤ Microsoft Windows Operating Systems and Services Architecture II

The elective exams offered are

➤ Microsoft Visual Basic

➤ Microsoft Access

➤ Microsoft SQL Server Database Implementation

➤ Microsoft Excel and Visual Basic for Applications

⇨ Microsoft Certified Product Specialist

❊ Audience

This certification is designed for individuals who are qualified to provide installation, configuration, and support for users of Microsoft desktop products.

Figure 7-11

Microsoft Certified Product Specialists	
Microsoft Certified Product Specialists are required to pass one operating system exam. In addition, individuals seeking to validate their expertise in an application must pass the appropriate elective exam.	
Operating systems requirements	Electives (optional)
Microsoft® Windows® OR	Microsoft Excel
Microsoft Windows® for Workgroups OR	Microsoft Word
Microsoft Windows NT™ Workstation	Microsoft Project

Microsoft Certified Product Specialist requirements

❊ Requirements

To become certified, the candidate is required to pass one operating system exam. In addition, a candidate seeking to validate experience in an application must pass the appropriate elective exam. Operating systems exams include passing any one of the following:

➤ Microsoft Windows

➤ Microsoft Windows for Workgroups

➤ Microsoft Windows NT Workstation

Elective exams include

➤ Microsoft Excel

➤ Microsoft Word

➤ Microsoft Project

Refer to the "Microsoft Roadmap to Education and Certification," available from Microsoft, for detailed information on current elective exams.

✳ Preparation

Microsoft offers a variety of training courses, self-study kits, video courseware, and other educational aids that might be helpful when preparing for a certification exam. Individuals can train at Microsoft Authorized Technical Education Centers, taking Microsoft Official Curriculum courses taught by Microsoft Certified Trainers, or they can prepare for certification using self-study instructional materials outside the classroom.

Microsoft does not require the completion of any course or other training to be certified as a Microsoft Certified Systems Engineer, Microsoft Certified Solution Developer, or Microsoft Certified Product Specialist.

✳ Examination details

Topics For information about the topics covered in each certification exam, refer to the "Microsoft Roadmap to Education and Certification" or contact Microsoft at 800-636-7544.

Length Microsoft certification exams are one hour and consist of approximately 50 to 65 questions.

Fees Each exam is $100 U.S. Fees might vary outside of the United States and Canada.

Registration To register for Microsoft Certified Professional exams, call 800-755-EXAM (800-755-3926).

 Recertification requirements

To keep up with product and technological changes, Microsoft Certified Professionals must occasionally meet continuing certification requirements. Certified individuals are notified by Microsoft of the need to meet additional requirements and given an appropriate amount of time to complete them.

Contact information

For additional information about the Microsoft Certified Professional program, call Microsoft at 800-636-7544.

Benefits and deliverables

The Microsoft Certified Professional program benefits an organization by providing a greater return on training investments. Certification gives an organization a standard method to determine training needs and measure results. It can also lead to greater customer satisfaction, improved service, and decreased support costs through greater productivity and increased organizational self-sufficiency.

Certification provides the technical manager with a reliable benchmark for hiring, promotion, and career planning. Organizations that outsource technical services benefit by using service organizations who employ Microsoft certified professionals because certification provides an assurance of quality and a standard of reliability.

The Microsoft Certified Professional program benefits technical professionals by enabling them to maximize the potential of new technologies through expanded knowledge. The program is designed to help the certified professional gain new career and business opportunities in an increasingly competitive marketplace. Through certification, the individual has the means to show employers and clients that he or she has proven knowledge and the skills required to build, implement, and support effective solutions.

Microsoft Certified Professionals receive a number of immediate and long-term benefits:

> *Recognition.* Microsoft Certified Professionals are instantly recognized as experts with the technical knowledge and skills needed to design and develop or implement and support solutions with Microsoft products. Microsoft helps build this recognition by promoting the expertise of Microsoft Certified Professionals within the industry and to customers and potential clients.

> *Access to technical information.* Microsoft Certified Professionals gain access to technical information directly from Microsoft and receive special invitations to Microsoft conferences and technical training events. Depending on the certification, Microsoft Certified Professionals also receive a prepaid trial membership to the Microsoft TechNet Technical Information Network or a discount for the Microsoft Developer Network; free incident support with Microsoft Product Support Services; and eligibility to participate in the Microsoft Beta Evaluation program.

> *Global community.* Microsoft Certified Professionals join a worldwide community of technical professionals who have validated their expertise with Microsoft products. Microsoft Certified Professionals are brought together through a dedicated CompuServe forum and local events; receive a free subscription to the Microsoft Certified Professional Magazine, a career and professional development magazine created especially for Microsoft Certified Professionals; and, depending on their certification, are eligible to join the Network Professional Association, a worldwide association of computer professionals.

⇨ Comments

"From my perspective as a consultant, I believe that certification is one of the ways our clients can be assured that the people they deal with know what they're doing. Most of the people I talk to have been particularly welcoming to my Microsoft certifications."

Vice president, Blakely-Signature Associates

 # National Association of PC Owners

 ## Company background

The National Association of PC Owners (NAPCO) is a not-for-profit association dedicated to the reform of the computer repair industry, including mandates for adequate training and testing for all computer technicians.

 ## NAPCO certification program

Working with National Advancement Corporation (NAC), a professional school that trains computer technicians for major corporate clients, NAPCO developed the Level 2 PC Certification to provide a high standard of competency for PC technicians. The Level 2 PC Certification has been very well accepted and demanded by users to ensure they receive high-quality service.

 ## Level 2 PC Certification

❋ **Audience**

This certification is directed toward all PC repair technicians.

❋ **Requirements**

There are no prerequisites required to take this certification test. However, the test focuses on the commonly misdiagnosed field problems, real-world PC problems, and troubleshooting skills that can only be acquired through years of field experience.

✳ Preparation

A number of courses offered by NAC can help the technician prepare for the certification exams. These courses include Advanced PC Maintenance, Printer Maintenance, Networking and Advanced Networking, and Macintosh. The classes range in length from three to five days and focus on cost-effectiveness and short cuts to repairing the most troublesome and repeated problems facing technicians.

The test focuses on the commonly misdiagnosed field problems, real-world PC problems, and troubleshooting skills that are acquired through years of field experience. Although a good training class is helpful, training is an ongoing need, not a one-time venture. Few courses available teach at the level required to pass this certification. It is a true measure of acquired technical knowledge and experience.

✳ Examination details

The test consists of multiple-choice and true/false questions relating to the most commonly misdiagnosed field problems. These questions make up the knowledge and experience levels that every technician should know.

Topics The following topics are covered on the Level 2 PC Certification exam:

➤ Component recognition

➤ Data recovery

➤ Diagnostics and troubleshooting

➤ Electronics

➤ General PC knowledge

➤ Industry knowledge

➤ Monitor knowledge

➤ Software

➤ Terminology

Length The test is one hour and consists of approximately 60 questions.

Fees The exam is $150 U.S. Fees might vary outside of the United States and Canada.

Registration To register for the Level 2 Certification exam, call 800-340-EXAM (800-340-3926).

 # Benefits and deliverables

The benefits of this certification for a service supplier lie in the statement it makes to both clients and potential clients. Certification can be very useful as a method of showing potential clients that your company is not interested in the status quo and that you use a different and more extensive measuring device for determining your technicians' skills. In addition, for the manager, it presents the opportunity to screen incoming applicants for technical ability and can be used to uncover developmental needs in the technicians already on staff.

When the test has been successfully completed, the technician receives a certificate and identification card to verify Level 2 PC Certification. The card is printed with a unique identification number that can be confirmed by calling NAPCO. In addition, Level 2 Certified technicians also receive a newsletter with information to help keep them on top of their industry.

✳ Recertification requirements

Certified technicians are required to pass the Level 2 exam every three years to maintain their certification status.

 # Contact information

For further information about Level 2 Certification, call NAPCO at 800-443-3384. National Advancement Corporation can be reached at 800-832-4787 or 714-754-7110.

 # Novell, Inc.

NOVELL®

 # Company background

Novell, Inc., which recently merged with WordPerfect Corporation, is a leading provider of network server operating system software and network applications that integrate desktop computers, servers, and minicomputer and mainframe hosts for businesswide information sharing. Novell is a market-driven company with a corporate vision to create, along with its partners, a world of pervasive computing that connects people with other people and the information they need, enabling them to act on it, anytime, anyplace.

 # Novell certification programs

Novell offers four certification programs targeted toward NetWare, UnixWare, and GroupWare professionals. By passing certification exams, these professionals demonstrate their ability to provide quality front-line support to Novell's customers. These programs include the following: Certified Novell Administrator (CNA), Certified Novell Engineer (CNE), Master Certified Novell Engineer (Master CNE), and Certified Novell Instructor (CNI).

Since Novell's 1994 merger with WordPerfect Corporation, WordPerfect's certification programs have been in transition. The

WordPerfect Certified Instructor program has been blended with Novell's CNI program. WordPerfect GroupWare (GroupWise, SoftSolutions, and InForms) certification is being integrated into Novell's CNA program. Call 800-233-3382 or 801-222-7800 for the latest information on WordPerfect and PerfectOffice certification information.

⇨ Certified Novell Administrator (CNA)

✳ Audience

The CNA program is designed to set a standard of competence for professionals who perform the day-to-day functions of NetWare, UnixWare, or GroupWare administration and user support. This certification is designed for people who handle routine network administration tasks, including adding and modifying user accounts, maintaining security, and loading applications. CNAs often manage a network in addition to other job responsibilities, such as managing an office.

CNA certification provides employers with the assurance that a network administrator has the knowledge required to manage a network on a day-to-day basis.

✳ Requirements

To become CNA certified, the successful candidate is required to pass one of the following proficiency tests. One exam is available for each version of the operating system:

➢ Certified NetWare 4 Administrator

➢ Certified NetWare 3 Administrator

➢ Certified NetWare 2 Administrator

➢ Certified UnixWare Administrator

➢ Certified GroupWise Administrator

➢ Certified InForms Administrator (available third quarter 1995)

➢ Certified SoftSolutions Administrator (available third quarter 1995)

After meeting CNA requirements, the candidate receives a certificate of recognition.

 # Certified Novell Engineer (CNE)

※ **Audience**

The CNE program is designed to set a standard of competence for professionals who provide technical support for Novell networks. Technicians who work with installing, configuring, and maintaining Novell networking products, including NetWare, UnixWare, and GroupWare can benefit from the CNE program. The CNE program has four areas of specialization: NetWare 3, NetWare 4, UnixWare, and GroupWare. Additional areas of CNE specialization may be added as business needs dictate.

Certified Novell Engineer candidates are employed in a variety of technical positions, including working for Novell resellers and Novell Authorized Service Centers (NASCs), working for organizations that use Novell networking products, and as independent consultants. (See figure on next page.)

※ **Requirements**

To become certified, the candidate is required to pass a series of required and elective proficiency tests specific to the desired area of specialization. Each test has associated credits. Candidates must earn and maintain 19 credits in their first area of CNE certification. Additional CNE certifications may be earned by passing nonredundant exams in any of the other available CNE specializations. For details about exams and credits, call 800-233-3382 or 801-222-7800 and order a CNE brochure and progress chart.

There is no time limit for completing the CNE proficiency tests. However, Novell reserves the right to change certification requirements at any time. It is the candidate's responsibility to make sure that the tests taken meet current certification requirements. For help in planning a training curriculum, call 800-233-3382 or 801-222-7800 and order a CNE brochure and progress chart.

In addition to passing the exams, all candidates are required to sign and return a Master CNE/CNE agreement.

After meeting CNE requirements, candidates receive a certificate of recognition, the right to use Novell's CNE logo in advertisements and business literature, two free technical support calls from Novell with a 50-percent discount thereafter, and discounts on Novell services.

Master CNE

✳ Audience

The Master CNE program is designed to set a standard of competence for professionals who provide high-level technical support for Novell's networking products. Master CNEs provide technical expertise similar to CNEs, but add value for organizations by providing in-depth understanding that enables them to readily manage issues related to system upgrade, migration, and integration. As Novell's highest-level technical certification, the Master CNE program represents the evolution of the original Enterprise CNE (ECNE) program into a more powerful, solutions-based certification.

CNEs can choose an appropriate Master CNE certification depending upon their CNE area of specialization. The three available Master CNE certifications are Network Management, Infrastructure and Advanced Access, and GroupWare Integration. Additional Master CNE areas of specialization may be added to Novell's Master CNE program as business needs dictate.

✳ Requirements

To become certified as a Master CNE, the candidate must have current CNE status. Candidates must then earn and maintain 10 additional credits by passing a series of proficiency tests to obtain a Master CNE certification.

There is no time limit for completing the Master CNE certification. However, Novell reserves the right to change certification requirements at any time. It is the candidate's responsibility to make sure that the tests taken meet current certifications requirements. For help in planning a training curriculum, call 800-233-3382 or 801-222-7800 and order a Master CNE progress chart.

After meeting all Master CNE requirements, candidates receive a certificate of recognition, a Master CNE lapel pin, a six-month subscription to *Novell Application Notes*, the *Novell Press Desk Reference* set, the *Novell Market Messenger* CD, and one free copy of the Network Support Encyclopedia Professional Volume (NSEPro) on CD-ROM.

Certified Novell Instructor (CNI)

✳ Audience

The CNI program is designed for people who want to make a career of teaching others how to install, configure, and use Novell network and network applications products.

✳ Requirements

CNI certification requirements include applying and being accepted into the program, attending courses, passing proficiency tests at a higher level than other certification candidates, and successfully completing a rigorous Instructor Performance Evaluation (IPE) conducted by Novell.

CNIs receive extensive, ongoing support from Novell to ensure they stay up-to-date on the latest products and technology. Novell also requires CNIs to meet continuing certification requirements, which include additional training and testing as Novell updates courses and releases new products.

✳ Preparation

Novell certification candidates are responsible for planning their own curriculums. Training is not required for certification. Novell does, however, strongly recommend plenty of hands-on experience to pass the certification exams. Candidates who want training may prepare for the certification exams through a Novell-authorized, hands-on training course. In addition to Novell-authorized training, candidates may choose from several self-study training options in preparing for Novell proficiency exams.

Instructor-led courses are available at any of more than 1200 Novell Authorized Education Centers (NAECs) and Novell Education Academic Partners (NEAPs) throughout the world. Novell-authorized education

sites include Novell distributors, resellers and consultants, national retail organizations, independent training centers, colleges, and universities. NAECs and NEAPs are carefully selected and authorized by Novell and must adhere to rigorous quality standards. Every authorized education provider must use Novell certified instructors, who are qualified through an intensive training and testing program, and student materials developed by Novell. Candidates should contact their local education center for course availability and prices, or call 800-233-3382 in the United States and Canada or 801-222-7800 elsewhere for the location of the nearest Novell Authorized Education Center.

Student kits contain material used in instructor-led courses to enable a student to study course materials independently. Student kits are available for purchase from local NAECs.

Novell offers a wide range of self-study materials, including computer-based training (CBT) courses, videos, and workbooks. These self-study products allow students to work at their own pace and focus study time on the information they really need. Self-study workbooks cover most of the exam material and are available for purchase at local NAECs worldwide. Workbooks are not available for all exams. Computer-based training (CBT) and video-based training (VBT) materials are available for a limited number of exams from local NAECs, Novell authorized resellers, or through Novell After Market Products group. Call Novell at 800-346-7177 for information on CBT or VBT availability and prices.

✳ Examination details

All Novell exams are administered on a personal computer, are "closed book," and are graded on a pass/fail basis. Candidates are informed of specific details pertaining to the exam they will take at the time of registration.

Topics Objectives for Novell certification exams are available from Novell Education, 800-233-EDUC (800-233-3382) or 801-222-7800.

Length Tests range from 30 to 180 minutes and vary in number of questions.

Fees Most Novell exams are $85 U.S. Fees might vary outside of the United States and Canada. WordPerfect exams that were released prior to the Novell-WordPerfect merger vary in price.

Registration To register for Novell certification exams, call 800-RED-EXAM (800-733-3926).

✳ Recertification requirements

Novell certification programs have continuing certification requirements that must be met from time to time to keep up with technological changes. Novell notifies certified individuals by mail of continuing certification requirements and deadlines.

 # Benefits and deliverables

Certified Novell professionals have proven ability to provide quality front-line support to Novell's customers. After meeting certification requirements, CNEs and Master CNEs receive

> ➢ A certificate of recognition

> ➢ Lapel pin identifying the designation earned

> ➢ Two free Novell technical support incidents and a 50-percent discount on all purchased support incidents

> ➢ A free issue of the Network Support Encyclopedia (NSEPro—an electronic information base)

> ➢ The right to use the logo of the earned certification designation in advertisements and business literature

 # Powersoft

Powersoft.™

 # Company background

Powersoft develops, markets, and supports client/server application development tools for Fortune 1000 companies and government agencies. Powersoft provides the Powersoft Enterprise Series, a family of client/server tools for enterprise productivity. These tools are

designed to allow professional developers and end users to work together in a collaborative relationship to meet all of an organization's development needs. Due to the success of PowerBuilder, its object-oriented client/server application development product, PowerSoft is cited by market researchers as the leading vendor of client/server application development tools and one of the fastest-growing companies in the software industry.

Powersoft certification program

Powersoft offers two certifications under its Certified PowerBuilder Developer (CPD) program. Certification under these programs ensures that application developers have the demonstrated skills and knowledge to create high-performance applications using PowerBuilder.

The two current Powersoft certification levels are CPD Associate and CPD Professional. The CPD Associate designation certifies that an individual is proficient with the fundamental and advanced concepts of PowerBuilder. A CPD Professional designation recognizes individuals who have achieved the CPD Associate level and developed an even higher standard of PowerBuilder development skill.

Certified PowerBuilder Developer Associate

❋ **Audience**
This certification is designed for application developers who create high-performance applications and client/server applications with the

PowerBuilder tool set. The candidate must demonstrate proficiency in a broad spectrum of PowerBuilder and client/server development topics.

✳ Requirements

To achieve certification as a CPD Associate, an individual must pass two examinations. The first is the CPD Fundamentals examination. Once the first level is passed, the candidate then moves on to the advanced concepts test.

Certified PowerBuilder Developer Professional

✳ Audience

This certification is designed for Certified PowerBuilder Developer Associates who want to move to the next level of development skill and recognition. In-depth understanding of PowerBuilder as a client/server application development tool and experience building PowerBuilder applications are both key to achieving CPD Professional status.

✳ Requirements

Certification as a CPD Professional requires a candidate to first obtain the CPD Associate certification. The individual must then pass an application test. The application test requires the candidate to demonstrate PowerBuilder skills by developing application modules that solve real-world problems.

✳ Preparation

To prepare for the CPD Associate certification, individuals are encouraged to attend PowerBuilder courses. Six different courses are recommended to provide the candidate with the base of knowledge covered by the certification exam. The following three courses cover the topics required to pass the Fundamentals test:

> ➤ Transition to the Client/Server Environment (one day)

> ➤ Introduction to PowerBuilder (four days)

> ➤ Effective GUI design for PowerBuilder (one day)

The PowerBuilder Advanced Concepts exam requires knowledge on a wide variety of application development topics, which are covered in these three additional courses:

➢ Mastering DataWindows (two days)

➢ PowerBuilder Performance Tuning and Techniques (two days)

➢ Object-Oriented PowerBuilder Development (three days)

In addition to these courses, PowerBuilder recommends the candidate gain an understanding of the underlying technologies that are covered in the Fundamentals portion of the exam. These technologies and concepts include the following:

➢ Client/server

➢ Relational databases

➢ SQL

➢ Object-oriented technology

➢ Graphical user interface (GUI) design

Preparation for the CPD Professional certification exam includes an in-depth understanding of all topics covered in the CPD Associate program. In addition, because the candidate is required to build a small application by solving a series of problems using PowerBuilder, it is recommended the candidate obtain additional hands-on experience using PowerBuilder to build advanced applications.

In addition to the courses described, books on PowerBuilder are available to assist the candidate with preparing for certification examinations.

✳ Examination details
Topics PowerBuilder Painters, PowerScript, Client/Server, Object-oriented concepts, GUI concepts, relational database concepts, and SQL are all topics included in the certification examinations for the CPD Associate designation. The CPD Professional exam requires the basic knowledge, plus requires the candidate to build a small application using the PowerBuilder tool set.

Length Each of the CPD Associate certification tests require about one hour to complete. Both are in a multiple-choice and true/false format. The Fundamentals test is comprised of approximately 50 to 100 questions. The Advanced Concepts exam has between 30 and 70 questions.

The CPD Professional certification exam is a hands-on application development test using PowerBuilder. The test takes approximately two and one-half hours to complete.

Fees CPD Associate level exams are $100 U.S and CPD Professional level exams are $250 U.S. Fees might vary outside of the United States and Canada.

Registration To register for Powersoft certification exams, call 800-407-EXAM (800-407-3926).

❋ **Recertification requirements**

Each year, CPD Associates and Professionals are asked to complete additional requirements to maintain certification. Powersoft contacts certified developers with information about recertification requirements.

 # Benefits and deliverables

Approximately two weeks after successfully completing certification requirements, candidates receive a kit containing

➤ An official CPD certificate

➤ CPD logo sheet

➤ Wallet-size membership card

➤ Gift from Powersoft

Certified PowerBuilder developers also receive a preferred rate for Powersoft's technical support. Annual technical support agreements are available at a 10-percent discount for CPD Associates and 20-percent discount for CPD professionals. Annual renewals for support at these discounted rates are contingent on maintaining annual certification requirements.

Both CPD Associates and CPD Professionals receive free issues of Powersoft's *PowerLine* newsletter. In addition to the newsletter, CPD Professionals can redeem a coupon that entitles them to receive a free one-year subscription to the Powersoft information base on CD-ROM.

The newly certified developer's name is placed in a CPD directory that is made available to clients as a preferred development resource. The list is posted on FaxLine and CompuServe.

 # Contact information

For additional information about training for PowerBuilder certification, call Powersoft at 508-287-1700, option 2. For other information, contact the CPD program administrator at 508-287-1807.

 # SCO

 # Company background

SCO is the world's leading developer and supplier of open systems software for business servers. SCO's strategy is to provide the most robust, multifunctional operating systems for cost-effective Intel-based servers. As the leading provider of UNIX system servers, SCO has a distinct technological edge and unique focus in this emerging market. The reliability, compatibility, interoperability, and ease of use of SCO systems make them the leading products in this market.

SCO supports end users and resellers with a broad range of support and service offerings, including a range of telephone support options, a CD-based SCO Support Library, online services, and high-level consulting and engineering services. SCO offers comprehensive education programs for end users and channels, including resellers.

 # SCO certification program

The SCO ACE certification program is designed for the technical professional who is responsible for the support and administration of

SCO installations and wishes to certify the skills required to maximize system performance. SCO offers two certification designations for the technical professional: SCO ACE and the SCO ACE+. To become SCO ACE certified, the candidate must pass four proficiency tests within one year of completing the first test. SCO ACE+ is the next level of program certification for the professional who requires higher-level, mission-critical, and enterprise-wide knowledge.

By passing proficiency tests in the SCO ACE designation, individuals demonstrate their competency in servicing and supporting SCO products. In addition to the basic competency demonstrated by SCO ACE certification, successful SCO ACE+ candidates also demonstrate competency in advanced network connectivity and graphical user interfaces.

SCO ACE certification

* **Audience**
The SCO ACE certification program is targeted toward technical professionals who provide support, consultation, integration, and education for SCO products in end-user and channel partner companies.

* **Requirements**
SCO ACE certification requires successful completion of four comprehensive examinations and certifies proficiency in the core technology required for administration and support of SCO UNIX systems.

Figure 7-12   SCO ACE Certification

SCO UNIX System V/386
Administration

Shell Programming for
System Administration

SCO TCP/IP and SCO NFS:
Administration and Configuration

Basic SCO System V
Communications: OR   Administration of Microsoft
uucp Administration*   LAN Manager for SCO Systems*

* Choose the exam most relevant to your SCO installations.

Required exams for SCO ACE certification

⇨ SCO ACE+ certification

✳ Audience
The SCO ACE+ certification program is targeted toward technical
professionals who need superior knowledge in mission-critical,
enterprise-wide systems implementation.

✳ Requirements
To become SCO ACE+ certified, the candidate must have current
ACE status, attend a practical workshop, and pass the three additional
tests for this program within a one-year period.

SCO ACE+ Certification

Figure 7-13

TCP and NFS Level II

SCO Graphical User
Interface/Desktop Administration
and Configuration 3.0

Administration of Microsoft
LAN Manager for SCO Systems*

Basic SCO System V
Communications:
uucp Administration

* Choose the exam not chosen for your ACE certification.

Required exams for SCO ACE+ certification

❋ Preparation

Classroom instruction is recommended but not required for certification. SCO offers a series of courses to prepare candidates for proficiency tests. The courses are offered at SCO Authorized Education Centers worldwide. For locations of authorized education centers, contact SCO at 800-SCO-UNIX (800-726-8649).

ACE preparation guides are available for candidates who are already knowledgeable in SCO products and wish to challenge the ACE exams without the recommended classroom preparation. To order preparation guides, call Drake Prometric at 800-775-EXAM.

❋ Examination details

Topics SCO provides prospective certification candidates with examination information free of charge. For a list of topics covered on SCO ACE or ACE+ exams, call SCO at 800-SCO-UNIX.

Length Most SCO ACE and ACE+ exams are one hour and consist of approximately 40 questions.

Fees The cost for each single exam is $125 U.S and the cost for the comprehensive recertification exam is $180 U.S. Fees might vary outside of the United States and Canada.

Registration To register for exams, call 800-775-EXAM (800-775-3926).

❋ Recertification requirements

Although ACE certification is a permanent status, SCO recommends that certified individuals pass one comprehensive recertification test at specified intervals to ensure that the individual maintains current knowledge of SCO products and technologies. Recertification is required to maintain SCO benefits.

⇨ Benefits and deliverables

After meeting requirements, certified individuals receive

> ➤ An official ACE certificate
> ➤ Lapel pin and desk trophy
> ➤ Right for personal use of the SCO ACE logo
> ➤ A subscription to *DISCOVER SCO* magazine

In addition, the individual's organization receives discounts on technical support calls and a free subscription to SOSCO, the online live database for SCO technical support.

⇨ Contact information

For additional information about the SCO ACE program, call SCO at 800-SCO-UNIX (800-726-8649).

⇨ Comments

"Even though I've had several years of practical SCO UNIX experience, I found that completing my SCO ACE certification courses increased my understanding of UNIX systems and helped me to more confidently and effectively provide assistance to our customers."

Student, San Jose, California

"The SCO ACE program provides an ideal framework for developing a comprehensive understanding of the SCO operating systems. It sets an industry benchmark for measuring the knowledge of system engineers."
Student, Sydney, Australia

"My SCO ACE certification has broadened our opportunities for sales into UNIX environments. Clients have expressed greater confidence in our expertise in providing them with UNIX solutions. Furthermore, our experience, coupled with SCO ACE status, has given us the qualifications we need to obtain reseller certification from manufacturers of high-end equipment."
Student, Westminster, Colorado

Software Publishers Association

Company background

The Software Publishers Association (SPA) is the principal international trade association of the personal computer software industry. Founded in April 1984 by 25 companies, the SPA has grown to a membership of more than 1100 firms. Its full members include business, consumer/leisure, and education software companies, as well as hardware systems manufacturers. Its associate members include firms with industry-related products and services that benefit from alliances with software publishers. The SPA is committed to promoting the industry and protecting the interests of its members.

 # Certified Software Manager program

The Certified Software Manager (CSM) program is designed for individuals responsible for the management of an organization's desktop software assets and for ensuring that the software licenses are in compliance. An organization invests in information technology to 1) increase productivity; 2) lower costs; and 3) gain a competitive edge. These benefits make information technology an indispensable asset— an asset that carries risks and responsibilities. An effective software manager is essential to gain the full benefits of software and avoid the penalties that can result from mismanaging it.

The CSM program defines the skills that enable a computer professional to manage software assets effectively, increasing productivity and lowering the organization's costs. Topics covered include understanding copyright law (United States and Canada); understanding license agreements; developing and implementing a software management program; the software audit process; managing and metering software on a network; and selling the importance of software management to every level of an organization.

✳ Audience

Individuals responsible for the management of an organization's desktop software assets and for ensuring software compliance are the intended audience for this program. Areas of responsibility might include microcomputing; MIS/DP; end-user computing; technical and

functional department managers; computer specialists; computer services; technical support; auditors; human resources; and legal counsel.

✳ Requirements

To become a Certified Software Manager, an individual must obtain a passing score on the required certification exam.

✳ Preparation

The SPA offers a comprehensive, six-hour training seminar to assist the candidate in preparing for the certification exam. If a candidate is unable to attend the seminar, he or she may prepare for the exam by purchasing a copy of the course materials.

✳ Examination details

Topics The exam covers topics presented in the CSM student manual.

Length The CSM exam is 60 minutes and consists of 50 to 59 questions.

Fees Each exam is $100 U.S. Fees might vary outside of the United States and Canada.

Registration To register for certification exams, call 800-804-EXAM (800-804-3926).

Benefits and deliverables

The new Certified Software Manager receives a certificate of recognition, a subscription to a quarterly newsletter on software management issues, and inclusion in a networking directory of CSMs in the United States and Canada. CSMs have acquired valuable skills that make them more effective in their present jobs and marketable to any organization with more than a few PCs.

 # Contact information

For more information about the Certified Software Manager program, call the CSM coordinator at 202-452-1600 (extension 367).

 # Comments

"This program will go a long way towards educating people about licensing and copyright procedures. I found it to be an interesting, well-presented course."
PC/LAN support technician, Cenlar Federal Savings Bank, Princeton, New Jersey

"Participation enhances the skills and knowledge of the organization's employees and provides the organization with an opportunity to improve their management of software assets."
Deputy director of budget analysis, Department of Budget and Fiscal Planning, State of Maryland

 # Solomon Software

 # Company background

Solomon Software, founded in 1980, is a leading international developer of Windows, Windows NT, NetWare and DOS-based accounting information systems software for middle-market companies. Solomon Software's mission is to improve the productivity

of middle-market business by providing accounting information systems and related services that support the changing needs of business.

 # Solomon IV for Windows Professional Skills certification

This certification program allows resellers and consultants to focus on their chosen areas of expertise and to receive formal recognition for their professional skill levels. Furthermore, certification provides a consistent and objective quality standard by which individuals are recognized for their level of technical expertise. The Professional Skills certification program is an integral component and requirement for becoming an Authorized Reseller or Certified Consultant for the Solomon IV product. For a complete description of the Reseller and Consultant Partner program, call 800-879-2767.

Solomon Software offers several professional certifications. Each of the certifications is built on five separate skill levels, or certification designations. These include:

➤ Solomon Certified Systems Engineer (SCSE)

➤ Solomon Certified Financial Specialist (SCFS)

➤ Solomon Certified Operations Specialist (SCOS)

➤ Solomon Certified Application Developer (SCAD)

➤ Solomon Certified Customization Developer (SCCD)

Professional Skills certification is independent of the process involved to become an Authorized Reseller or a Certified Consultant of Solomon Software products.

Figure 7-14

Certification Title	Designation	Exam I.D. #
Solomon IV Certified Systems Engineer	SCSE	370-001
Solomon IV Certified Financial Specialist	SCFS	370-002
Solomon IV Certified Operations Specialist	SCOS	370-003
Solomon IV Certified Customization Developer	SCCD	370-004
Solomon IV Certified Application Developer	SCAD	370-005

Exam numbers for Solomon certification levels

✳ Audience

The Solomon IV for Windows Professional Skills certification was designed for resellers, consultants, and clients who implement, support, and use the Solomon IV for Windows product line.

✳ Requirements

Certification is awarded based upon successful completion of a series of examinations.

✳ Preparation

Solomon Software offers a variety of education services, including on-site training and classroom seminars taught in hands-on format. Course prerequisites include a working knowledge of Novell NetWare 3.X and Microsoft Windows. While these courses can help the candidate prepare for the certification examination, course attendance in itself is not a guarantee that a candidate will pass the test.

It is also possible for prospective resellers or consultants to obtain Solomon IV certification by passing the certification tests without taking the training courses. However, given the nature of the material covered in many Solomon IV training courses and the prerequisite knowledge and skills required, it is difficult to pass the certification tests without having attended a given training course.

Solomon Software recommends that candidates review the Solomon IV test preparation guidelines, which are available on SolomonFAX in the Training Data Sheets Catalog (Document #2959). SolomonFAX, a document retrieval system, allows you to request documents by telephone and receive them by fax. Call 419-424-5060.

✳ Examination details

Topics Solomon Software will provide additional information on course details, exam preparation, and prerequisites free of charge, or call SolomonFAX at 419-424-5060 for a catalog of course details.

Length Most exams for the Solomon IV Professional Skills certification program are approximately one hour long. All tests are closed-book.

Fees The testing fee for each exam is approximately $100 for tests taken in the United States; $152 if the exam is taken outside the United States.

Registration To register for Solomon certification exams, call 800-307-EXAM (800-307-3926).

✳ Recertification requirements

To enable its certified professionals to keep up with advances in accounting information system technology and to ensure quality platform support, Solomon IV Authorized Resellers and Certified Consultants must meet continuing certification requirements.

When Solomon software introduces a major new product, or if there has been a major technological advance in the industry, certified individuals might be required to pass a proficiency test on the subject. Solomon Software mails notification of continuing certification requirements to Solomon certified professionals and then allows them six months to complete the requirements.

Benefits and deliverables

Upon successful completion of the Solomon IV Professional certification, the candidate receives an exam certificate from Solomon

Software. Solomon Software also provides these additional benefits to Solomon IV certified professionals:

➤ Authorization plaque

➤ Personal rights to use the authorized logo

➤ Priority access to technical support

➤ Access to Solomon Flyte; BBS; Support Forum on CompuServe

➤ Technical publications & telefax communication

➤ System Evaluation Kit (SEK)

➤ Pre-release beta software (one-year subscription)

Contact information

Solomon Software will provide additional information on course details, exam preparation, and prerequisites free of charge. The Solomon Fax document retrieval system allows you to request documents by phone and receive them by fax. Call 419-424-5060 to receive the latest catalog.

For more information about training, call Solomon Software's seminar department at 800-879-2767.

Comments

"Please keep certification for Solomon IV for Windows. It's the best thing you've done."
Consultant

"I strongly believe certification will separate the knowledgeable and experienced from those that say they know it all and can't support the product."
Consultant

Sun Microsystems, Inc.

 # Company background

Sun Microsystems, Inc. is an integrated portfolio of businesses that supply distributed computing technologies, products, and services. Its innovative open client-server computing solutions include networked workstation and multiprocessing servers, operating systems software, silicon designs, and other value-added technologies.

Sun Microsystems certification programs

Sun Microsystems offers a system administrator and a reseller certification targeted toward professionals who support, administer, and sell Sun Microsystems products in end-user and reseller environments. By meeting certification requirements, individuals have demonstrated proficiency in support of Sun Microsystems products.

Solaris System Administration certification

✳ **Audience**

This certification is designed for professionals who perform the system administration functions for a network of Sun workstations.

✳ Requirements

To become certified, the candidate is required to pass the following proficiency tests:

- ➤ Solaris Fundamentals
- ➤ Solaris System Administration

✳ Audience

As a part of Sun's VAR agreement, sales and technical staff are required to complete training certification courses or certification proficiency tests. Sun's reseller certification program is called Sun Competency 2000 and has three Expert Levels of training.

✳ Requirements

Each expert level has its own requirements and reward for sales representatives and system engineers. All resellers with training certification requirements must reach at least Expert Level 1000.

✳ Preparation

Training for Sun certification programs is offered through SunService Educational Services. Instructor-led courses, self-study courses, and computer- and video-based training are available. For details, candidates should call 800-422-8020 and request a copy of the SunService Educational Services catalog.

✳ Examination details

Topics Test objectives can be obtained from Drake as they become available. Call 800-795-EXAM (800-795-3926).

Length Most tests are 60 to 90 minutes and have 35 to 85 questions.

Fees Each exam is $150 U.S. Fees might vary outside of the United States and Canada.

Registration To register for certification exams, call 800-795-EXAM (800-795-3926).

Benefits and deliverables

✳ Certified Solaris System Administrator

Professionals who are Certified Solaris System Administrators have proven they have the expertise to develop, administer, and service mission-critical systems. The Certified Solaris System Administrator receives a certificate confirming her or his status.

✳ Sun Competency 2000

The Sun Competency 2000 reseller certification program ensures that Sun resellers have the sales and technical knowledge to effectively sell and support Sun Microsystems products.

Contact information

For additional information about the Certified Solaris Administrator program or the Sun Competency 2000 program, contact Sun at 800-422-8020.

Sybase Inc.

The Enterprise Client/Server Company™

Company background

Sybase, Inc., develops and markets a leading family of client/server-based software products and services for online, enterprise-wide applications and is a leader in open client/server technology. The SYBASE integrated family of software includes servers, tools, connectivity, and administration/control products that provide complete desktop to mainframe solutions. Headquartered in

Emeryville, California, Sybase markets its products worldwide through its direct sales force, telesales, distributors, OEMs, VARs, and systems integrators.

⇨ SYBASE Professional certification program

The Certified SYBASE Professional (CSP) program enables Sybase customers, partners, and technical professionals to demonstrate competence in the SYBASE architecture and product suite. The CSP program is targeted at client/server architects, designers, developers, systems and database administrators, and support engineers.

⇨ Certified SYBASE Professional Database Administrator (CSPDBA)

Figure 7-15

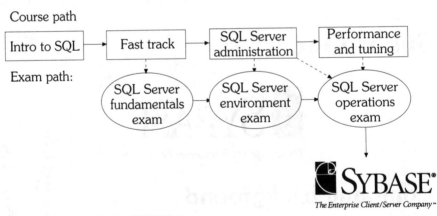

Curriculum path for CSPDBA

✳ Audience

The Certified SYBASE Professional Database Administrator program is specifically designed for professionals who design, administer, and support SYBASE SQL Server databases.

✻ Requirements

Candidates are required to pass the following three exams within six months to become a CSPDBA:

- SQL Server Fundamentals
- SQL Server Environment
- SQL Server Operations

Sybase offers a certification upgrade exam to enable CSPDBAs to easily upgrade their certification to a new release level without having to retake all three CSPDBA exams.

Certified SYBASE Professional Open Interfaces Developer (CSPIFD)

Figure 7-16

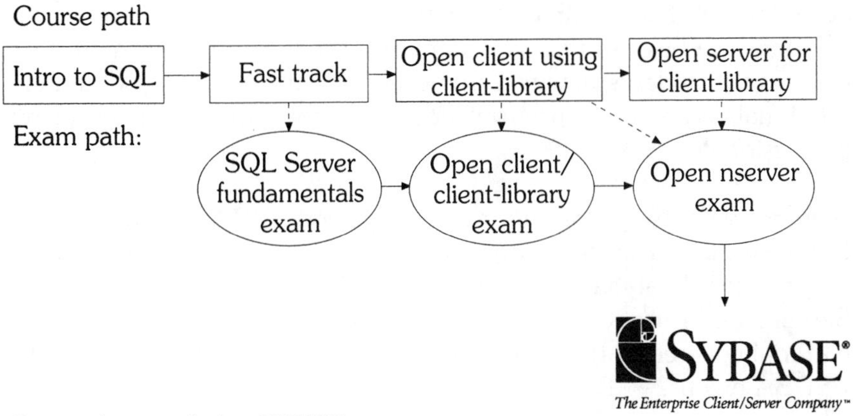

Curriculum path for CSPIFD

✻ Audience

The Certified SYBASE Professional Open Interfaces Developer (CSPIFD) program is geared toward the application developer who uses the SYBASE Open Client and Open Server interfaces. This program provides these technical professionals with an opportunity to earn a credential that objectively verifies their knowledge and skill level in using these Sybase products.

✻ **Requirements**

Candidates are required to pass the following exams within six months to become a CSPIFD:

➤ SQL Server Version 10 Fundamentals

➤ Open Client/Client-Library Version 10

➤ Open Server Version 10

SQL Server Version 10 Fundamentals is a required first examination for both SYBASE certifications. Candidates who want to use this first exam as a stepping stone toward both certifications need not repeat this test for their second certification program.

✻ **Preparation**

Although there are no formal requirements to attend Sybase education courses before taking exams, Sybase has a complete curriculum to support the certification program and encourages students to take advantage of this resource to prepare for certification. Course offerings are tailored to the student and range from introductory courses for students new to Structured Query Language (SQL) and relational databases to programs designed for more advanced technical professionals.

Students who are preparing for the Certified SYBASE Professional Database Administrator program and are already familiar with at least one relational database should take the Fast Track to SYBASE, SQL Server Administration, and Performance and Tuning classes. The material covered in these courses helps students prepare for the three CSDBA exams.

Students preparing for the Certified SYBASE Professional Open Interfaces Developer exams also have a number of course options. To prepare for the Open Client/Client-Library Version 10 exam, students should take the Open Client Using Client-Library course. To prepare for the Open Server Version 10 exam, students should take the Open Server for Client-Library course.

Training for both of these certification programs is available through a worldwide network of Sybase learning centers. Sybase has 16 North

American learning centers and an additional 14 Sybase Authorized Education Providers throughout the United States. Classes cost $375 U.S. per student per day. On-site and customized education services are also available. Education discount packages for courses leading to certification are available. Call 800-8-SYBASE for more information.

❋ Examination details

Topics To receive a list of test objectives, call Sybase at 800-8-SYBASE (800-879-2273) in North America. Outside of North America, call your local Sybase Education Center.

Length Tests for both certification programs are approximately one to one and a half hours and have between 60 and 90 questions.

Fees Each exam is $150 U.S. Fees might vary outside of the United States and Canada.

Registration Call 800-792-EXAM (800-792-3926) to register for Sybase certification exams.

Benefits and deliverables

The Certified SYBASE Professional receives an array of special services from Sybase. A licensing agreement is included with the certificate that allows the candidate to display and use the Certified SYBASE Professional service mark (logo) in the office and on business cards. Individuals with CompuServe accounts are given access to a private section of "Sybase OpenLine," a new technical forum on CompuServe. If the individual's company is an Open Solutions partner, certification is acknowledged by the appearance of the CSP logo with the company's name in the Open Solutions Directory.

Contact information

For more information about Sybase products, services, or programs, call Sybase at 800-8-SYBASE (800-879-2273). Further information on the Certified SYBASE Professional program can also be found on CompuServe and the WorldWide Web. CompuServe users should

access the SYBASE forum (GO SYBASE). The education forum is section 6. WorldWide Web users should use (URL://www.sybase.com/).

 # WIFI

 # Company background

WIFI is the educational division of the Austrian Chamber of Commerce and provides a wide variety of secondary and tertiary education. The office in the province of Steiermark has a particularly strong information technology department and has developed the concept of the PC Users (PCU) and PC Administrator (PCA).

 # WIFI certification program

The objectives of the PC Users (PCU) is to establish an entry-level desktop computing standard, leading to the work-group computing standard, PCA, and the first step in an IT career.

PC User (PCU) 95 Exam

✳ Audience

The candidates for the PCU 95 exam are individuals competent in the introductory use of MS Windows, MS Word for Windows, MS Excel, and MS Access.

Requirements

The exam is currently given in German text only in Germany, Switzerland, and Austria. Plans to publish the exam in French and English are in progress.

PC Administrator (PCA) 95 Exam

Audience

The candidate for the PCA 95 exam is an individual competent as a super-user operating in a work-group computing environment who is able to provide first-level support to other users.

Requirements

The exam is currently given in German text only in Germany, Switzerland, and Austria. Plans to publish the exam in French and English are in progress.

Examination details

Topics The exam focuses on the use of the software applications rather than installation. Both exams are closed-book, which means that examinees cannot refer to notes or reference materials during the exam.

Length The PCU 95 exam is 60 questions and candidates have up to 60 minutes to complete the exam. The PCA 95 exam is still under development, but it is expected to be 60 questions given in 60 minutes.

Fees Candidate fee for PCU 95 is 1.680,00 Austrian schillings, including 15 percent VAT.

Registration Candidates interested in taking either exam should contact the Drake Regional Service Centre in Düsseldorf, Germany, at 49 (0)211 500 99-0.

 # Benefits and deliverables

WIFI plans to build the PCU/PCA certifications into an entry-level desktop standard recognized by employers throughout German-speaking Europe. It is already promoted by the Austrian Chamber of Commerce as a measure of employee competence. Holders of the certification receive employer recognition in the workplace and job market. Recognition takes the form of a certificate, badge, and access to WIFI's Internet service.

 # Contact information

For more information about the WIFI PCU/PCA certification program, contact:

> Drake's Regional Service Centre in Düsseldorf, 49 (0)211 500 99-0

> Wolfgang Schinagl at WIFI, 43 (0)316 602-0

Index

Ilustrations are in **boldface**.